*Oracle Press*™

Everyday Oracle DBA

About the Author

April Wells has a BS degree from University of Pittsburgh's School of Information Sciences and an MBA from West Texas A&M.

She is a database administrator, currently working as an Oracle Apps DBA for TEK Systems, in Austin, Texas, where she lives with her husband and two children. With over seven years IT experience to her credit, including as a COBOL and Visual Basic programmer, SQLServer DBA, Web Master, Oracle DBA, Oracle APPS DBA, Disaster Recovery team member, and Linux System Administrator, she has a varied background on which to draw.

April has spent time teaching and training, not only in her companies, but also as a guest lecturer for Database Administration and Introduction to Information Systems classes at West Texas A&M University and as an invited speaker to the Prentice Hall IT conference and International Oracle User's Group. She has to her credit several books, including *Oracle E-Business Suite 11i From the Front Lines* (CRC Press, 2003), *Grid Database Design* (CRC Press, 2005), *Grid System Application Design* (CRC Press, 2006), *Exam Cram2 Oracle 9i Fundamentals 1* (2005), and she was a contributing author of MORE Simple Internet Activities (Teacher Created Materials, 2003). She is currently working on *Disaster Recovery* for Prentice Hall and a number of e-learning classes. Further, April has authored several articles for *InformIT*, was the editor for the South Central Oracle Users Group's E-magazine, and founded the TriState Oracle Users Group.

ORACLE®   *Oracle Press*™

Everyday Oracle DBA

April Wells

McGraw-Hill/Osborne

New York   Chicago   San Francisco
Lisbon   London   Madrid   Mexico City   Milan
New Delhi   San Juan   Seoul   Singapore   Sydney   Toronto

The *McGraw-Hill* Companies

McGraw-Hill/Osborne
2100 Powell Street, 10th Floor
Emeryville, California 94608
U.S.A.

To arrange bulk purchase discounts for sales promotions, premiums, or fund-raisers, please contact
McGraw-Hill/Osborne at the above address.

Everyday Oracle DBA

1234567890 FGR FGR 0198765

ISBN 0-07-226208-7

Acquisitions Editor	**Proofreader**
Lisa McClain	Paul Tyler
Project Editor	**Composition**
Claire Splan	Eurodesign
Acquisitions Coordinator	**Illustrator**
Alex McDonald	Lyssa Wald
Technical Editor	**Series Design**
Rachel Carmichael	Jani Beckwith
Tom Kyte	Peter F. Hancik
Copy Editor	**Cover Series Design**
Mike McGee	Damore Johann Design, Inc.

This book was composed with Corel VENTURA™ Publisher.

Contents at a Glance

1 Making It Work 1

2 Getting Things Done 47

3 Saving It and Bringing It Back 97

4 Database Tuning: Making It Sing 145

5 Database Down! Bring It Back Alive! 201

6 High Availability 223

7 Other Stuff 249

8 Will It Work? 299

Glossary 323

Index 337

Contents

ACKNOWLEDGMENTS xv
INTRODUCTION xvii

1 Making It Work **1**
Checking Space 4
    Checking Object Status 10
    Monitoring the Alert Log 13
    Automating Tasks 17
Creating a Database 18
    Optimal Flexible Architecture (OFA) 18
    Oracle DBCA 18
    PFILE 19
Starting and Stopping a Database 20
    Shutdown Options 20
    Startup Options 21
Managing Users 23
    Profiles 23
    Resource Group Directives 25
    Password Group Parameters 26
    The CREATE USER Statement 28
Working with Roles 29
    Control of Data Access 31
Summary 45

2 Getting Things Done **47**
Database Connections 48
    Connection Basics 48

Connecting as a User 52
Connecting as SYSDBA or SYSOPER 56
Connecting with a Script 63
Disconnecting Users 63
Auditing Database Connections 65
Using Oracle's Auditing Feature 68
Limiting User Connection Time 73
PL/SQL 73
Handy Oracle-Provided PL/SQL Facilities 74
PL/SQL Procedures 77
PL/SQL Functions 87
Using Packages in PL/SQL 88
Wrapping PL/SQL Code 91
Triggers 93
Summary 96

3 Saving It and Bringing It Back **97**
Some Concept Definitions 101
User-Managed Backup vs. RMAN-Managed Backup
and Recovery 104
User-Managed Backup and Recovery 105
RMAN-Managed Backups 107
Strategy 108
Requirements 108
Failures 109
Cold Backups 111
Shutdown 111
Copying Files 114
Startup 114
Restoring from Cold Backups 115
Disadvantages 115
Warm Backups 116
Differences 116
Putting Tablespaces into Backup Mode 116
Scripting 118
Recovering from Warm Backups 123
An Aside 124
Real-Time Backups 125

Suspended Backup 126
RMAN 127
   Vocabulary 129
   To Catalog or Not to Catalog 131
   Creating a Catalog 133
   Connecting 134
   REGISTER DATABASE 134
   Allocating Channels 134
   Creating Backup Sets 135
   Restoring and Recovering from Backup Sets 135
   Reporting 137
   Scripting 137
   Extras 139
Backing Up Parts and Pieces 141
   Backing Up Your Control File 141
   Backing Up with Exports 142
Summary 143

4 Database Tuning: Making It Sing **145**
Database Design 146
   Application Tuning 147
   Memory Tuning 147
   Disk I/O Tuning 147
   Database Contention 148
   Operating System Tuning 149
Finding the Trouble 149
   EXPLAIN Please 149
   Traces 149
   Statspack 169
   Users 172
Fixing the Trouble 173
   Tuning Database Parameters 173
   Tuning the Database Structure 179
   What, More? 181
   Oracle 10*g* 185
Making It Sing 193
   Materialized Views 194
   Clusters 197

Summary 199

5 Database Down! Bring It Back Alive! **201**
   Database Down 202
      Restarting 202
      If It Doesn't Start 203
      If It Doesn't Stop 203
      Finding Out Why 204
   Tools 212
      Alert Log Monitors 212
      Database Monitoring 213
      History 216
   Panic Mode 216
   Hot Standby Database 217
   Problem Resolution 217
      No Oracle Connectivity 218
      Database Links 218
   RDA 220
   Test Cases 221
   Summary 221

6 High Availability **223**
   High Availability 224
      Simple High Availability 224
      Hardware Failure and High Availability 227
   What It Isn't 229
      Grid 229
      The Only Answer 230
      For Everyone 231
   What It Is 232
   Want to Try It Out? 232
      No Need for Fencing 233
      No Need for Oracle Cluster File System or Raw Devices . . 234
      No Need for Multiple Oracle Homes 234
      Init File 235
      Parameters 237
   Single-Node RAC on Linux 237
   RAC on a Single VMware Node 238

RAC on Multiple VMware Nodes 239
RAC with Network Block Devices 239
What, There's More? 241
Data Guard 242
    Protection Modes 244
    Oracle 10*g* 246
Maximum Availability Architecture 246
Grid 247
Summary 248

7 Other Stuff **249**
OEM 250
    Standalone Use 251
    Intelligent Agents 253
    Blackouts 254
    Using Jobs 255
    Setting Events 257
OAM 258
    Configuration Information 258
    Oracle Workflow Mailer Management 258
    System Alerts 259
    Diagnostic Log Viewer 259
    Patch Advisor 260
    License Manager 260
    Init.ora Parameters 261
    Monitoring and Analysis 261
Other Oracle Systems 266
    Express 266
    Oracle 9*i* Lite 271
    Warehouse Builder 274
    Discoverer 275
    Oracle Text 276
    HTML DB 279
    Ultra Search 282
    Spatial 283
    How Does It Do That? 286
    XML DB 286
    Collaboration Suite 288

E-Business Suite 289
    Oracle i*AS* 290
    Concurrent Managers 291
    ADI 293
    FSG 293
    Workflow 294
    Customization 294
    Passwords 296
Summary 297

8 Will It Work? **299**
Planning and Organization 300
    Develop a Test Plan 301
    Requirements-Based Testing 303
What Testing Is 304
    Important 304
    A Tool 304
What Testing Is Not 305
    What Good Testing Does 305
Functional Testing 306
    The Proper Environment 306
    Limiting Variables 307
    Collecting Results 307
Unit Testing 307
Component Testing 309
Integration Testing 310
An Example and a Counter Example 311
Load Testing 314
    How to Determine Possible Loads 315
Regression Testing 316
    Clone 316
    Building a Library 318
Tools 319
    Mercury WinRunner 319
    OUNIT 319
Optimization 320
    Collection 320
    Analysis 320

Configuration 320
Testing Again 321
Summary 321

Glossary **323**

Index **337**

Acknowledgments

his book, if nothing else, has been a labor of love and determination. It has been my one true constant. It has been with me through the death of my stepson (Marine Sgt. Lonny Wells) in the initial battles in Fallujah, my mom's diagnosis of cancer, three jobs, and a big move. It has been through a lot with me.

I would like to thank Rachel Carmichael and Tom Kyte for their work in tech editing the book; their comments and humor kept me centered on the project.

Lisa McClain and Alexander McDonald, thank you for all of your help and hard work on this project. I hope that we can go down this road again, albeit a little more smoothly the next time.

Most importantly, to my family … My husband, Larry, and my kids, Adam and Amandya, thank you for sticking by me and seeing me through this. It has been a long tunnel, but there is always a light at the end of the tunnel, even if it is a very long tunnel with a lot of twists and turns and you can't actually see the light most of the time. You had the faith, and gave me the faith, that the light was there even when it couldn't be seen.

Mom, I wish for you a pocket full of heart-shaped rocks and lucky stones. Now more than ever, it is time to take the time to do the important things (watch little people jump in the leaves, listen to the wind chimes, watch the dragonflies dance, enjoy a quiet cup of Chai tea).

Finally, a word to those of you who are just bored enough to be reading this part of the book. We are a hardy bunch, we in the technology field, and if I can do it (break out of the mold, follow my dream), so can we all. I hope that this book will inspire just one person to think outside of the box, to look at the technology that we have been handed and see it through different lenses, from a different perspective, and apply it to a different set of circumstances.

Introduction

here are a lot of good Oracle books out there. If you're a beginner there are books like *Oracle 9i DBA 101* from Oracle Press. If you're an advanced DBA there are always things like *Oracle: The Complete Reference*. But what if you're somewhere in between? You've been working as a DBA for a while and you know how to do the basics but you're nowhere near an expert at tuning or user management. Where do you turn then? You can't turn to your mother; she probably can't help you, although she may be able to offer you a shoulder to pound on when you get frustrated enough to want to chew rocks. You can't turn to your boss; heck, she probably thinks you are the greatest thing in the world and we know we don't want to disillusion her! You might be able to turn to some of your peers, but what happens when they just look at you and roll their eyes? I mean really, someone of your experience asking a question like that? But we all ask questions like that. Sometimes we ask them out loud, sometimes we ask them in our own heads (we don't want to look crazy talking to ourselves, do we?), but we all ask them.

The book you hold here before you is one thing that I hope will answer the questions that you ponder. What I've tried to do here is provide a mix of things I've either used or seen used, things I've read on the net or in a listserv, things I've groveled and begged for from other people (and gave them credit for), and general stuff served up for your enjoyment

Some of the stuff here I have played with for years; other stuff I am in the process of playing with and learning day by day. I have tried thoughout to keep things in a format that can be used in all supported Oracle versions. In short, it's a general compendium of stuff to make your everyday job easier and more productive, maybe even a little more fun.

If you're a real beginner, thank you for your support in buying this book and your faith that it will bring you knowledge. If you are reading it at your favorite bookstore, enjoy, but you might be better off looking towards something more easily digested and lower level in some cases. I can highly recommend either *DBA 101* or *Effective Oracle by Design*. Both are very good books—one will help you in your day-to-day life as a DBA; the other will help you with understanding how to best design your system(s).

If you are a member in good standing of the Oak Table Network, I am deeply honored that you believe that you can learn something from me.

This book assumes that you have some working knowledge of how to do a DBA's job and are looking for ways to make it easier. I assume that you have access even to a playground environment and that you can pick up SQL*Plus and play to your heart's content if you see something that interests you.

Okay then, sit back, relax, grab a cup of coffee (no, don't put it in the cup holder on your computer, that is where you hide your music CDs when the boss is coming) and let's take a look at what's coming up. In Chapter 1, "Making It Work," we will look at the day-to-day mundane tasks that you face. Things like checking space usage, user management, basic security, starting and stopping, creating a database, and other everyday tasks. The things we have to do every day to keep things running and interacting somewhat smoothly and to keep people from actually knowing that we exist.

In Chapter 2, "Getting Things Done," we'll discuss writing code, connecting, creating packages and procedures and using the built-in ones, and when to wrap your code and when not to. We'll also take a look at tuning your code whenever you have the ability to tune.

Chapter 3, "Saving It and Bringing It Back," will deal with backup and restoration and the various ways to do both. Remember, a backup isn't any good if you can't restore from it. We'll cover point-in-time recovery and other ways to bring back, clone, or otherwise copy your databases.

Chapter 4, "Database Tuning: Making It Sing," will take us on a magic carpet ride through the wonderful world of database and query tuning. We'll look at the various methods to find and fix problems and when to use each. We will take a brief look at changing the initialization parameters, various kinds of traces and how to figure out what the traces are telling you.

Chapter 5, "Database Down! Bring It Back Alive!," deals with troubleshooting both end user problems and database problems—things like what to do if it doesn't restart, how to recover, and how to deal with user panic. We don't, however, cover how to deal with your panic. For that, you will need to deal closely with your friendly neighborhood therapist.

Chapter 6, "High Availability," looks fleetingly into the wonderful world of high availability, from simple things that you can do every day to make your life easier and your users happier (like online table reorganization) to architectural changes (like RAC and Data Guard).

Chapter 7, "Other Stuff," takes a look at things outside the database itself, like OEM and OAM, Apps servers, and other front ends. While not strictly DBA tasks, they do impact how we do our jobs and how easy those jobs are. Besides, the friendly voice of experience tells us that you never can tell when you will be called upon to be the expert in one of these areas, and having some working knowledge of them will make you sound like you know what you are talking about.

And finally in Chapter 8, "Will It Work?," we take a look at testing: what it is and isn't, the various kinds of testing, and what they can and cannot tell you about your database and your applications. And maybe how it can help you find out where things will break before they break in real life.

This book is an adventure. It is more than a reference, it is a way to discover what you knew you knew but forgot you knew, and a way to discover what you didn't know you didn't know or to find new ways of thinking about things. Hang on, and have fun. This is only the beginning.

CHAPTER
1

Making It Work

racle, for the most part, just works. It has gotten more and more reliable as time has gone by, and at the same time, it has gotten bigger, more complicated, more robust, and more all-encompassing. The definition of what database administrators do, who they are, and what they can affect and influence in the database has evolved at the same time. This chapter will look at the DBA's typical day-to-day tasks, the mundane things that tend to fill up our time whenever we aren't answering questions, responding to emergencies, or helping users and developers to better understand this product that they love to hate.

One of the banes of a DBA's existence is the early morning call that proclaims, "The database is broken and we need it now. Fix it!" You know the calls, the ones where a user calls you or has you paged way before you would ever dream that any of them could possibly be at work. The ones informing you that *your* database is horribly broken; they of course had nothing at all to do with the current broken situation ("It was like this when I got here") and imply that you are somehow less of a person because of this current situation.

This chapter will help you keep those calls from happening, or at least lessen their frequency or their severity. Keeping the database operational and efficient involves tasks that you don't just do once and then forget about—it involves a series of tasks, some that have to be handled on a daily (some days it seems hourly) basis, others that can be scheduled weekly, monthly, or even annually in the case of adding additional partitions to a partitioned tablespace. Sometimes it means planning based on informed reasoning, and taking action to ensure simpler maintenance in the future. Sometimes it means making your own notes in your own notebook or, gasp, taking the proper care to document for yourself those things that you do.

Documentation takes some effort (okay, let's be realistic, it often takes considerable effort), but it makes things easier for you later. There is no sense in doing something really well once, and then realizing that you can't remember what you did or why you did it six months down the line when you need to do it again. Making it easy on yourself in the long run sometimes requires a little extra work at the front end. Then you can take that week's vacation to the Grand Canyon knowing that your colleagues will be able to keep things running until you get back and won't need to track you down halfway down the Colorado River. Knowing that the database is running smoothly, both when we're in the office and when we're not, is the mark of a good DBA. Technologists (okay, in many cases, it is probably more appropriate to say "geeks") aren't necessarily extroverts. We usually know what a computer is going to do way more often than we can predict what people will do. We don't go out of our way to draw attention to ourselves, and are usually just as happy living in our office or even our cube as long as there is an ample supply of coffee and periodic access to food. However, in every big race, the pit crew is just as critical to the outcome as the driver. If we can keep the wheels on the wagon, and if we can make the wagon run well and look pretty in the process, we might just get that recognition that we really do have coming in the end.

Doing magic effortlessly and on command, however, requires preparation, some skill, a lot of hard work, and, often, considerable practice. The more you do to make it easier on yourself along the way, the better you will feel in the long run.

The topics discussed in this chapter aren't anything even approaching a complete list of day-to-day tasks for a typical DBA. Some may be done more or less frequently than others, but all are things that we have to do, usually on a repetitive basis. You can find such lists (daily tasks for the Oracle DBA, routine tasks for the Oracle DBA) on the Internet easily; Google is your friend, as are MetaLink (http://metalink.oracle.com) and Tahiti (http://tahiti.oracle.com). Of course, none of these lists is complete either, as the definition of DBA is a fluid one, varying from company to company and often from DBA to DBA, and just when you have the quintessential list of tasks a DBA does, the definition of DBA changes and the list is out of date. Neither are there any lists that will actually tell you what to do all the time. The best you can hope for is a general task list that you can customize to your situation and follow when the database is running smoothly. Every day is different; every day is an adventure. And be honest—isn't that one of the reasons that many of us do what we do?

The tasks discussed in the following sections are the ones I have found will give you a good feel for the status of your databases and will alert you to any problems before the users do. And it is always good to know things before the users do. That way you can answer complaints with, "Yes, I know about that, and I'm working to fix it right now. It should be fixed in five minutes." Or better yet, you can send out a courtesy e-mail letting everyone know what happened and what actions you took before they get the chance to notice anything is wrong.

Checking Space

The main reason a database exists, whether it is an online transaction processing (OLTP) database or a data warehousing (DW) database, is to hold data. How much space you have to hold that data is one of the primary things the DBA needs to check. So how do you go about it?

Well, you can use a product like Oracle Enterprise Manager (OEM) or Toad that shows you the remaining space graphically. But what happens if you are sitting with a UNIX prompt blinking at you and you don't have access to a graphical interface? You could write a SQL script that checks the used and remaining space in the tablespaces and run it. Better yet, if your databases are on a Unix-like operating system, use cron to run it for you and have your script e-mail you the results. You can take it even further by storing the results in administrative tables in the database and analyzing the data for trends at your leisure (whatever that is). This can give you projections on when you will need to add space, and how much you'll need to add to each tablespace.

In any case, knowing how much space you have, and how much is being used, is key to keeping your databases up and going. The following SQL*Plus script, written by Tim Gorman of SageLogix, will check how much space is being used, both by autoextensible datafiles as well as those that have autoextend off, in the database.

```
/*****************************************************
 * File:     spc.sql
 * Type:     SQL*Plus script
 * Author:   Tim Gorman (SageLogix, Inc.)
 * Date:     10-Oct-97
 *
 * Description:
 *     SQL*Plus script to display database space usage.
 *
 * Modifications:
 *     TGorman 11mar02 added support for
 *                     AUTOEXTENSIBLE data files
 *****************************************************/
col tablespace format a25
col owner format a20
col type format a19
col sort1 noprint
col mb format 999,990.00
clear breaks
```

```
clear compute
break on report on tablespace on owner on type
set echo off
set feedback off
set timing off
set pagesize 66
set verify off
set trimspool on
col instance new_value V_INSTANCE noprint
SELECT instance FROM v$thread;
spool spc_&&V_INSTANCE
SELECT tablespace_name tablespace,
       owner,
       'a' sort1,
       segment_type type,
       SUM(bytes)/1048576 mb
FROM dba_segments
GROUP BY tablespace_name, owner, segment_type
UNION ALL
SELECT tablespace,
       username owner,
       'b' sort1,
       segtype type,
       SUM(blocks)/128 mb
FROM v$sort_usage
GROUP BY tablespace, username, segtype
UNION ALL
SELECT tablespace_name tablespace,
       '' owner,
       'c' sort1,
       '-------total-------' type,
       SUM(bytes)/1048576 mb
FROM dba_segments
GROUP BY tablespace_name
UNION ALL
SELECT tablespace,
       '' owner,
       'd' sort1,
       '-------total-------' type,
       SUM(blocks)/128 mb
FROM v$sort_usage
GROUP BY tablespace
UNION ALL
SELECT tablespace_name tablespace,
       '' owner,
```

```
       'e' sort1,
       '-----allocated-----' type,
       SUM(bytes)/1048576 mb
FROM dba_data_files
GROUP BY tablespace_name
UNION ALL
SELECT tablespace_name tablespace,
       '' owner,
       'f' sort1,
       '-----allocated-----' type,
       SUM(bytes)/1048576 mb
FROM dba_temp_files
GROUP BY tablespace_name
UNION ALL
SELECT tablespace_name tablespace,
       '' owner,
       'g' sort1,
       '----allocatable----' type,
       SUM(DECODE
(autoextensible,'YES',maxbytes,bytes))/1048576 mb
FROM dba_data_files
GROUP BY tablespace_name
UNION ALL
SELECT tablespace_name tablespace,
       '' owner,
       'h' sort1,
       '----allocatable----' type,
       sum(decode
(autoextensible,'YES',maxbytes,bytes))/1048576 mb
FROM dba_temp_files
GROUP BY tablespace_name
UNION ALL
SELECT tablespace_name tablespace,
       '' owner,
       'i' sort1,
       '' type,
       TO_NUMBER('') mb
FROM dba_tablespaces
UNION ALL
SELECT tablespace,
       owner,
       sort1,
       type,
       SUM(mb)
FROM (SELECT'' tablespace,
```

```
                    'Total' owner,
                    'a' sort1,
                    'Used' type,
                    SUM(bytes)/1048576 mb
            FROM dba_segments
            UNION ALL
            SELECT '' tablespace,
                    'Total' owner,
                    'a' sort1,
                    'Used' type,
                    SUM(blocks)/128 mb
            FROM v$sort_usage)
GROUP BY  tablespace, owner, sort1, type
UNION ALL
SELECT tablespace,
        owner,
        sort1,
        type,
        SUM(mb)
FROM (SELECT'' tablespace,
                    'Total' owner,
                    'b' sort1,
                    'Allocated' type,
                    SUM(bytes)/1048576 mb
            FROM dba_data_files
            UNION ALL
            SELECT   '' tablespace,
                    'Total' owner,
                    'b' sort1,
                    'Allocated' type,
                    SUM(bytes)/1048576 mb
            FROM dba_temp_files)
GROUP BY tablespace, owner, sort1, type
UNION ALL
SELECT tablespace,
        owner,
        sort1,
        type,
        sum(mb)
FROM (SELECT '' tablespace,
                    'Total' owner,
                    'c' sort1,
                    'Allocatable' type,
                    SUM(DECODE
(autoextensible,'YES',maxbytes,bytes))/1048576 mb
```

```
       FROM dba_data_files
       UNION ALL
       SELECT '' tablespace,
               'Total' owner,
               'c' sort1,
               'Allocatable' type,
               SUM(DECODE
(autoextensible,'YES',maxbytes,bytes))/1048576 mb
         FROM dba_temp_files)
GROUP BY tablespace, owner, sort1, type
ORDER BY 1, 2, 3, 4;
spool off
```

Here is sample output from the spc.sql script:

```
TABLESPACE  OWNER          TYPE                    MB
----------  -----------    -----------------   ---------
DRSYS       CTXSYS         INDEX                322.81
                           LOBINDEX               0.13
                           LOBSEGMENT             0.19
                           TABLE                113.56
                 -------total-------            436.69
                 -----allocated-----          1,024.00
                 ----allocatable----          1,024.00
SYSTEM      OUTLN          INDEX                  0.19
                           TABLE                  0.19
            SYS            CACHE                  0.06
                           CLUSTER                8.25
                           INDEX                 32.31
                           LOBINDEX               1.75
                           LOBSEGMENT             4.19
                           ROLLBACK               0.38
                           TABLE                122.75
            SYSTEM         INDEX                  8.31
                           INDEX PARTITION        1.50
                           LOBINDEX               1.31
                           LOBSEGMENT             1.31
                           TABLE                  6.31
                           TABLE PARTITION        1.69
                 -------total-------            194.19
                 -----allocated-----          1,024.00
                 ----allocatable----          1,024.00
```

As you can see, the spc.sql script provides you with a listing of all the tablespaces in your database, every user who owns objects with segments allocated in those tablespaces, the segments they own, and the space allocated for each segment type and for the tablespace itself. In this way, you can see what objects are taking up space in your tablespaces so that you can plan better for growth and future placement of objects. At the end of each tablespace listing is a summation of all of the segment space: how much space is allocated to the tablespace, and how much of that space is available to be allocated from that total.

NOTE
The spc.sql script can be found on the book's companion web site, so you don't actually have to type in all this code but can copy and paste instead. (Keep in mind that you might want to paste it into Notepad first. You never can tell what kind of unprintable characters will suddenly appear in SQL*Plus from a straight copy and paste. These characters come from the translation from HTML or word processing or even RTF text to the interface you are using for your SQL*Plus session. By pasting the script into a straight ASCII text editor first, you can check for and eliminate any weird characters that might get translated badly.)

If you want to see what percent of available space is being used by data in a tablespace, on a tablespace-by-tablespace basis, you can use the following script. It will give you a quick overview so you know where you may need to add datafiles in the near future.

```
SELECT tablespace_name, TO_CHAR
(100*sum_free_blocks/sum_alloc_blocks, '999.99')
AS percent_free
 FROM
(SELECT tablespace_name, SUM(blocks)
AS sum_alloc_blocks
 FROM dba_data_files
 GROUP BY tablespace_name),
 (SELECT tablespace_name
AS fs_ts_name,MAX(blocks)
```

```
AS max_blocks,
 COUNT(blocks)
AS count_blocks, SUM(blocks) AS sum_free_blocks
 FROM dba_free_space
 GROUP BY tablespace_name)
 WHERE tablespace_name = fs_ts_name
 ORDER BY percent_free DESC;
```

The output from this script may look something like this:

```
TABLESPACE_NAME                      PERCENT_FREE
--------------------------------     -------
UNDOTBS1                               99.96
USERS01                                99.75
SYSTEM                                 81.03
DRSYS                                  57.35
TOOLS01                                17.24
```

Checking Object Status

Everything in the Oracle database is one kind of object or another, so checking the status of those objects stands high on any preventative maintenance list. There are a number of ways that objects can become invalid. For example, when you make changes to objects underlying a package or procedure, the package or procedure becomes invalid. Similarly, making changes to a table will, in some cases, invalidate any indexes. (For example, a function-based index on a column or set of columns can become invalid if the definition or size of the column changes.) Sometimes simply validating some objects will cause others to become invalid for a period of time. There are many ways that objects in the database can be invalidated.

Finding and fixing these invalid objects is sometimes necessary and sometimes not. If a package or procedure is invalid, it will throw an error the next time it is called. This can be prevented (or resolved) by running utlrp.sql, found in the $ORACLE_HOME/rdbms/admin directory. This script will find invalid packages and recompile them if they are able to recompile.

NOTE
The utlrp.sql script has had substantial changes between Oracle versions 8i and 9i. Read the script before running it.

You can find out which objects are invalid by looking in ALL_OBJECTS, DBA_OBJECTS, or USER_OBJECTS. These views will tell you which objects are invalid, and look... ...sponding error tables will tell you why ...RORS, DBA_ERRORS, or USER_ERRORS ...number and error associated with the ...fore running utlrp.sql to determine what ...e compilation script, to determine what, ...d objects like indexes requires a different ...n-based indexes need to be either ...h of these options can impact database ...ls.

...ever, utlrp.sql
...ate function-
...ving table
...not had

...etermine the name, type, and status

```
SELECT owner, object_name, object_type, status
FROM all_objects
ORDER BY owner;
```

Tom Kyte, of "Ask Tom" fame, has a SQL script that will return a list of invalid objects, sorted by owner, type, and object name, so that you can more elegantly determine what invalid objects you have in your database, who owns them (which is often of great importance in an Oracle 11*i* instance), and what kind of objects they are:

```
break on object_type skip 1
column status format a10
SELECT owner, object_type, object_name, status
FROM all_objects
WHERE status = 'INVALID'
ORDER BY owner,
```

```
OWNER                     OBJECT_TYPE
--------------------- -----------------------------
\          OBJECT_NAME STATUS
----------------- -------
SCOTT                     PACKAGE
SCOTTS_PACKAGE1              INVALID
SCOTT                     PACKAGE BODY
SCOTTS_PACKAGE1           INVALID
```

You can then run the following query on the ALL_ERRORS view as a user with DBA privileges. This will allow you to see what the errors are in the objects that have a status of "INVALID".

```
SELECTline, position, text
FROM all_errors WHERE name = 'SCOTTS_PACKAGE1';
```

The preceding script might produce the following output:

```
     LINE    POSITION
---------- ----------
TEXT
--------------------------------------------------------
        10          19
PLS-00201: identifier 'EMPLOYER' must be declared
         9           2
PL/SQL: Declaration ignored
        15          37
PLS-00201: identifier 'JOB' must be declared
```

While this will identify most errors associated with program units, views, and other similar constructs, it will not provide you with an explanation of what happened to the code if a column's data type changed, or if it is an index that is invalid.

Don't forget that when you attempt to recompile an invalid object directly, with the following statement, if Oracle finds syntactic errors, it will tell you that your program unit compiled with errors:

```
ALTER PACKAGE my_package COMPILE;
```

If you show errors at this point, Oracle will tell you what was wrong with the last program unit compiled:

```
SHO ERR
```

Monitoring the Alert Log

Oracle will tell you when it finds things wrong with its inner operations—all you have to do is look in the *alert log*. Oracle keeps a log of events in this special type of trace file. It is a chronological record of events that occur in the database. This file is written to the bdump destination specified in the initialization file. You can manually go and read the file (or more precisely, the end of the file), or there are several ways to automate the practice.

But no matter how you manage this task, watching the alert log is a must for any DBA. Here is where you'll find problems with log switches and archiving, internal errors, and any other significant events that happen within the database instance. Often you can catch problems in the alert log long before they become apparent to users. Setting up monitoring and notification for the alert log should be at the top of any DBA's list of things to do. This can be done with automated scripts that parse through the alert log and raise an alarm (via e-mail or pager notification) if something is amiss. But there is nothing that is better, or more reliable, than manually looking in the database's bdump directory at the alert logs, at least on a daily basis, and making note of anything that looks like it is out of the ordinary.

If you don't know where your alert log can be found, you can find out with the following query:

```
SELECT value
FROM v$parameter
WHERE name = 'background_dump_dest';
```

Using a Shell Script

You can set up a shell script, via cron in Unix or Linux, to check the log file for errors. The following is a simple example of just such a script:

```
#! /bin/ksh
# remarks go here.
cd $ORACLE_HOME/bdump
# or where your alert log lives.
files="alert_*.log"
for file in $(find $files)
do
DT=$(date)
awk '
BEGIN   {Flg=0}
```

```
NR==1    {R=split(DATE,TMP," ")
          Day=TMP[1]
          Month=TMP[2]
          NoDay=TMP[3] }
{NoDayM=NoDay-1}
NF==5 && $2==Month && ( $3==(NoDayM) || $3==NoDay ) {Flg=1}
Flg==1  {print $0}
' DATE="$DT" $file  | awk '
/^ORA-/ || /cannot/ {print DATE
print $0}
NF==5 {DATE=$0}
'
done
exit 0
```

This script can be set up to run in cron and to e-mail the results to the user under whose ID the script was run. A blank response will be sent if there are no errors. In order to send the e-mail to someplace other than the server on which the script is run, you can put a ".forward" file in the home directory of the user that runs the file. This .forward file should have the address or addresses to which you would like the message sent (something along the lines of my.address@gmail.com, with one address per line, should be included in the .forward file).

A similar script can be called on Windows if you install Cygwin (http://www.cygwin.com/), a free piece of software that will allow you to run Unix utilities (cron, awk, grep, etc.) under the Windows operating system. Or, if you want to spend a good deal of money (or you have to maintain compliance for Oracle E-Business Suite) you can invest in MKS Toolkit (http://www.mkssoftware.com/) to accomplish the same thing.

Using an External Table

Alternatively, you can make use of Oracle's external table feature to query the alert log directly with SQL. By running the following script as the SYS user, or a user with CREATE ANY TABLE and CREATE ANY DIRECTORY privileges granted, you can create a procedure that will read the alert log into the database. You can then view the information produced as a quick way to find alert log errors. You can use SQL scripts to parse through the alert log and find the errors or the situations that would make you stop and think. You can even take this information and insert it into another table along with your notes on troubleshooting, degugging, and resolution, again using simple SQL commands. This is much simpler than having to parse throuh the file manually, and even easier than using find or grep to locate errors. You can use SQL to find things that are like a string and be as broad or specific as you like.

NOTE
I found this script on René Nyffenegger's site, ADP—Analyse, Design & Programmierung GmbH (http://www.adp-gmbh.ch/), where you can find many very elegant scripts.

```
CREATE OR REPLACE PROCEDURE external_alert_log AS
  path_bdump varchar2(4000);
  name_alert varchar2(100);
BEGIN
  SELECT
    value INTO path_bdump
  FROM
    sys.v_$parameter
  WHERE
    name = 'background_dump_dest';
  SELECT
    'alert_' || value || '.log' into name_alert
  FROM
    sys.v_$parameter
  WHERE
    name = 'db_name';
  EXECUTE IMMEDIATE 'create or replace
directory background_dump_dest_dir
as ''' ||  path_bdump || '''';
  execute immediate
    'CREATE table alert_log_external '           ||
    ' (line  varchar2(4000) ) '                  ||
    ' ORGANIZATION EXTERNAL '                     ||
    ' (TYPE oracle_loader '                       ||
    ' DEFAULT DIRECTORY background_dump_dest_dir '||
    ' ACCESS PARAMETERS ( '                       ||
    '   RECORDS DELIMITED BY  newline '           ||
    '   nobadfile '                               ||
    '   nologfile '                               ||
    '   nodiscardfile '                           ||
    '   FIELDS TERMINATED BY ''#$~=ui$X'''        ||
```

```
     '    MISSING FIELD VALUES ARE NULL '                ||
     '    (line) '                                       ||
     '  ) '                                              ||
     ' LOCATION ('''  || name_alert || ''') )'           ||
     ' REJECT LIMIT UNLIMITED ';
end;
/
```

You can execute the external_alert_log procedure with the following anonymous block:

```
begin
   external_alert_log;
end;
/
```

And to read the alert log's content, use the following:

```
select * from alert_log_external;
```

Writing to and Backing Up the Alert Log

There may be times when you want the ability to insert your own comments into the alert log, in an error-handling routine, for example, or when you are debugging code. You can use the following anonymous block (or the same statement inserted into PL/SQL code) to accomplish this.

CAUTION
The following code is uncommented, undocumented, and unsupported by Oracle. Extreme caution should be exercised if you decide to use this procedure, since no one knows for sure exactly what it is doing.

```
BEGIN
   SYS.DBMS_SYSTEM.KSDWRT(2, 'Put my message into the log');
END;
/
```

It is important to note that the alert log can get very large, because most events are written to the log. It is one of the things that Oracle Support always asks about when you open an iTAR (Technical Assistance Request). If you want to keep the alert log to a manageable size, you can simply rename the current version to a backup name, and the next write to the log (a log switch, shutdown, startup, ORA-00600, or whatever) will cause a new iteration of the alert log to be started.

For one client, my colleagues and I automated the rename of the alert log from alertSID.log to alertSID.date every time the database was restarted (which was every week, to facilitate a cold backup of all instances and of the server itself). By simply renaming and moving the alert log to a backup location, we were able to keep past logs, but we also maintained a small active log that we could upload to Oracle Support with little trouble. While this is not strictly necessary for maintenance purposes, it is handy to keep these logs around. You can never tell when you will need to have the logs to go back to, and it is much easier to parse a week's worth of logs rather than five years' worth of logs that we would have had if we had left it just as alertSID.log. Also, Oracle Support doesn't always appreciate having to handle huge log files when all they need to see is in the last couple of days' worth of entries.

Automating Tasks

As the standard Oracle wisdom goes, "If you do something more than once, write a script for it." Taken a step further, even if you don't think you will ever end up doing it more than once, write a script for it anyway. You will undoubtedly have to do it again and again and again, and if you write a script for it the first time, you will save time rewriting it later. If you don't ever do it again, it is quicker to delete a script after a period of time than it is to keep rewriting it.

Automated tasks can take many forms, and they fall into two general classes. The first class is jobs that are scheduled on the database using either OEM or DBMS_JOB, shell scripts on Unix systems to be run by cron, or batch jobs to be scheduled and run on Windows servers. The common thread among these is that they are self-contained enough to run on their own via a scheduler. The other class is scripts written to perform common tasks and that are run manually at the DBA's command. Accumulating your own libraries of scripts that you use to perform various tasks is to your advantage. Most of us have gathered our own libraries of scripts that we can use in various combinations to make all the tasks we do simpler and easier to finish.

Creating a Database

While not exactly a day-to-day opportunity for most database administrators, creating databases is a job that many enjoy, yet many others face with dread. What parameters do I set? What values should I pick? Some decisions are easy (take the defaults and finesse them later), while others have more lasting ramifications and should be chosen before you actually start the creation script, or before you launch the Database Creation Assistant (DBCA).

Optimal Flexible Architecture (OFA)

Oracle has suggested that the Optimal Flexible Architecture (OFA) is a good way to maintain different binaries associated with different versions of the database and with different Oracle products (Discoverer, E-Business Suite, and Developer, for example). It also is a means to allow you to separate database files for one instance from those of another instance simply and elegantly, and to allow you to logically separate redo logs from data files from control files. Most of the installers are set up to allow you to do this without having to give much thought to most decisions.

However, there are often reasons that you won't want to simply take Oracle's default settings (for example, if you have to house both test and development instances of the E-Business Suite on the same server, and you want to be sure that you separate all traces of each instance from the other). You can make your own choices on the naming of the file systems (they don't have to be /data01/oradata/instance1 and /data02/oradata/instance1 or e:\u1\oradata\test and f:\u2\oradata\test). You really can decide for yourself what you want to call the file systems, and employ your own conventions.

Oracle DBCA

The Oracle Database Creation Assistant (DBCA) is the supported means by which you can create a database. It is a GUI interface that allows you to click your way through the windows, making choices about creation decisions. You can pretty much start to kiss command-line creation goodbye in Oracle Database 10*g* anyway, particularly if you are using Automatic Storage Management.

PFILE

Once you find a configuration, or set of configurations, that perform reasonably well, you can duplicate the configuration, parameter file to parameter file.

While it is true that the SPFILE is a valuable tool for the DBA, because it allows you to make many database parameter alterations to a running instance, it is always a good idea to back up your SPFILE to a static PFILE whenever you make changes to the system (or before you make any changes to the system, and again after you have accepted the changes that you want). I have often been glad to have that static backup to go back to, so that I can undo something that has broken the database. You can always edit out changes from the PFILE, where you can't in the SPFILE.

You can create a PFILE from an SPFILE at any time. The database doesn't have to be started or the instance even mounted. Simply log into SQL*Plus as SYSDBA and issue the following command:

```
CREATE PFILE FROM SPFILE;
```

or this one:

```
CREATE PFILE \path\to\pfile\withname
FROM SPFILE \path\to\spfile\withname;
```

Either of these commands will create a parameter file from your server parameter file as quick as you please. This is sometimes really important, especially when you have messed something up and can't get your database to start because of it.

Did you know that you can't use a 32KB block size in a Red Hat AS 2.1 environment? No, neither did I. I learned quickly the advantage of having a backup PFILE when I altered the database to use 32KB block sizes for tablespaces and had to use the PFILE to start the database. Granted, there are other ways around this problem, but being able to edit out the mess I made felt good.

I actually should have created a backup PFILE before I started tinkering with the database. It isn't necessary, even when you have a crashed system— you just create the new PFILE from the old SPFILE and do the necessary editing—but it would have been nice to have on hand. It would then just have been a matter of issuing the startup command referencing the PFILE, and once I had verified that I was happy with the way the database was running, I could have issued the `CREATE SPFILE FROM PFILE` command so that the errors I had introduced into the SPFILE were eliminated.

I really like the freedom and flexibility the SPFILE allows for changing parameters in the system, but knowing that I have an out if I mess something up is good too.

Having the ability to go back in and edit out mistakes that I have made has proven handy to me on a couple of occasions. It served me particularly well on a Linux system when I was trying out multiple block sizes and went beyond Linux's limitations.

Starting and Stopping a Database

In a perfect world, your database would hum happily forever and ever, and would never need to be shut down or restarted for any reason. Of course, this is neither practical nor logical. You have to maintain your databases. You have to perform database upgrades, and operating system upgrades, and even occasionally take a cold backup of the server.

You can start up and shut down the database as SYSDBA or as SYSOPER. If you have given the ability to shut down and restart the database to computer operators in your data center, you probably should set up your database with a password file and provide these people with their own userid and password that has been granted SYSOPER role, in order to perform the shutdown and restart operations. The SYSOPER role has less potential to damage the system than the SYSDBA role. In this way, you can limit the potential damage that could be done accidentally by people. Sometimes a little knowledge is a dangerous thing. Allowing the computer operators this amount of control is better than their shutting down the database with `kill -9` to the background processes.

Giving each person their own userid also means that you can track what each of them does as SYSOPER in terms of stopping and restarting the database. This can mean added security and increased accountability.

Shutdown Options

Yes, `SHUTDOWN ABORT` is a valid shutdown option. Oracle Support assures me that this is true. No, it isn't usually the best option, but it is an option.

Contrary to some opinions, if you do have to do a SHUTDOWN ABORT, and you follow it with a STARTUP and a SHUTDOWN IMMEDIATE and another STARTUP, you will have your database in a stable, recovered state when you are finished.

One of the reasons that I know that SHUTDOWN ABORT is a valid shutdown option for the database is that occasionally the emn0 process goes to sleep and forgets what it is supposed to do, and when you SHUTDOWN IMMEDIATE, it takes hours and hours to not shut down. The only way to shut down the database in that case is to SHUTDOWN ABORT and then go through the restart, shutdown, restart process.

Startup Options

If you want to automate the startup (and shutdown, for that matter) of the database, follow these steps:

1. Edit the ORATAB file to include the instance that you want to have restarted. Something approximating the following line should be included:

   ```
   PROD:/prodoracle/oracle/database/9.2.0:Y
   ```

   The translation of this is <SID>:<ORACLE_HOME>:<Y/N>, where Y states that the database SID in question can be started and stopped using DBSTART and DBSHUT.

2. While logged in as root, create the dbora service script in the init.d directory on Unix or Linux, as follows:

   ```
   case "$1" in
     'start')
       # Start the Oracle databases
       su - $ORA_OWNER -c $ORACLE_HOME/bin/dbstart
       # Start the TNS Listener
       su - $ORA_OWNER -c "$ORACLE_HOME/bin/lsnrctl start"
       touch /var/lock/subsys/dbora
     ;;
     'stop')
       # Stop the TNS Listener
       su - $ORA_OWNER -c "$ORACLE_HOME/bin/lsnrctl stop"
       # Stop the Oracle databases
   ```

```
su - $ORA_OWNER -c $ORACLE_HOME/bin/dbshut
rm -f /var/lock/subsys/dbora
;;
esac
```

The previous bash script (the dbora script contents) starts and stops the Oracle processes and assumes that you have set ORACLE_HOME and ORA_OWNER (the Unix owner of the binaries) for the given instance.

Now you can register the services and make sure that the symbolic links are created in the right rc directories (rc<runlevel>.d) so that it gets picked up when the server shuts down or is started.

3. Set the permissions for dbora using the following command:

```
$ chmod 755 dbora
```

4. Register the dbora service using the following command:

```
$ /sbin/chkconfig --add dbora
```

5. Make sure the symbolic links are created in the right rc directories (rc<runlevel>.d) so that the service gets picked up when the server shuts down or is started:

```
$ cd /ect/rc.d
$ ls -l */*dbora
  init.d/dbora
  rc0.d/K10dbora -> ../init.d/dbora
  rc1.d/K10dbora -> ../init.d/dbora
  rc2.d/K10dbora -> ../init.d/dbora
  rc3.d/S90dbora -> ../init.d/dbora
  rc4.d/K10dbora -> ../init.d/dbora
  rc5.d/K10dbora -> ../init.d/dbora
  rc6.d/K10dbora -> ../init.d/dbora
```

Once you have created the symbolic links, make sure if you try to follow the links that they work.

6. Edit the dbshut script so that you have the database shutdown immediate based on the environment variables and the entries in the /etc/oratab file:

```
$ cd $ORACLE_HOME/bin
$ vi dbshut
```

Change the shutdown command at the end of the script from simply
SHUTDOWN to SHUTDOWN IMMEDIATE.

7. Most importantly, test your script. To do this, log in as root, and start
   the Oracle database server:

```
$ cd /etc/init.d
$ ./dbora start
```

Then stop the Oracle database server:

```
$ ./dbora stop
```

Make sure that everything looks okay during this process.

Managing Users

It is amazing how much more efficient a database can be when you don't
have to put users into the mix. Of course, without users, the database would
also be nearly useless, but it would be very efficient.

Profiles

All database users have a profile; if you didn't deliberately assign them one
(either at user creation time, or later), they receive the profile named "default."
In the words of Rachel Carmichael, "Do not mess with the default profile,
for you will break things badly!" We'll see why that is so in a bit.

Think that profiles are too good to be true? Well, maybe a little. To use
profiles, there is some background setup work that needs to be done. You
need to set the RESOURCE_LIMIT initialization parameter to TRUE so that
profiles will work. You also have to decide what kind of profiles you want
(what distribution of resources you want to be able to enforce at the database
and server level, and the quantity that you will be able to maintain and still
stay within the constraints of your organization's hardware configuration). It
is important to note that ALTER SYSTEM SET RESOURCE_LIMIT=TRUE
only sets the parameter for the currently running database—once the database
is restarted, whatever initialization parameter is in force will take precedence.
If you are using a PFILE and can't restart the database, you can ALTER the
system to start using profiles, and you can then set the initialization parameter
to keep using them successfully.

Profiles are used to limit users' use of resources and to control password selection, expiration, reuse, and locking. Let's take a quick look at the `CREATE PROFILE` statement:

```
CREATE PROFILE <profile name> LIMIT
     SESSIONS_PER_USER           UNLIMITED or <number>
     CPU_PER_SESSION             UNLIMITED or <number>
     CPU_PER_CALL                <number>
     IDLE_TIME                   <number>
     CONNECT_TIME                <number>
     LOGICAL_READS_PER_SESSION   <number>
     LOGICAL_READS_PER_CALL      <number>
     PRIVATE_SGA                 <number>
     COMPOSITE_LIMIT             <number>
     FAILED_LOGIN_ATTEMPTS       <number>
     PASSWORD_LIFE_TIME          <number>
     PASSWORD_REUSE_TIME         <number>
     PASSWORD_REUSE_MAX          <number>
     PASSWORD_VERIFY_FUNCTION    <verify function>
     PASSWORD_LOCK_TIME          <number>
     PASSWORD_GRACE_TIME         <number>;
```

As you can see, there are a lot of parameters that you can customize for each type of user you create. Do you need to specify all of them every time? Well, no, not really. Not all of them every time, but what you don't specify in your `CREATE PROFILE` statement gets filled in from the default profile, so beware. Hence the words of Rachel Carmichael: "Do not mess with the default profile!" If you mess with it, you mess with a lot more than you are bargaining for.

The directives are basically divided into two groups:

- **Resource group**   These directives (from the first through COMPOSITE_LIMIT) deal with limiting the resources available to the user assigned the profile.

- **Password group**   These directives deal with password security and checking.

Why would you want to limit any of these things? Each profile can be custom tailored to make the given user set assigned to it more efficient in its use of hardware resources or more secure or both. Limiting resource usage by one group will make more resources available for other groups to use.

And setting high security standards will protect the contents and operation of your databases. So tailoring profiles to how a group does its work will improve things for each group.

Resource Group Directives

The first set of directives deals with the often-scarce resources on a system. Let's take a look at the resource group of parameters. These directives limit the amount of resources that a given user can take up.

- SESSIONS_PER_USER sets the number of concurrent sessions that the user is allowed to have open.

- CPU_PER_SESSION sets the CPU time limit for a session, expressed in hundredths of a second.

- CPU_PER_CALL sets the CPU time limit per call (parse, execute, fetch, or stored procedure call), expressed in hundredths of a second.

- IDLE_TIME sets the length of time the session is allowed to be idle, expressed in minutes.

- CONNECT_TIME sets the amount of elapsed time a session is allowed, expressed in minutes.

- LOGICAL_READS_PER_SESSION sets the permitted number of data block reads per session. This includes blocks read from memory or disk.

- LOGICAL_READS_PER_CALL sets the permitted number of data blocks read per call (parse, execute, fetch, or stored procedure call).

- PRIVATE_SGA specifies the amount of space a private session can allocate in the System Global Area (SGA), expressed in bytes.

- COMPOSITE_LIMIT sets the total amount of resources for a session, expressed in service units. Service units are calculated as a weighted sum of CPU_PER_SESSION, CONNECT_TIME, LOGICAL_READS_ PER_SESSION, and PRIVATE_SGA.

Password Group Parameters

The rest of the parameters deal with password checking and security. While it is apparently often attractive to use default passwords, or to allow users to set their own basic passwords, having a set policy, even if it isn't required by the organization, is a much better practice. You may have to (on occasion) reset user passwords, but you will have the assurance that there will be some rules in place so that anyone trying to break in to the database has a harder time. Even if everyone else thinks that you really should leave the APPS password set to "apps" so they don't have to think too much when they are programming, or when they are trying to run queries (or worse, updates) in E-Business Suite, changing and taking control of changes that are made in the E-Business Suite data through SQL*Plus is a good thing.

The following parameters allow you to take as fine-grained control of the password situation as you choose:

- FAILED_LOGIN_ATTEMPTS sets the number of failed login attempts permitted before the account is locked.

- PASSWORD_LIFE_TIME sets the number of days the same password can be used for authentication. If you also set PASSWORD_GRACE_TIME, the password expires at the end of the grace period, and further connections are refused. If PASSWORD_GRACE_TIME is not set then, the default of UNLIMITED is in effect, and the database will issue a warning but continue to allow logins.

- PASSWORD_REUSE_TIME and PASSWORD_REUSE_MAX must be set together. PASSWORD_REUSE_TIME sets the number of days before a password can be reused, and PASSWORD_REUSE_MAX sets the number of password changes that must occur before a password can be reused. For these to be effective, you must set both to an integer. If you set the value of one of these parameters to an integer, and then set the other parameter to UNLIMITED, a user can never reuse a password. If you set both to DEFAULT, the value gets filled in from the default profile, and since those are all set to UNLIMITED, the database ignores both of them.

NOTE
*In Oracle 8i, if you set PASSWORD_REUSE_
TIME or PASSWORD_REUSE_MAX to
UNLIMITED, the user could reuse the password
whenever they chose to do so. In Oracle 9i, the
intended use is the behavior that is in place.
This behavior was "fixed," so that setting
PASSWORD_REUSE_TIME or PASSWORD_
REUSE_MAX to UNLIMITED means that you
can never reuse the password again. While this
fixed the behavior of these directives to what
they intended it to be originally, this change
likely means that some applications using
profiles with these parameters set may start
behaving differently after upgrading to Oracle
9i. Want more information? Sure you do, and
you can get that information as well as tests and
examples in Metalink note 228991.1.*

- PASSWORD_LOCK_TIME sets the number of days that the account will be locked after the number of failed login attempts. This can be set to something like 1/24 to lock the account for an hour.

- PASSWORD_GRACE_TIME sets the number of days after the grace period begins in which the database issues a warning but still allows logins. If the password is not reset within that grace time, it expires and logins are refused.

- PASSWORD_VERIFY_FUNCTION is used to specify the password-complexity-verification function. Oracle provides one named VERIFY_FUNCTION. You specify the name of the function if you are using one, or null if a function is not used. Oracle provides guidelines for writing your own function in the *Oracle Database Security Guide* (http://www.oracle.com/pls/db102/show_toc).

If you decide to write your own password-verification function, it needs to adhere to some standards. It needs to take in the username, the new password, and the old password, and return a Boolean. An example of a simple function is given in Chapter 7 of the *Oracle Database Security Guide*. As usual in these situations, simple is better than complex, since complex functions can tie up system resources and take extra time. The nature of your testing will, most likely, be determined by the security policy at your company.

The CREATE USER Statement

You can create a user with the CREATE USER statement like this:

```
CREATE USER username IDENTIFIED BY password;
```

But this is only the basics of user creation. You know all of the details: you can only use legal special characters in passwords, you should always use profiles and roles (discussed in the next section), and you should never grant privileges that aren't required just because it is convenient. But what does all of this really mean, practically speaking?

Most DBAs use the default profile, because it is easier and requires less thought and trouble. But this does not mean that this is the right decision. Considering security when you create user accounts can mean the difference between having a hacked database and having one that only legitimate users can access. Unauthorized users tend to try sets of common passwords to gain access to the database. Even now that Oracle tries to make it more difficult to use the defaults, DBAs can still choose to shoot themselves in the foot. I have seen "very secure" databases created deliberately with old default passwords because they were the passwords that were easiest to remember.

Setting a profile like this, using unusual passwords that are difficult to guess will go a long way toward securing your environment:

```
CREATE PROFILE secure_profile LIMIT
    FAILED_LOGIN_ATTEMPTS 3
    PASSWORD_LOCK_TIME 1;
```

Coupling unusual (strong) passwords and making those passwords difficult to guess will go a long way to helping you to secure your environment. Assign this profile to all your users, and their accounts will be locked after three failed login attempts, and they will remain locked for a day afterwards or until intervention by the DBA. In this way, you can keep an eye on those accounts that may be ripe for hacking and determine what steps to take to make sure the system is more secure than before.

Working with Roles

Rolls? Oh, man … hot ones with melted butter all over them? Or maybe cinnamon ones that are sticky with sugar? OOOOOOHHHHHHHHH. Or the ones that the Grove City High School cafeteria ladies used to call sticky buns. Um … no. *Roles*, not rolls.

Roles are the means by which DBAs can assign different privileges *en masse* to a given user or, more often, set of users. Roles can be granted system privileges and object privileges, and they can be granted to other roles. Object privileges granted through roles do not work within procedures, functions, and packages unless your stored program units are created with invoker's rights. Those permissions must be granted explicitly to the user if the program units involved are written so that they leverage definer's rights instead of invoker's rights.

Think through what roles you really need and what privileges or sets of privileges the given user group definition likely needs. You can determine whether or not a given role really needs the added security of possibly requiring another password.

There are several predefined roles that most of us either know or have heard of. One is CONNECT, another is RESOURCE, and the most widely know is DBA. Recall again, you should never change the default behavior of the Oracle-supplied components—not the profiles, nor the roles. However, it is important to understand what is connected with the roles that Oracle provides, and when they are appropriate to use.

The DBA role is automatically created when you create your database. It is by virtue of this role and its associated privileges that you can log on to the database as a user other than SYS and administrate the database. Because this role has been granted most system-level privileges (and has them granted with admin option, so that anyone with the DBA role can grant the DBA role to anyone else), it is important that only administrators be granted this role. While it is important for some users to be granted the DBA role, and it is particularly useful to grant the DBA role to your development DBA or maybe your head developer in their own development instance, it is just as critical to keep a tight reign on who has this role.

The other two roles are slightly more dangerous to use, and quite honestly should never be used if you can help it. Oracle grants the CREATE SESSION, ALTER SESSION, CREATE SYNONYM, CREATE VIEW, CREATE TABLE, CREATE CLUSTER, CREATE DATABASE LINK, and CREATE SEQUENCE privileges to the CONNECT role. While many of these are handy privileges to have, you likely don't want everyone who logs in to your database to be able to create database links, tables, clusters, or sequences without your knowledge and complete understanding of who needs what, and why. The RESOURCE role has been granted UNLIMITED TABLESPACE, CREATE TABLE, CREATE CLUSTER, CREATE SEQUENCE, CREATE TRIGGER, CREATE PROCEDURE, CREATE TYPE, CREATE INDEXTYPE, and CREATE OPERATOR privileges. Again, many of these might be exactly what you want, but it really isn't difficult to create your own role that allows users exactly the privileges you want them to have while doing away with the ones that make you cringe.

Most users will never need to create anything other than a session, and maybe temporary tables if they are calling stored programs. The unlimited_ tablespace privilege is just wrong, fundamentally. While the APPS user in Oracle Financials might need that much power, the normal user will not, and APPS has DBA role, so RESOURCE even in this case is overkill. You are the DBA, and you should assist anyone in creating the objects they need. You, and only you, should be able to move those objects into production.

The following code will create the "ap clerk" role and grant it the appropriate privileges.

```
CREATE ROLE ap_clerk;
GRANT SELECT ON general_ledger TO ap_clerk;
GRANT INSERT ON ap_master TO ap_clerk;
GRANT UPDATE ON ap_master TO ap_clerk;
GRANT INSERT ON ap_detail TO ap_clerk;
GRANT UPDATE ON ap_detail TO ap_clerk;
CREATE ROLE ap_manager IDENTIFIED BY appwd;
GRANT ap_clerk TO ap_manager;
GRANT DELETE ON ap_master TO ap_manager;
GRANT DELETE ON ap_detail TO ap_manager;
GRANT SELECT any table TO ap_manager;
```

Control of Data Access

Roles give you control over what users can do; the next step is to keep users from getting to information they shouldn't have the privilege to see, and to prevent them from altering information that they should only be looking at. While it might be nice to be able to provide raises or promotions to whomever you think ought to have them, and to demote those who really don't deserve to be where they are, that level of data access should not be given to everyone.

Discretionary Access Control (DAC)

Discretionary Access Control isn't one of the really cool buzz words that people are throwing around. It kind of sounds a little familiar, but you can't quite put your finger on just what it is. Maybe one of the new 10*g* features that you haven't had a chance to look into yet? Or one of those extras that were there in 9*i* but you never got around to using. Nope.

DAC has been around nearly from Oracle's beginnings—it is the level of access that every user must pass when they access the database. You may know it better (at least conceptually) as role-based access control. User access is controlled through the granting of access privileges to objects in the database by using system and object privileges, and it is based on the premise that no user should have more access than they need in order to do their job adequately. It's the principle of *least privilege*.

Oracle gives you the tools to exercise a great deal of control over what users can do and see in the database, even in the standard version: data encryption, a robust set of privileges that can be mixed and matched to exactly meet the needs of any given user to access information in the database, and the ability to group privileges into roles and roles into other roles. There's no extra licensing necessary, and no additional cost. You can group object privileges with system privileges and allow everyone to view the data dictionary, if you like, while limiting them to selecting only information from certain tables and only updating a select few.

I have never had a problem with granting SELECT ANY DICTIONARY privilege to a role, and granting that role to every other role, or automatically to every user whenever they were created. I created a generic EVERYONE role and gave it the CREATE SESSION and SELECT ANY DICTIONARY privileges. Granting these privileges to PUBLIC would probably have been easier (no need to remember that I had to grant the role, no need to create the role, and no need to go back and clean up after myself when I forgot to grant that role to a user), but if I granted SELECT ANY DICTIONARY to PUBLIC, and someone unauthorized got access to the database by nefarious means, they would also be able to see the data dictionary, which could be dangerous.

Of course, you must sit down and plan what privileges each user, or at least each kind of user, needs. (And this isn't something that you can do on your own—you need to seek help from the security administration in your organization and the management of the departments to which the users belong.) No matter what you might think, it isn't easier in the long run to just grant DBA to all of your developers even in the development database.

It might seem like a good idea to some people to keep everyone from being able to see the data that is in the database. Some people might think that it is better for only those people in HR and Accounting and the developers, for example, to be able to see salary information for everyone in the organization (the developers so they can assure that their code is working correctly and the others for obvious reasons). However, it is counterproductive to hobble DBAs by not allowing them access to the data in the database. While it is possible to obfuscate the information in the database through encryption, there are times when encryption isn't practical or even possible. For example, the information storage characteristics for the Oracle 11*i* E-Business Suite are pretty much predefined, and altering those characteristics is frowned upon and unsupported in most cases. It isn't practical for anyone to suggest that the DBAs should be able to maintain the database but that they not actually be able to log in to the database to do their job, or that they not be allowed to see select columns in a set of tables. Often it is a DBA's job to help figure out if there is corruption and if the code that is being implemented is correct. Nondisclosure agreements are a better way of assuring that no one tells anyone what the CEO makes.

Fine-Grained Access Control

If you want to limit access to information to an even greater extent than the standard version of Oracle allows, you can invest in the Enterprise Edition and gain access to the even more robust security features included in Fine-Grained Access Control (FGAC). FGAC, or row-level security, allows you to control which exact rows a given user can access. FGAC automatically bases its security on the setting of an application role whenever a user logs in. FGAC dynamically and transparently modifies SQL statements by adding a condition (in the WHERE clause) that will restrict the rows returned to any given user.

To use FGAC, follow these steps:

1. Create the DBMS_RLS package as SYS:

```
cd $ORACLE_HOME/rdbms/admin
sqlplus /nolog
conn / as sysdba
@dbmsrlsa.sql
@prvtrlsa.plb
```

2. Grant the proper privileges to the users as the owner of the tables:

```
GRANT EXECUTE ON DBMS_RLS TO owner1;
GRANT CREATE CONTEXT TO owner1;
GRANT CREATE  TRIGGER TO owner1;
GRANT ADMINISTER DATABASE TRIGGER TO owner1;
```

3. Create the context:

```
CREATE CONTEXT mycontext USING opc_ctx;
```

4. Create the package to set up the context:

```
 # Create the package as SCOTT
CREATE OR REPLACE PACKAGE ocp_rls
AS
  PROCEDURE set_ctx;
END ocp_rls;
/
CREATE OR REPLACE PACKAGE BODY ocp_rls
AS
  PROCEDURE set_ctx
  AS
  BEGIN
 -- create the context and
 --    store the context variables
 -- create a dummy variable if

 -- you don't have any to store
   DBMS_SESSION.SET_CONTEXT('ocp_ctx','dummy','dummy');

END set_ctx;
END ocp_rls;
/ Create the logon trigger to set up the context when a user
logins
```

```
CREATE OR REPLACE TRIGGER fgac_security_trigger
AFTER LOGON ON DATABASE
call owner1.ocp_rls.set_ctx
/
```

5. Create the access-control package:

```
# This package will limit
# the user to access his own record
# in the EMP table
# Modify this package to fit your needs
CREATE OR REPLACE PACKAGE ocp_predicate
AS
   FUNCTION set_emp_predicate
           (obj_schema VARCHAR2,
            obj_name   VARCHAR2)
             RETURN VARCHAR2;
END ocp_predicate;
/
CREATE OR REPLACE PACKAGE BODY ocp_predicate
AS
   FUNCTION set_emp_predicate
           (obj_schema VARCHAR2,
            obj_name   VARCHAR2)
             RETURN VARCHAR2
   IS
     x_username  VARCHAR2(50);
     x_predicate VARCHAR2(2000);
   BEGIN
     -- you can also get the
     -- user-defined context variables here
     x_username := sys_context('USERENV', 'SESSION_USER');
     -- this is where the magic
     -- you can also use the 'ename IN ( ... )' format
     x_predicate := 'ename = ''' || x_username || '''';
     RETURN   x_predicate;
   END set_emp_predicate;
END ocp_predicate;
/
```

6. Add the access-control policy:

```
# Before adding the access control policy
# SCOTT can access all the EMP records
```

```
SQL> SELECT * FROM emp;
...
14 rows selected.
# Add the access control policy as a user
# with EXECUTE ON DBMS_RLS privilege
BEGIN
  DBMS_RLS.ADD_POLICY('<your given user>',
                'EMPLOYEE',
                'VPD_EMP_P1', -- Policy Name
                'USER1',
                'OCP_PREDICATE.SET_EMP_PREDICATE');
END;
/

# After adding the access control policy
# any given user can only access
# his or her own record in the EMP table
SQL> connect scott/tiger
SQL> SELECT * FROM emp;

   ...
1 row selected.
# Other users cannot access
# the record in the EMP records
SQL> conn system/manager;
SQL> SELECT * FROM scott.emp;
...
0 row selected.
```

Through this mechanism, it is possible to allow every user to have their own virtual private database (VPD) without having to go to the trouble of creating a new database every time a new user group is added. This can be particularly attractive in an application service provider (ASP) model environment, where many different users could potentially use the same database, but would need to know that there is no way that their data could be seen by any other user of the system.

While setting up and maintaining the FGAC or VPD can be time consuming, it can also be very useful in the long run. You can combine the row-level security of FGAC with public key/private key encryption to add another layer of security to the mix. By using different keys to encrypt the data that you are storing in the database, and by allowing users access to only their assigned public keys, you can assure almost anyone that their data is as secure as possible. Even if someone did find a way around the row-level security, the different keys used to encrypt the different pieces of data would mean that any compromise would be limited at best and any data retrieved would be unreadable.

But what do you do if something goes wrong and FGAC doesn't work? You have pretty effectively tied even your own hands at this point in many cases.

You can expect the following kinds of errors if FGAC is not quite configured correctly:

- **ORA-28110: policy function or package <function name> has error.** This error indicates that the package or function that the policy is bound to has an error and cannot be recompiled. If you issue show errors function <function name> or show errors package body <package name>, you will discover what the errors are. If you simply run SHO ERR after the package or function fails to compile, you will see the errors. Or, you can look at the ALL_ERRORS view later to see the errors.

- **ORA-28112: failed to execute policy function.** This error will typically occur if your predicate function encounters an error during execution. For example, this will happen if you have a SELECT INTO statement in the PL/SQL function that fails to find a row to select into the record, and the function has no exception handling built in.

- **ORA-28113: policy predicate has error.** This error typically occurs when the predicate function successfully returns values to a WHERE clause, but when the WHERE clause itself has an error when placed into the SQL query. This can happen if you return a WHERE clause such as :x = 5, and the table to which this WHERE clause is associated does not have a column named "x".

- **ORA-28106: input value for argument #2 is not valid.** You will receive this error from a call to dbms_session.set_context whenever the attribute name is not a valid Oracle identifier.

The following utility, suggested by Tom Kyte (of "Ask Tom" fame) for when you are writing and debugging predicate functions, is a simple debug package that was authored by Christopher Beck (also of Oracle). The package allows you to simply instrument your code with `print` and `put` statements.

```
create or replace package debug as
  type Argv is table of varchar2(4000);
  emptyDebugArgv Argv;
  procedure init(
    p_modules      in varchar2 default 'ALL',
    p_file         in varchar2
          default '/tmp/' || user || '.dbg',
    p_user         in varchar2 default user,
    p_show_date    in varchar2 default 'YES',
    p_date_format in varchar2
          default 'MMDDYYYY HH24MISS',
    p_name_len     in number   default 30,
    p_show_sesid  in varchar2 default 'NO' );
  procedure f(
    p_message in varchar2,
    p_arg1     in varchar2 default null,
    p_arg2     in varchar2 default null,
    p_arg3     in varchar2 default null,
    p_arg4     in varchar2 default null,
    p_arg5     in varchar2 default null,
    p_arg6     in varchar2 default null,
    p_arg7     in varchar2 default null,
    p_arg8     in varchar2 default null,
    p_arg9     in varchar2 default null,
    p_arg10    in varchar2 default null );
  procedure fa(
    p_message in varchar2,
    p_args     in Argv default emptyDebugArgv );
  procedure status(
    p_user in varchar2 default user,
    p_file in varchar2 default null );
  procedure clear(
    p_user in varchar2 default user,
    p_file in varchar2 default null );
end debug;
/
create or replace package body debug as
g_session_id varchar2(2000);
procedure who_called_me(
  o_owner  out varchar2,
  o_object out varchar2,
```

```
    o_lineno out number ) is
--
  l_call_stack long default
          dbms_utility.format_call_stack;
  l_line varchar2(4000);
begin
  for i in 1 .. 6 loop
    l_call_stack := substr( l_call_stack,
                 instr( l_call_stack, chr(10) )+1 );
  end loop;
  l_line := ltrim(substr( l_call_stack,
                   1,
                   instr(l_call_stack, chr(10)) - 1);
  l_line := ltrim( substr
                 ( l_line, instr( l_line, ' ' )));
  o_lineno := to_number(substr
                 (l_line, 1, instr(l_line, ' ')));
  l_line := ltrim(substr
                 (l_line, instr(l_line, ' ')));
  l_line := ltrim( substr
                 ( l_line, instr( l_line, ' ' )));
  if l_line like 'block%' or
     l_line like 'body%' then
     l_line := ltrim( substr
                 ( l_line, instr( l_line, ' ' )));
  end if;
  o_owner := ltrim( rtrim( substr( l_line,
                   1,
                   instr( l_line, '.' )-1 )));
  o_object  := ltrim( rtrim( substr( l_line,
                     instr( l_line, '.' )+1 )));
  if o_owner is null then
    o_owner := user;
    o_object := 'ANONYMOUS BLOCK';
  end if;
end who_called_me;
function build_it(
  p_debug_row in debugtab%rowtype,
  p_owner     in varchar2,
  p_object    in varchar2,
  p_lineno number ) return varchar2 is
--
  l_header long := null;
begin
  if p_debug_row. session_id = 'YES' then
```

```
      l_header := g_session_id || ' - ';
   end if;
   if p_debug_row.show_date = 'YES' then
      l_header := l_header ||
                   to_char( sysdate,
                   nvl( p_debug_row.date_format,
                   'MMDDYYYY HH24MISS' ) );
   end if;
   l_header :=
             l_header ||
             '(' ||
      lpad( substr( p_owner || '.' || p_object,
      greatest( 1, length
               ( p_owner || '.' || p_object ) -
      least( p_debug_row.name_length, 61 ) + 1 ) ),
      least( p_debug_row.name_length, 61 ) ) ||
      lpad( p_lineno, 5 ) ||
       ') ';
   return l_header;
end build_it;
function parse_it(
  p_message        in varchar2,
  p_argv           in argv,
  p_header_length in number ) return varchar2 is
--
  l_message long := null;
  l_str long := p_message;
  l_idx number := 1;
  l_ptr number := 1;
begin
   if nvl( instr( p_message, '%' ), 0 ) = 0 and
      nvl( instr( p_message, '\' ), 0 ) = 0 then
      return p_message;
   end if;
   loop
      l_ptr := instr( l_str, '%' );
      exit when l_ptr = 0 or l_ptr is null;
      l_message := l_message ||
          substr( l_str, 1, l_ptr-1 );
      l_str :=  substr( l_str, l_ptr+1 );
      if substr( l_str, 1, 1 ) = 's' then
        l_message := l_message || p_argv(l_idx);
        l_idx := l_idx + 1;
        l_str := substr( l_str, 2 );
      elsif substr( l_str,1,1 ) = '%' then
```

```
        l_message := l_message || '%';
        l_str := substr( l_str, 2 );
      else
        l_message := l_message || '%';
      end if;
   end loop;
   l_str := l_message || l_str;
   l_message := null;
   loop
     l_ptr := instr( l_str, '\' );
     exit when l_ptr = 0 or l_ptr is null;
     l_message := l_message
            || substr( l_str, 1, l_ptr-1 );
     l_str :=  substr( l_str, l_ptr+1 );
     if substr( l_str, 1, 1 ) = 'n' then
       l_message := l_message || chr(10) ||
       rpad( ' ', p_header_length, ' ' );
       l_str := substr( l_str, 2 );
     elsif substr( l_str, 1, 1 ) = 't' then
       l_message := l_message || chr(9);
       l_str := substr( l_str, 2 );
     elsif substr( l_str, 1, 1 ) = '\' then
       l_message := l_message || '\';
       l_str := substr( l_str, 2 );
     else
       l_message := l_message || '\';
     end if;
   end loop;
   return l_message || l_str;
end parse_it;
function file_it(
  p_file    in debugtab.filename%type,
  p_message in varchar2 ) return boolean is
--
  l_handle utl_file.file_type;
  l_file long;
  l_location long;
begin
  l_file := substr( p_file,
            instr( replace( p_file, '\', '/' ),
            '/', -1 )+1 );
  l_location := substr( p_file,
               1,
               instr( replace( p_file, '\', '/' ),
               '/', -1 )-1 );
```

```
    l_handle := utl_file.fopen(
                location => l_location,
                filename => l_file,
                open_mode => 'a',
                max_linesize => 32767 );
   utl_file.put( l_handle, '' );
   utl_file.put_line( l_handle, p_message );
   utl_file.fclose( l_handle );
   return true;
   exception
     when others then
       if utl_file.is_open( l_handle ) then
         utl_file.fclose( l_handle );
       end if;
   return false;
end file_it;
procedure debug_it(
  p_message in varchar2,
  p_argv    in argv ) is
--
  l_message long := null;
  l_header long := null;
  call_who_called_me boolean := true;
  l_owner varchar2(255);
  l_object varchar2(255);
  l_lineno number;
  l_dummy boolean;
begin
  for c in ( select *
               from debugtab
              where userid = user )
 loop
   if call_who_called_me then
    who_called_me( l_owner, l_object, l_lineno );
    call_who_called_me := false;
   end if;
   if instr( ',' || c.modules || ',',
               ',' || l_object || ',' ) <> 0 or
     c.modules = 'ALL'
   then
     l_header :=
         build_it( c, l_owner, l_object, l_lineno );
     l_message :=
         parse_it( p_message, p_argv, length(l_header) );
     l_dummy :=
```

```
            file_it( c.filename, l_header || l_message );
       end if;
     end loop;
  end debug_it;
  procedure init(
    p_modules      in varchar2 default 'ALL',
    p_file     in varchar2
         default '/tmp/' || user || '.dbg',
    p_user         in varchar2 default user,
    p_show_date    in varchar2 default 'YES',
    p_date_format in varchar2
           default 'MMDDYYYY HH24MISS',
    p_name_len     in number   default 30,
    p_show_sesid  in varchar2 default 'NO' ) is
  --
    pragma autonomous_transaction;
    debugtab_rec debugtab%rowtype;
    l_message long;
  begin
    delete from debugtab
      where userid = p_user
      and filename = p_file;
    insert into debugtab(
      userid, modules, filename, show_date,
      date_format, name_length, session_id )
    values (
      p_user, p_modules, p_file, p_show_date,
      p_date_format, p_name_len, p_show_sesid )
    returning
      userid, modules, filename, show_date,
      date_format, name_length, session_id
    into
      debugtab_rec.userid,
      debugtab_rec.modules,
      debugtab_rec.filename,
      debugtab_rec.show_date,
      debugtab_rec.date_format,
      debugtab_rec.name_length,
      debugtab_rec.session_id;
    l_message := chr(10) ||
       'Debug parameters initialized on ' ||
        to_char( sysdate, 'dd-MON-yyyy hh24:mi:ss' )
                          || chr(10);
    l_message := l_message || '            USER: ' ||
        debugtab_rec.userid || chr(10);
```

```
  l_message := l_message || '          MODULES: ' ||
      debugtab_rec.modules || chr(10);
  l_message := l_message || '         FILENAME: ' ||
      debugtab_rec.filename || chr(10);
  l_message := l_message || '        SHOW DATE: ' ||
      debugtab_rec.show_date || chr(10);
  l_message := l_message || '      DATE FORMAT: ' ||
      debugtab_rec.date_format || chr(10);
  l_message := l_message || '      NAME LENGTH: ' ||
      debugtab_rec.name_length || chr(10);
  l_message := l_message || 'SHOW SESSION ID: ' ||
      debugtab_rec.session_id || chr(10);
  if not file_it( debugtab_rec.filename, l_message )
  then
    rollback;
    raise_application_error(
        -20001,
        'Can not open file "' ||
        debugtab_rec.filename || '"' );
  end if;
  commit;
end init;
procedure f(
  p_message in varchar2,
  p_arg1    in varchar2 default null,
  p_arg2    in varchar2 default null,
  p_arg3    in varchar2 default null,
  p_arg4    in varchar2 default null,
  p_arg5    in varchar2 default null,
  p_arg6    in varchar2 default null,
  p_arg7    in varchar2 default null,
  p_arg8    in varchar2 default null,
  p_arg9    in varchar2 default null,
  p_arg10   in varchar2 default null ) is
begin
  -- return;
  debug_it( p_message,
          argv( substr( p_arg1, 1, 4000 ),
                substr( p_arg2, 1, 4000 ),
                substr( p_arg3, 1, 4000 ),
                substr( p_arg4, 1, 4000 ),
                substr( p_arg5, 1, 4000 ),
                substr( p_arg6, 1, 4000 ),
                substr( p_arg7, 1, 4000 ),
                substr( p_arg8, 1, 4000 ),
```

```
                    substr( p_arg9, 1, 4000 ),
                    substr( p_arg10, 1, 4000 ) ) );
end f;
procedure fa(
  p_message in varchar2,
  p_args    in Argv default emptyDebugArgv ) is
begin
  -- return;
  debug_it( p_message, p_args );
end fa;
procedure clear( p_user in varchar2 default user,
  p_file in varchar2 default null ) is
  pragma autonomous_transaction;
begin
  delete from debugtab where userid = p_user
          and filename = nvl( p_file, filename );
  commit;
end clear;
procedure status(
  p_user in varchar2 default user,
  p_file in varchar2 default null ) is
--
  l_found boolean := false;
begin
  dbms_output.put_line( chr(10) );
  dbms_output.put_line( 'Debug info for ' ||
                        p_user );
  for c in ( select *
             from debugtab
             where userid = p_user
             and nvl( p_file, filename ) = filename )
  loop
    dbms_output.put_line( '----------------' ||
             rpad( '-', length( p_user ), '-' ) );
    l_found := true;
    dbms_output.put_line( 'USER:            ' ||
             c.userid );
    dbms_output.put_line( 'MODULES:         ' ||
             c.modules );
    dbms_output.put_line( 'FILENAME:        ' ||
                          c.filename );
    dbms_output.put_line( 'SHOW DATE:       ' ||
                          c.show_date );
    dbms_output.put_line( 'DATE FORMAT:     ' ||
                          c.date_format );
```

```
      dbms_output.put_line ( 'NAME LENGTH:          ' ||
                             c.name_length );
      dbms_output.put_line ( 'SHOW SESSION ID:    ' ||
                             c.session_id );
      dbms_output.put_line ( ' ' );
   end loop;
   if not l_found then
      dbms_output.put_line ( 'No debug setup.' );
   end if;
end status;
begin
   g_session_id := userenv('SESSIONID');
end debug;
/
```

Calling the debug.f function (the code we just created) can be done from within another calling program unit, as follows:

```
create function foo . . .
as
    . . .
begin
    debug.f ( 'Enter procedure foo' );
    if ( some_condition ) then
        l_predicate := 'x=1';
    end if;
   debug.f ( 'Going to return the
        predicate "%s"', l_predicate );
    return l_predicate;
end;
```

Debug.f works very similarly to the 'C' printf function and in this example is implemented using UTL_FILE. This version creates a programmer-managed trace file on the database server containing all of your debug statements so that you can see exactly what is happening in your code.

Summary

And we have come to the end of the first chapter. We have created the database and set up some monitoring. We can start up and shut down the database, and we are protecting the users from the data and (more importantly) the data from the users.

We have nowhere now to go but up.

CHAPTER
2

Getting Things Done

I n Chapter 1 we looked at the basics of getting the database up and running—now we will look at how to get stuff done in the running database. Starting to feel better yet? More confident? Maybe even starting to feel like you can run faster than a locomotive and dodge speeding bullets? Nah, me neither. But we still have to see about getting stuff done.

Users generally want to be able to get information into and out of the database, and to make changes to what is already there Users are funny that way. Databases would run much smoother and more efficiently if it weren't for users muddying the waters. But then, the database wouldn't be much good either if users couldn't use it, so in this chapter, we will look at efficient and effective ways to safely allow users to manipulate and look at data while protecting the integrity of the data and the database.

We will start where the users start, with connecting to the database. Once connected, we will look at the building blocks of the code and how they are put together and get built. Finally, we will look at how to hide all the intricate code details from the inquisitive eyes of users who really shouldn't see the internal workings of the database or the program units that do the work that they take for granted, especially when the code really shouldn't be changed.

Database Connections

Before you can get anything done, you first have to connect to the database. Users really have no concept of how the interface to the database works. They only know, and honestly should only care, that when they click on an icon, the interface starts and works. We, on the other hand, need to, at least on some level, have an understanding of what happens (and to a degree how it happens) when a connection is made. There are many ways and tools that can be used to connect. SQL Navigator, Toad, SQL*Plus, or any number of other front ends that will allow you to construct queries can be used to get into the database. There are even tools that allow users to simply drag and drop components onto a pane and that construct the query in the background (BusinessObjects, Cognos, Discoverer).

Connection Basics

So, just what is a connection? A connection is simply a communication pathway between a user, or a user process, and an Oracle instance. The connection path starts being created when the user clicks the mouse button or presses the ENTER key at the end of a command-line command, and is completed when the database effectively says, "Oh, you want to talk to me? Great, I want to talk to you too. Let's chat." The pathway is established using Oracle's communication protocols (either interprocess communication or network communication mechanisms). Oracle Net Services is the set of pieces (historically known by *many* other names, such as Net8 and SQL*Net) that allows a network session to be established from a client machine or a client application to an Oracle database.

The term "session" is often used interchangeably with "connection." This is like the way people often use the terms "database" and "instance" interchangeably. But confusing the terms can lead to confusion and fundamental misunderstanding of the underlying concepts. Let's look at the vocabulary involved:

- **Connection**   A physical communication pathway between a user's client (whatever that client may be) and the Oracle instance.

- **Session**   A purely logical entity that exists within the database. It is associated with a specific user's connection and is typically what people are talking about when they say "database connection." You execute SQL statements in this session. Sessions last from the time a connection is created to the time the user disconnects or exits from the program. It is possible to have one connection associated with more than one session (particularly if you are doing something like using AUTOTRACE to trace SQL statements to see what your SQL is really doing).

- **Process**   Oracle jobs that perform specific tasks or functions. These can be either *user processes* that execute application or Oracle tool code, or Oracle *server or background processes.* User processes execute application code. Oracle processes run the Oracle server code. Server processes are Oracle processes that communicate with user processes and Oracle to carry out the user requests; background processes are Oracle processes that consolidate functions (such as I/O and monitoring) that would otherwise require each connection to have multiple dedicated Oracle programs running.

- **Database**   A construct that stores a collection of (usually related) data that is treated as a unit and is ready for retrieval and manipulation. In the case of Oracle, the database consists of the datafiles and supporting physical structures.

- **Instance**   The set of memory structures and processes that support the database, its access, and its inner workings. This includes virtual memory, the software code area, the System Global Area (SGA), the Program Global Area (PGA), and sort areas:

  - **Virtual memory**   Not available on all operating systems, but, where it is available, it allows the database to access more memory than is physically available on the system. Oracle recommends keeping the SGA sized so that it fits completely within main memory, but the ability to use extended memory is sometimes handy.

  - **Software code area**   A protected area of memory that stores the code of the Oracle database. This is a separate and more protected area of memory than where the user's code is running. This area, located physically on disk, is static in size and changes only when you install new software or when you update existing software. Many different instances can use the same software code area. (This is the $ORACLE_HOME or %ORACLE_HOME% area.)

  - **System Global Area (SGA)**   A group of memory structures that, taken together, contain the data and control information necessary to maintain one Oracle instance:

    - **Database buffer cache**   This is where the copies of data blocks that have been read from datafiles are held. All connected users share the database buffer cache.

    - **Redo log buffers**   These are the circular buffers holding information on changes made to the database. Entries in the redo log buffers (called *redo log entries*) are necessary for the database to reconstruct changes made to the data or the structures holding the data if database recovery is necessary.

    - **Shared pool**   The shared pool consists of the library cache, the dictionary cache, and control structures:

- **Library cache** This has a shared SQL area and a private SQL area. The *shared SQL area* is a memory area that contains the parse tree and execution plan for a single SQL statement. Whenever more than one user is executing the same SQL statement, the shared code (SQL, PL/SQL, triggers) is stored here once. The *private SQL area* contains data such as bind information and runtime buffers. Each session that issues any SQL statement uses its own private SQL area to store values for bind variables. Many private SQL areas can be associated with the same piece of code in a single shared SQL area. It is just the values associated with the code that are stored in the private SQL area.

- **Dictionary cache** This is a collection of database tables and views containing reference information about the database, its structures, and its users. This is where the information comes from for the volatile V$ views that give you real-time information about the structures and users of the currently running instance and database.

- **Control structures** There are many control structures in the SGA. Some support interprocess communication, locking information, character-set conversion, and network security attributes, among other functions.

- **Program Global Area (PGA)** An area allocated by Oracle when a user process connects to an Oracle database and a session is created. It contains a stack area, in which memory is allocated to hold a session's variables, arrays, and other information necessary to support the connection's processing.

- **Sort areas** Portions of memory in which Oracle sorts data, provided that the area is sufficient to hold all of the data being sorted. If the sorted data does not fit into the SGA, it will be sorted on disk. If you use automatic memory management with either Oracle 9*i* or 10*g*, this area is also known as the *work area*, and there are sort areas, hash areas, and bitmap areas dedicated for manual memory management.

Multiple sessions can coexist concurrently for any single Oracle username (this is the way that Oracle E-Business Suite works, for example). Oracle is robust. It isn't a little single-user database running on somebody's PC. A single Oracle instance can be the background to countless applications, and each application can be the interface for numerous simultaneous users. This is handy to remember when you are trying to troubleshoot database problems, or when you are trying to tune queries. None of the processes exists in a vacuum. The entire environment plays a part, and other users have processes going on at the same time. Everything can impact everything else. You pretty much have to trace a session to know what that session is doing. But doing so doesn't necessarily give you the full picture.

Connecting as a User

Users don't connect the same way that DBAs (who connect as SYS or SYSTEM or AS SYSDBA) do, all the time. The powers that be decided a long time ago that it would probably be safer if the end users and programmers were kept somewhat separated from the internals of the database—the data dictionary and the program units that make up the standard processes of the database. In their early wisdom, they were right.

Let's start with the simple and work towards the more complex. We'll start off looking at how "normal" users log into the database, since most of us probably started out that way anyway. Getting us back to our roots may be the best way to start, so we all have the same foundation on which to build. I'll bet you remember logging in to your databases early on as Scott/Tiger, don't you? You may not remember much about your early days working with the Oracle database (I know I certainly don't), but Scott/Tiger is infamous. It stays with us through all of our classes, all of our books, all of our fond and not so fond memories.

Connecting Normally

Normally, all of the connectivity pieces are in place when you or your users log in to the database; all you have to do is log in and the magic happens. When you log on as a user, you don't usually need an in-depth understanding about how the connection happens, or what pieces are involved in the connection. You just sit down at the terminal (the PC, console, etc.) and connect:

```
Connect awells/mypass@mytnsentry
```

Even if you are logging in through a tool or an application, the back end of the tool is still sending this kind of login string to the database to connect.

It is important to note that you don't connect @the_database_sid—you connect with the TNSNAMES.ORA entry associated with that SID (or one of them—there are many situations where a TNSNAMES.ORA file will have multiple TNS entries associated with each SID because different users and different tools have different conventions for each SID).

Connecting Without a Password

You can log in quite easily if you know the password, but what if you need to log in to one of the schemas on the database, but you don't know the password? Developers hide hard-coded passwords in some pretty weird places, so if you simply change the password, the applications may break. Yes, we all know that hard-coding passwords in applications isn't good form and it breaks all of the security rules, but in all reality, there are times when this does happen. The password is kept in configuration files that the developers maintain in protected directories and update when the passwords change on their schedule. Or it is kept in a special file that is read into the program when it is time to allow that program to log in to the database, so it is external to the code, but still hard-coded into a file. Anyone who works with Oracle E-Business Suite can probably cite many examples of where different passwords are kept. Changing a password in these situations without knowing for sure what the password was to begin with can cause issues that are difficult at best to resolve.

The following script will allow you to alter the password temporarily, saving the original password, and when you are done, you can change the password back:

```
set head off
Set echo off
Set pagesize 0
spool restore_password.sql
SELECT 'alter user ' || username
||' identified by values '''
|| password || ''';'
FROM dba_users
WHERE username = 'your_user';
SPOOL OFF
ALTER USER your_user IDENTIFIED BY your_new_password;
```

Yes, it is a bit chancy to use that particular procedure. If everything goes well, it will work fine, but there are several opportunities for errors, and there is always the possibility that you may lose the password and be unable to reset it to what it was before. A better method that many DBAs use is as follows:

```
WHENEVER SQLERROR EXIT
column password new_value pw
DECLARE
    l_passwd varchar2(45);
BEGIN
    SELECT password INTO l_passwd
      FROM sys.dba_users
     WHERE username = upper('&1');
END;
/
SELECT  password
  FROM  sys.dba_users
 WHERE  username = UPPER ( '&1' )
/
ALTER  user &1  IDENTIFIED BY Hello;
CONNECT  &1/hello
ALTER  user &1 IDENTIFIED BY VALUES '&pw';
SHOW  user
WHENEVER SQLERROR CONTINUE
```

This script starts out by testing your access to the sys.dba_users table (which means you must have access to that table for the script to work, but you really should be doing this with full DBA privileges anyway; you have to have the ALTER USER privilege too, but since you will be logging in as a privileged user, that won't be an issue). If the test fails, you get kicked out of SQL*Plus. If you pass the all-important test, the script selects the user's password from the dba_users table and stores it in the &pw variable. Once the value is safely stored, the script alters the target user's password. If that fails, the script exits.

After you have logged in to the other user's schema, you can fix the password, replacing it with the original value. Run the command that was output into the spool file to set it back.

NOTE
If you have set profile limits on password reuse,
the preceding script will not work.

Connecting Without a TNSNAMES.ORA File

You know you can connect to the database if all the pieces are in place. But what happens if there isn't a TNSNAMES.ORA file available to your computer? For example, suppose you are trying to log in to a remote computer for which you have a userid, but that you don't seem to have a TNSNAMES.ORA entry for? Can't be done, you say? Not so. While it requires significantly more typing, you can still log in to the database with the following syntax:

```
sqlplus
   your_id/password@//myhostmachine.mydomain:listeningport/MYSID
```

An alternative to the preceding command is as follows:

```
sqlplus id/password@(myhostmachine.mydomain:listeningport/MYSID)
```

Of course, you can always create a TNSNAMES.ORA file or set the TNS_ADMIN environment variable to point to your own file located somewhere else on the system.

This command, in effect, tells the database that you're connecting, and exactly where you are connecting to. The connection string ends up being the same as it would have been had the information come from the TNSNAMES.ORA file. The host, domain, and port, along with the SID of the instance that you are trying to connect to, are all in place, and you can make use of them.

This method also works if you think everything is okay with your database and client software, but you still find that a user is not able to connect. If this command allows you to connect, then something is likely wrong with the copy of the TNSNAMES.ORA file, and not the database.

Keep in mind, though, that if you can connect this way, so can other people. This makes it all the more obvious that you need to ensure the security of your database to protect it from unwanted intrusion.

Connecting as SYSDBA or SYSOPER

There are things that just anyone can't be allowed to do. For example, it would be bad practice to allow just anyone to start up and shut down the database or to change database-wide or system-wide parameters. That means we need another way to connect to the database. These functions are only permitted if you have the Administrator privilege (better known as SYSDBA). When you need to see things inside the database at a deeper level, with a broader range of details, you can log in as SYS or as SYSDBA. Also, there are times that you might want some people (such as those on the operations team) to have a little higher privileges than regular users but not as high as a DBA. For that purpose, Oracle provides SYSOPER.

The SYSOPER role allows some database administrators to successfully issue the following commands: STARTUP, SHUTDOWN, ALTER DATABASE OPEN or MOUNT, ALTER DATABASE BACKUP, ALTER DATABASE END BACKUP, ARCHIVE LOG, and RECOVER. SYSOPER also includes the RESTRICTED SESSION privilege that allows the user to start the database in restricted-session mode. As SYSOPER, however, you cannot go around granting the same privilege to other people. It does not have the WITH ADMIN option.

SYSDBA, on the other hand, contains all of the system privileges, and has also been given the WITH ADMIN option as well as the ability to perform time-based recovery, and also to create the database in the first place. SYSDBA contains the SYSOPER system privilege (isn't it great how roles work to help make your life easier?).

There are two different ways to authenticate a user to log on with these privileges. The one that DBAs and SYSADMINs alike prefer is the operating system authentication. The other, which requires a little extra work, is password-file authentication.

Using Operating System Authentication

If you are administering a local database and you want the operating system to be responsible for authentication, or you are administering a remote database and you have a secure connection, you could opt for operating system (OS) authentication. When you allow the OS to be responsible for authentication, you tell it that a particular user (lwells, for example) is a member of a particular group (the DBA group, for example), and that that group has the right to administer the database. In this example, when lwells logs in to the network with the correct password, the authentication is done, and he or she can simply launch SQL*Plus or another tool of choice and connect / as sysdba.

This method of authentication is usually chosen in smaller shops where a limited number of administrators have access to the database. The control that you have over the level of connectivity, and your ability to audit who is doing what, is coarser with OS authentication.

Using Password-File Authentication

If you want finer control over who is doing what, or you want the ability to see who has done what later, or you do not have a secure connection, you will likely want to have your administration accounts authenticated by a password file.

Creating a Password File   Keep in mind that the password file is used to maintain information about database administrators for the purpose of allowing them to manage databases remotely or for the purpose of allowing SYSOPERs as well as SYSDBA users to start up and shut down the database. The only users whose authentication will be managed using the password file will be those to whom the role of SYSOPER or SYSDBA has been assigned.

You can create the password file for your instance using Oracle's password-file creation utility (ORAPWD). When you install your database on certain operating systems, the creation of the password file is automatic.

The required parameters for ORAPWD are file (mandatory), password (mandatory), and entries (optional). Here is the command syntax (with no spaces around the equal signs):

```
orapwd file=<password file name>
password=<password for SYS>
entries=<number of distinct entries to be stored in the file>
```

Here is an actual working example:

```
Orapwd file=mysid.pwd password=change_on_install entries=100
```

NOTE
When you invoke ORAPWD, if you do not supply the necessary parameters, you will receive the help messages that explain the proper use of the command.

This command will create a password file (the mysid.pwd file), which can contain a maximum of 100 distinct entries, and the default SYS password will be change_on_install. If you are running Real Application Clusters (RACs), the environment variable on each server should point to one single password file. The contents of this file are encrypted so they cannot be read from an operating system or through a text editor. The name allowed, location, and format for the password file are typically dependent on the operating system. This operating system dependence can mean that you have to follow certain naming conventions, or that the operating system takes the naming out of your hands completely and names it per its Oracle conventions.

NOTE
It is critical that you protect the password file and that you obscure the environment variables that point to the location of the password file. While the contents of the file are not readable through a text editor, a user with nefarious intentions could use the file and the variables to compromise the security of the database.

The `password` parameter in the `orapwd` command sets the password for user SYS. It is, of course, still possible for the user SYS to log in to the database as SYSDBA locally, even if the password file gets lost or damaged. But if the password file is lost or damaged, it will be impossible for anyone who is SYSDBA to log in remotely.

The `entries` parameter specifies the number of entries that you need the password file to accept. This will be the maximum number of distinct users allowed to connect to the database as either SYSOPER or SYSDBA. The actual number of allowed entries can be higher than the number of users specified as either SYSOPER or SYSDBA, because Oracle will continue to add users to the password file until it fills the last operating system block (each entry takes up 128 bytes). This means that if you have an OS that uses 512 bytes per block, every block in the file will hold four password entries, so the number of entries allocated will always be a multiple of four—if you set up the file to hold 97 entries, it will in reality hold 100.

Oracle suggests that you can reuse the space taken up in the password file as users are deleted from the SYSDBA or SYSOPER role.

If you are going to set REMOTE_LOGON_PASSWORDFILE to EXCLUSIVE and you will be granting users the SYSDBA and SYSOPER privilege, the `entries` parameter is also required.

Once the password file has been created, connecting to the database and issuing the `ALTER USER` statement to change the password for SYS will change both the password stored in the data dictionary and the password in the password file.

Maintaining a Password File   Now that you have created the password file and started adding users to it, you will need to start to learn how to maintain the file. You may find that you start to get errors because you are trying to add more users than you initially specified in the `entries` parameter. The database will give you an ORA-01996 error when you try next to grant SYSOPER or SYSDBA to a user. To solve this problem, you need to re-create the password file, larger this time, re-grant privileges to the existing users, and then add the new users. This means that you will need to know who has been granted SYSOPER and SYSDBA at the time the password file ran out of space and re-grant these privileges to these users again once the new file is in place.

You may also find that you need to replace or remove the password file, or change the file's state. The following sections will help you with these maintenance tasks.

Replacing a Password File   Okay, so we know how to fix the ORA-01996 error, but how do we get rid of the old password file before we create the new one without breaking anything? Before you replace a password file, you need to find out what users are already in the password file. Check the V$PWFILE_USERS view and make a list of these people to make sure that you put all the right people back in the new file.

Once you've done that, shut down the database and delete the old password file, or better yet, rename it to something innocuous so that you can get it back if you have to. Then create a new password file the same way that you created the original password file, but this time make sure that the setting for the `entries` parameter is significantly larger than the previous time. Count the number of people on your list, and add a margin of error (10 percent, 25 percent, or add a hundred or a thousand users so you know that you won't run out of space).

Once you've created the new file, add the existing users to the file again, and then start adding the new ones.

NOTE
I would never suggest that you have a thousand people with SYSDBA privileges in any database. However, the number of users who actually end up in the password file is usually more an organizational decision than a technological one. Having sufficient space in the password file to guarantee that you can add anyone else who comes into the company and needs to be added will make your maintenance simpler.

Removing a Password File   If, for some reason, you decide that you no longer require a password file to authenticate users, you can reset the REMOTE_LOGIN_PASSWORDFILE initialization parameter to NONE, and then you can delete the password file.

NOTE
Never remove or modify (other than to modify the file with the GRANT SYSDBA or GRANT SYSOPER or REVOKE the same privileges to or from users) the password file while the database is mounted or open and the REMOTE_LOGIN_ PASSWORDFILE parameter is set to either EXCLUSIVE or SHARED. If you do, you will no longer be able to connect using the password file authentication method because the timestamp and checksums will be wrong.

Changing the Password File State   The password file's state is stored within the file itself. When you first created the password file, its default state was SHARED. You can change this state by setting the REMOTE_LOGIN_PASSWORDFILE initialization parameter to something else.

What else might you want it to be and why, you ask? Good question, glad you brought it up. There are several states that the initialization parameter can be set to, and each of these states means something entirely different to the database. The default state is NONE. When REMOTE_LOGIN_PASSWORDFILE is set to none, Oracle will simply ignore any password files that might exist, and all authentications are taken from the operating system for those who are trying to log in as SYSOPER or SYSDBA.

If you set the value of the REMOTE_LOGIN_PASSWORDFILE to SHARED you intend for more than one database to use the same password file for its authentication. Think that sounds real handy? Just wait before you rush out and make that change on your systems. The only user that is recognized by the password file in the case of SHARED as the value is SYS, so if you have other people logging in as SYSDBA or SYSOPER on your various databases, you may be causing yourself issues if you take this route.

EXCLUSIVE is what we have been dealing with here. EXCLUSIVE means that the password file can only be used by one database but it also means that other users (other than just SYS) can be contained in the file. If you are working with RAC, then you have to set the REMOTE_LOGIN_PASSWORDFILE to EXCLUSIVE and you have to create a password file on each node that is running an instance.

Oracle retrieves the value of this parameter from the parameter file on your database server when you start the instance. When you mount the database, Oracle compares the value of this parameter to the value stored in the password file. If the values do not match, Oracle overwrites the value stored in the file.

CAUTION
*Make sure that the password file parameter REMOTE_
LOGIN_PASSWORDFILE is not changed accidentally
(or deliberately without the person doing the changing
having an understanding of what they are doing) from
EXCLUSIVE to SHARED. If you want to allow the
instance to start up from any of several servers, each of
those servers has to have the initialization parameter file
with the REMOTE_LOGIN_PASSWORDFILE parameter
set to the same value. If you do not ensure that every
computer's initialization file has the same value, you
may find that your use of the password file is dependent
directly on the server from which you started the instance.*

Making the Connection

Administrative users can connect and be authenticated to either a local or
remote database by using the SQL*Plus CONNECT command, using the
password files of that database. Users connected in this way must connect
using their username and password (as usual), but they also have to add the
AS SYSDBA or AS SYSOPER clause, depending on which privilege they
have been granted and which authorization they want to connect with. For
example, user awells may have been granted the SYSDBA privilege, so she
can connect as follows:

```
CONNECT awells/mypass AS SYSDBA
```

However, since she has not been granted the SYSOPER privilege, the following
command will fail, even though SYSDBA is a superset of SYSOPER privileges:

```
CONNECT awells/mypass AS SYSOPER
```

It is important to note that OS authentication takes precedence over
password-file authentication. This means that a user who is a member of the
DBA group on the operating system can still connect AS SYSDBA, even if
they have not been granted SYSDBA privileges in the database, simply by
issuing the following command:

```
Sqlplus '/ as sysdba'
```

Connecting with a Script

Suppose you need to have someone connect from the operating system in a shell script, but you don't necessarily want the users to know the passwords that they are using. You can create the connection strings in a shell script that is executable but not readable. The following script will connect to the database and run as much embedded SQL within the script as you need:

```
#!/bin/sh
sqlplus -s /nolog << EOF
    CONNECT scott/tiger
# insert SQL commands here to get what you need
# from the database...
    EXIT;
EOF
```

Note that the userid and password are in plain text in this file. While this will allow you to connect to the database without this information showing up when you run `ps -ef` on a Unix or Linux system, it still puts the password in a location that is easily read if anyone has access to the script at the file system level. While you have to have some level of trust in your system administrators and database administrators, it is very important that the script be set so that only the proper people can see this information. If this is a script that anyone can run, set the file to be executable by everyone, but readable and writeable only by the owner. This will allow you the tightest security, and everyone who needs to get that information can either find someone who knows how to become the owner, or can justify finding out. It is better, in every case, to err on the side of caution.

Disconnecting Users

So your users have connected, and stayed connected for weeks on end. It is likely that those users who log in to the system and never log out are simply leaving their sessions open and locking their computer when they leave. You know what I mean: CTRL-ALT-DELETE and then lock computer from the Windows Security screen. That way they don't have to close all of the open programs and lose time the next morning re-launching the applications. And they don't have to remember where they were in their process—they can just pick up where they left off. Or maybe they even have a SQL statement running, one that is now running away and eating up resources and not necessarily doing what they thought it would be doing. Not that this happens in every shop, but I have had the privilege of having to track down a runaway statement in the database, then track down the user who submitted it only to find out that the user had locked the computer on Friday and went on a week's vacation out of the country. As you may, or may not, be aware, there is a handy little V$ view called V$SESSION. This view allows you to peek into the database and see just who is poking around in there. It is also handy when you need to turn on tracing for a given session, and for determining just how long someone has been in the database.

The STATUS column in V$SESSION will tell you whether a user is doing things that are consuming database resources. If its value is ACTIVE for a given user, you can assume that the user is doing something (running SQL, a procedure, or a package).

A lesser known, and ever less documented, column in the view is the LAST_CALL_ET column. The documentation simply says that the column tells you the last call, and that the type is number. A more accurate description for the column might well be the number of seconds that have passed since the issuance of the last call. Therefore, if you want to see just how idle the idle session is, and which program isn't out there doing anything, you can look at the output from this query:

```
SET VERIFY OFF
SELECT sid||','|| serial# session_num,
       USERNAME,
       LAST_CALL_ET seconds_idle,
       status,
       sql_address,
       program
FROM v$session
WHERE status != 'ACTIVE';
```

Once you have the results from this query, you can make an informed decision about whether or not to kill particular processes and on what basis to kill them (for example, processes that have been idle for more than a day). You can kill them with a command like this:

```
ALTER SYSTEM kill session 'sid,serial#';
```

Auditing Database Connections

There are times when you will need to track when users log in to and out of the database. There are many reasons that you will want to do this—often to determine from when and where someone is connecting, who is connecting, and what program they are running. Simply turning auditing on will not really accomplish this. However, creating an auditing table that you populate and maintain with logon and logoff triggers will allow you to capture the information needed.

You will want to protect the table from prying eyes and from data manipulation, since those you are seeking to audit might prefer to modify this data. For this reason you will want to create the table in a protected area where no one but those who are trusted can access the data, and where no one can alter that information, other than the trigger, without your knowledge. Here's how to create the table:

```
CONNECT control/control_pwd;
/**/
CREATE TABLE user_connections
(user_id          varchar2(32),
 session_id       number(8),
 host             varchar2(32),
 last_program     varchar2(48),
 last_action      varchar2(32),
 last_module      varchar2(32),
 connection_id    varchar2(32),
 logon_day        date,
 logon_time       varchar2(10),
 logoff_day       date,
 logoff_time      varchar2(10),
 elapsed_minutes  number(8)
);
```

Once you have the table created, you can create the system-level logon trigger. This trigger will fill in the information that is available at logon time. While there will be a delay added to the time it takes each session to connect, the delay will be nearly unnoticeable to the end user, and the information gathered will prove invaluable. Here's how you create the trigger:

```
CREATE or REPLACE TRIGGER
     user_connect_audit_trigger
AFTER LOGON ON DATABASE
```

```
v_ipaddr varchar2(20);
v_host varchar2(20);
BEGIN
SELECT SYS_CONTEXT('userenv', 'ip_address')
     INTO v_ipaddr FROM SYS;
SELECT SYS_CONTEXT ('userenv', 'host')
     INTO v_host FROM DUAL;
INSERT INTO user_connections VALUES(
   user,
  SYS_CONTEXT('USERENV','SESSIONID'),
   v_host,
   null,
   null,
   null,
   v_ipaddr,
   SYSDATE,
   TO_CHAR(SYSDATE, 'hh24:mi:ss'),
   null,
   null,
   null
);
COMMIT;
END;
/
```

Now let's look at the information that you will want to collect at logoff time using a `before logoff` trigger. We will update the user_connections table to include the very last actions performed by the given user. This can be accomplished using SYS's context function to go after the information in the V$SESSION view. Here's how to create the trigger:

```
CREATE or REPLACE TRIGGER user_disconnect_audit_trigger
BEFORE LOGOFF ON DATABASE
BEGIN
/***************************************************
* Update the table with the last action accessed
***************************************************/
UPDATE user_connections
SET last_action = (SELECT action FROM V$SESSION
WHERE SYS_CONTEXT('USERENV','SESSIONID') = AUDSID)
WHERE SYS_CONTEXT ('USERENV','SESSIONID') = SESSION_ID;
/***************************************************
* Update the table with the last program accessed
***************************************************/
```

```
UPDATE user_connections
SET last_program = (SELECT program FROM V$SESSION
WHERE SYS_CONTEXT ('USERENV','SESSIONID') = AUSID)
WHERE SYS_CONTEXT ('USERENV','SESSIONID') = SESSION_ID;
/*****************************************************
* Update the table with the last module accessed
*****************************************************/
UPDATE user_connections
SET last_module = (SELECT module FROM V$SESSION
WHERE SYS_CONTEXT('USERENV','SESSIONID') = AUDSID)
WHERE SYS_CONTEXT('USERENV','SESSIONID') = SESSION_ID;
/*****************************************************
* Update the table with the logoff day
*****************************************************/
UPDATE user_connections
SET logoff_day = SYSDATE
WHERE sys_context('USERENV','SESSIONID') = SESSION_ID;
/*****************************************************
* Update the table with the session's logoff time
*****************************************************/
UPDATE user_connections
SET logoff_time = TO_CHAR(SYSDATE, 'hh24:mi:ss')
WHERE SYS_CONTEXT('USERENV','SESSIONID') = SESSION_ID;
/*****************************************************
* Compute the elapsed minutes and update the table with this.
* While this is something that can be computed later,
* on select from the table,
* we can save time and processing doing it now.
*****************************************************/
UPDATE user_connections
SET elapsed_minutes = ROUND((logoff_day - logon_day)*1440)
WHERE SYS_CONTEXT('USERENV','SESSIONID') = SESSION_ID;
COMMIT;
END;
/
```

So what can we learn from this auditing table?

- How long each user was logged on each day

- How long the database was logged in to in total in a day (indicating just how much the database is used)

- What IP addresses are in use to access the database

- What hosts and IP addresses go together (not always very useful, but we can also see if some spoofing might be going on)

- What programs are being run (or at least the last program that was run by each user who logged in)

With a little alteration, we could also gather information on how long (roughly) each program was running.

Using Oracle's Auditing Feature

If you find the previous type of auditing a little convoluted, Oracle does provide a handy little auditing feature that logs information based on criteria that you can customize. Enabling database auditing is as simple as setting the AUDIT_TRAIL initialization parameter. The parameter should be set to OS so that you can make use of the operating system's file system to store the audit information. Alternatively, you can set the parameter to DB and store the auditing information in the SYS.AUD$ table.

NOTE
Many people have suggested that if you use the DB option, you should move the SYS.AUD$ table out of the system tablespace so that you don't fragment the tablespace or overtax it with the additional overhead. It is very important to note that this is not supported and can lead to severe issues that may occur whenever you upgrade, or during backup and recovery.

In order to set up auditing by using the AUDIT statement, you need to be logged in to the database as a user that has been granted the ALTER SYSTEM privilege. Further, you not only need to have this privilege, you have to either own the object on which you are attempting to enable auditing, or you need to have been granted the AUDIT ANY privilege. This implies that you must be logged in as someone who has been granted the DBA role.

If you have AUDIT_TRAIL=OS set, you can elegantly separate responsibilities and add an additional layer of security and auditing by setting the AUDIT_FILE_DEST initialization paramter to an OS location to which the database administrators do not have access, but to which Oracle can write (but not necessarily read). This tends to help satisfy auditors that there is separation of responsibility and the ability to have different people answerable for different aspects on several different levels.

Oracle-provided auditing can be customized to meet the needs that you have for auditing to answer the difficult questions asked by auditors. Because it is so customizable, those in your organization responsible for the setting of auditing rules (often the business subject-matter experts (SMEs), system administrators, and the DBA) need to take care and time to plan what can be done, what needs to be done, and what it makes sense to do in the way of auditing. A balance needs to be struck between the need to capture critical information (and what is defined as critical) and the need to actually be able to use the database to get the organization's work accomplished. Auditing is just another kind of processing that can occur on the database, and on the operating system by extension. Too much auditing can slow the database down significantly and adversely impact performance.

Anyone who has ever paid any attention to the alert logs has noticed that there are a couple of things that Oracle audits by default. Database startup and database shutdown (provided it isn't a crash or shutdown abort) are audited and written to the alert logs. Not only is the time of the command audited, but the identifier of the terminal used to issue the command is written, as is the auditing state of the database at the time of startup. This can be of assistance in auditing the administrators, because you can, at a glance, see if someone has started a database that had previously been audited with auditing disabled—if there is no justification for the action, there may be some less than honorable actions taking place on the database during this time.

Oracle also automatically audits any connection that is made as SYSOPER or as SYSDBA. The operating system ID of the user making the connection, along with the time of the connection, is automatically audited. This provides a means of accountability and can be a tool to determine who did what, if something happened to the database during a given period of time that could only been done using a privileged account.

The following sections discuss the various types of auditing information that can be captured. The nice thing about setting auditing up in the database is that the commands to set up auditing are similar regardless of the level of auditing you want to employ. You simply execute the AUDIT command at a SQL prompt with the kind of auditing you want to do.

Auditing by Session

Setting auditing up by session causes Oracle to write a single record for all statements of the same type (INSERT, for example) issued in the same session.

The following command will audit all successful or unsuccessful connections and disconnections with the following statement:

```
AUDIT SESSION;
```

Alternatively, you can selectively audit certain users:

```
AUDIT SESSION BY scott;
```

Auditing by Access

Setting auditing up by access causes Oracle to write a single record for each access of the audited type to the audited object.

```
AUDIT TABLE emp BY ACCESS;
```

Auditing Transaction Success

You need to decide, as a part of the planning process, whether you want to audit whenever the audited action is successful or when it is not successful. This decision is best made when you understand what you are trying to accomplish. Are you trying to find out who successfully inserts information into a table so you can see who is succeeding in doing their job (or succeeding in getting data into the table, at any rate), or do you want to find out who is using the production database as a learning environment and failing over and over again when trying to enter data? There are times when you can set up auditing for failures as a means to detect when someone is trying to do something that they aren't supposed to do. It is true that you will capture information that you don't care about (those users who accidentally mistype something) but you will be able to determine when something fishy is going on, and it is better to catch too much than to not catch what is necessary.

```
AUDIT DELETE ANY TABLE
BY ACCESS
WHENEVER NOT SUCCESSFUL;
```

Statement Auditing

Statement auditing can be used to audit statements, or groups of statements, that affect a particular kind of database object. You can audit any statement that in any way alters the state of a table (by auditing ALTER, INSERT, UPDATE, DELETE, TRUNCATE or even COMMENT ON statements). Statements made by proxy can be audited; statements on schema objects or directories on multitiers are often statements that we want to keep an eye on.

Another kind of statement auditing is the auditing of connections and disconnections. You can granularly audit only certain users' connections and disconnections, as in this example:

```
AUDIT SESSION BY april, larry, adam, amandya;
```

Another special case of statement auditing is auditing SQL statements that fail because the target object does not exist. This is NOT EXISTS auditing.

You need the AUDIT SYSTEM privilege to set up statement auditing.

Privilege Auditing

Privilege auditing sets up auditing for particular system privileges. When auditing privileges, it is often to your advantage to audit by access rather than by session, because a lot of damage can be done without being tracked otherwise.

Consider this example:

```
AUDIT DELETE ANY TABLE
BY ACCESS
WHEN SUCCESSFUL
```

This example generates an audit record for any DELETE TABLE statement every time the statement is issued and is successful. You may not care if someone tries unsuccessfully to delete a table. But you probably will care if someone successfully deletes a table. You may also care if someone is out there deleting many tables. Granted, there may be times when tables need to be deleted. You may have an application that is no longer being used, and you have archived off the schema by exporting it, and now you want to drop the old tables from the database. Auditing won't keep you from doing what you need to do in the database. It just keeps you honest and makes sure that what is done in the database is traceable.

The AUDIT SYSTEM privilege is necessary for anyone setting up privilege auditing, and it should really only be done as the security administrator or as a database administrator.

Object Auditing

Object auditing audits specific statements on specific objects. This is the only auditing option that doesn't require any special system-level privilege to enable it. Any user can set object auditing on objects that he or she already owns. Of course, if you are trying to set object auditing on someone else's objects, you still have to have the AUDIT SYSTEM privilege. AUDIT SYSTEM is also necessary when setting default object auditing.

Suppose you need to keep track of who is altering the emp table (since it is where salaries are kept). Just log in and issue the following command:

```
AUDIT INSERT, UPDATE, DELETE ON emp
BY ACCESS
WHENEVER SUCCESSFUL;
```

Alternatively, you as the DBA could always enable the same auditing as follows:

```
AUDIT INSERT, UPDATE, DELETE ON scott.emp
BY ACCESS
WHENEVER SUCCESSFUL;
```

Auditing the Keepers of the Kingdom

While it is true that Oracle audits connections to the database whenever someone logs in as SYSOPER or as SYSDBA, this is where the automatic auditing ends. If you need to make sure that anyone connecting with a privileged account is behaving, you can enable this level of auditing by setting AUDIT_SYS_OPERATIONS to TRUE. Of course, since these people are the keepers of the kingdom and can manipulate the data in any table of the database, regardless of the setting that is used for AUDIT_TRAIL, the records generated by anything that SYSDBA or SYSOPER does get written to the operating system audit file.

This audit trail can be particularly useful as well, because as a general rule, for day-to-day database maintenance and typical day-to-day work DBAs should be using their own IDs that have been granted SYSDBA privilege. You can use SYSDBA and SYSOPER auditing to make special note of those times or people who make use of the ability to leverage this powerful account. While most situations may not call for auditing the SYS or SYSDBA accounts, different organizational auditing protocols will require different solutions. With the evolution of Sarbanes-Oxley, SAS-70, and ISO audits, the proof that is called for to satisfy the auditors will likely continue to evolve as well.

Turning Auditing Off

You can turn off all statement auditing with the following command:

```
NOAUDIT ALL;
```

Use this command to turn off privilege auditing:

```
NOAUDIT ALL PRIVILEGES;
```

Or you can selectively turn auditing off just as you can selectively turn it on:

```
NOAUDIT SESSION BY larry, amandya;
```

For object auditing you can turn it off simply by undoing whatever you did to enable auditing:

```
NOAUDIT INSERT, UPDATE, DELETE ON scott.emp;
```

Limiting User Connection Time

Don't forget, it is possible, and preferable, to use profiles as a means to limit connection time. You can limit the time that a user sits idle (IDLE_TIME) or the total time that a user is connected (CONNECT_TIME). While there are other ways to accomplish the same thing, this is the preferred method.

If a user reaches the limit in the user profile, the user's session will appear with the status of KILLED in the V$SESSION view, and all associated resources that were being used by that session will be released (locks will be released, and so forth).

PL/SQL

PL/SQL is Oracle's completely portable, high-performance transaction-processing language. PL/SQL provides support for SQL and object-oriented programming concepts, improved performance over simply using ANSI SQL, and a framework for higher productivity. PL/SQL is fully portable (PL/SQL program units will run the same, regardless of operating system or database), it is tightly integrated with the Oracle database, and using PL/SQL programs provides the facility for tightening security.

While many people have the impression that PL/SQL is only for professional programmers and developers, and that shell-driven SQL statements are written by people who are interested in direct control over the code and who don't want the code stored in the database (such as many database administrators), PL/SQL is a powerful tool for database administration. You can use PL/SQL to store your SQL library within the database.

Handy Oracle-Provided PL/SQL Facilities

Okay, so is there anything else we might need to know in the venue of PL/SQL programming as an everyday DBA? There are things that DBAs, depending on what exactly their job title is, don't typically consider. To a great extent, PL/SQL isn't typically considered to be the bailiwick of a DBA. The following, however, are things that most DBAs, even those who do PL/SQL programming at some level, don't think about.

BULK COLLECT and FORALL

In Oracle 8*i*, two new data manipulation language (DML) statements for PL/SQL were introduced: BULK COLLECT and FORALL. Both of these statements implement a form of array processing inside the PL/SQL code. BULK COLLECT facilitates high-speed retrieval of data. FORALL greatly improves performance of INSERT, UPDATE, and DELETE operations.

You can achieve significant performance gains using these statements because, with their use, Oracle significantly reduces the number of context switches between the PL/SQL and SQL statement engines. With BULK COLLECT, you fetch multiple rows at a time into one or more collections (a collection being an ordered group of elements, all of the same type or an array of similarly typed elements), rather than into individual variables or records. FORALL transfers all of the data from a PL/SQL collection to the specified table using collections—it instructs the PL/SQL engine to bulk-bind the input collections before sending them to the SQL engine.

BULK COLLECT and FORALL not only improve performance (something with which nearly every DBA is concerned), but they also help to simplify code that is written for SQL operations embedded within PL/SQL program units.

In Oracle Database 10*g*, these constructs are even more robust than they were in previous releases. Oracle's 10*g* PL/SQL now provides two new clauses that are associated with the FORALL statement: INDICES OF and VALUES OF. These added clauses allow you to be very selective about which rows from the collection (the array that is driving the FORALL statement) should be processed by the extended DML statement. Previously, you could only process the FORALL constructs as a whole, processing every row in the collection. With these new clauses, you can skip some rows of the collection and only process those that meet your criteria.

The INDICES OF clause comes in very handy when your binding array is sparse or contains gaps. The VALUES OF clause allows you to be selective as to what subset of the rows in the collection you want to process.

IEEE Floating-Point Types

Oracle Database 10*g* now supports two new data types: BINARY_FLOAT and BINARY_DOUBLE. These new data types represent floating-point numbers in the IEEE 754 format, and they are particularly useful for scientific computation. Because many computer systems support IEEE 754 floating-point operations through native processor instructions, Oracle's ability to make native use of the types is much more efficient for intensive computations involving floating-point data.

Even better, the rules for subprogram overloading are more robust. This means that you can now write math libraries with different versions of the same function operating on PLS_INTEGER, NUMBER, BINARY_FLOAT, and BINARY_DOUBLE parameters.

While it is possible to see significant performance gains in some operations by making use of these features, there is also a huge loss of precision. For that reason, these new types should never be used in financial applications.

PL/SQL Native Compilation

PL/SQL, as of Oracle 9*i*, has been able to be natively compiled, but it was often difficult to get set up correctly. This feature now requires less setup and maintenance.

A package body and its specification no longer need to be compiled with the same settings for native compilation. This means that a package body can be compiled natively while its specification is interpreted, or vice versa.

Natively compiled subprograms are stored in the database, and their corresponding shared libraries are extracted automatically as needed. There is no need to worry about backing up or loading the shared libraries, or cleaning up old ones when they are no longer needed. That is all taken care of centrally.

The initialization parameters and command setup for native compilation have also been greatly simplified. The only required parameter, as of version 10*g*, is PLSQL_NATIVE_LIBRARY_DIR. The Oracle 9*i* parameters related to the compiler, linker, and make utility have been obsoleted. The file that controls compilation is now a command file rather than a makefile, and any errors that occur during native compilation are reflected in the USER_ERRORS or ALL_ERRORS dictionary view and are accessible by the SQL*Plus SHOW ERRORS command.

Invoker's Rights

One frequently misunderstood feature of Oracle in recent releases is invoker's rights. Prior to Oracle 8*i*, all stored program units (packages, functions, triggers, and procedures) were always executed with the privileges of the definer of the object (the set of privileges that were granted directly to the definer, and therefore owner, of the stored object). This meant that, at compile time, it was necessary for Oracle to figure out not only what objects to access but also whether the owner of the procedure was allowed to access them.

Beginning in version 8*i*, however, Oracle provided a feature called invoker's rights to provide finer-grained security to code. Invoker's rights allow anyone to create stored procedures that don't necessarily have to follow the old rules. Programmers can now develop stored procedures that are able to execute with the privilege set of the *invoker* (the currently logged-in user that is calling the program) at runtime rather than the programmer having to predetermine everything. This is possible because the access to the underlying objects is not predefined at compile time but is gathered from the login at runtime. Even with program units created to have invoker's rights, however, the owner of the procedure must have access to the underlying objects at compile time, or to objects with the same names; otherwise the program code will fail.

Invoker's rights means that someone with DBA privileges can own all of the packages in the database, and only the privileges necessary to actually perform one's job need to be granted to any given user. The program units will be allowed to process exactly the way they should for that given user. A single program will perform SELECT-only functionality for a user with that level of privilege, it will allow INSERT, UPDATE, and DELETE access for someone else, and it will permit UPDATE-only for someone else. Only one version of the source needs to be maintained, and the security that you would have provided anyway will apply to those who use the program.

PL/SQL Procedures

A *procedure* is a program unit (often used as a subprogram) that can be invoked and that can, but doesn't have to, take parameters. A procedure usually performs an action, and the action can produce one, many, or no return values.

A procedure usually has two parts: a specification and a body. The specification begins with the keyword PROCEDURE (actually, something along the lines of create or replace procedure <procedure name>), and it ends with the procedure name if there are no parameters (either input or output parameters) or with a parameter list (if parameters are needed). The parameter declarations are optional, depending on what you are trying to accomplish. The name of a procedure that takes no parameters is written without parentheses.

The procedure's body begins with the keyword IS (or AS), and it ends with the keyword END (optionally followed by the procedure name for style or clarity reasons). The procedure body can have three parts, only one of which is required:

- ■ **Declarations**   The declarative part is optional. This section contains the declarations of cursors, constants, types, user-defined types, variables, user-defined exceptions, and any subprograms that the procedure might call. These declared objects live only within the boundaries of the procedure.

- ■ **Executable statements**   This section contains the executable statements that make up the meat of the program. These statements assign values, control the execution of the program logic, and manipulate the Oracle data.

■ **Exception handling** The exception-handling section is optional, but it is very important to include this section if the code relies on having exceptions caught. Any code that deals with data needs to have a means to trap errors. No matter how careful you are, errors will happen.

Loops

Loops are very powerful and useful constructs in any programming language. They are typically not the most complicated structures, logically and mechanically, to construct, but they are among the most complicated control structures in PL/SQL. Loops allow you to execute the same code repeatedly, with execution controlled in different manners. Oracle provides you with different looping controls that offer you the flexibility to write efficient straightforward code that can handle any situation.

Oracle provides simple or infinite loops, numeric for loops, and while loops. The differences are in how the loops are terminated and whether there is a test to provide for termination conditions.

Regardless of which type of loop you use, every loop structure has two parts: a loop boundary and a loop body. The boundary is made up of the keywords that initiate the loop and control the loop's progress, the conditions that cause the loop to terminate, and the END LOOP statement that officially terminates the loop structure. The loop body consists of the executable statements that are processed with every iteration of the loop.

Simple Loops The simple, or infinite, loop starts with the LOOP keyword, ends with the END LOOP keywords, and has the executable statements in between (there must be at least one executable statement). The loop terminates when an EXIT statement is executed in the body of the loop. If this EXIT statement never executes, the loop turns into an infinite loop, which can cause unwanted side effects and usually should be avoided at all costs.

CAUTION
Using resource profiles in the development database can prevent infinite loops from really running away. Even if you don't use them anywhere else, their use in the development database can be very helpful.

The loop is terminated by the success or failure of a test. This means that the code inside of a simple loop must execute at least once.

You should use a simple loop when you don't know how many times you need the loop to execute, but you know you want it to execute at least once. Here is a simplified example of a simple loop declaration:

```
LOOP
      IF <insert condition>

      THEN
            EXIT;
      END IF;
END LOOP;
```

And here is another version of a simple loop:

```
LOOP
      Statements;
      EXIT WHEN condition;
END LOOP;
```

You can also write code to imitate a repeat-until condition loop, which is where the condition is tested not at the beginning of the loop, but after the body of the loop is executed. This guarantees that the loop always executes at least once, and it can use a Boolean condition that evaluates to TRUE when you want to exit. The loop will repeat continuously until the condition evaluates to TRUE:

```
LOOP UNTIL
      Statements to execute
      EXIT WHEN boolean_condition;
END LOOP;
```

I often use a simple loop when I need to recursively execute an ALTER statement or a CREATE TABLE statement in each of several schemas. While it isn't likely that this is what the people who developed the PL/SQL constructs intended as its use, it is a very handy use for it.

Numeric For Loop   The numeric for loop is the one that people typically recognize from other programming languages. It is a traditional counted loop that executes exactly as many times as the counter lets it. The iterator is set in the loop's boundary, and the loop has the following general syntax:

```
FOR loop_index IN lowest_number..highest_number LOOP
Executable statements
END LOOP;
```

This loop terminates unconditionally when the number of iterations reaches the upper bounds of the loop iterator. You can also force it to end with an EXIT clause, and there are occasions when you will likely need to do this, but for elegance and simplicity it usually isn't recommended.

As in the simple loop, you must have at least one executable element between the LOOP and END LOOP statements. However, the NULL statement is considered to be executable, and it is a good way of getting past this requirement if you are just working on debugging the structure of your code rather than its logic.

After each execution of the loop body, PL/SQL checks the value of the loop index. If it hasn't *exceeded* the upper limit yet, it runs through the process again. If it has exceeded the upper limit, it stops. (Remember, both end limits are inclusive—if you use 1..10 it will execute the tenth time and automatically exit before the eleventh.) If the lower bound is higher than the upper bound (even if you have set up the loop in reverse order), the loop will never execute.

NOTE
You can use the REVERSE keyword to force the loop to decrement rather than increment the counter, but you still have to have the lower boundary number on the left and the upper boundary number on the right, or the reversed loop will not execute.

```
FOR i IN REVERSE 1..10 LOOP
    -- statements that you want to execute 10 times
END LOOP;
```

The loop variable (the iterator) is one construct that you don't want to declare anywhere else in your code. PL/SQL does that for you. This variable's whole purpose is to be the iterator—don't use it for anything else. And don't try to change it with any of the code inside the loop, because nothing will happen—Oracle protects it. In other programming languages you often have to increment or decrement the iterator within the logic, but not in PL/SQL. Similarly, don't change the upper boundary or the lower boundary within your code. This can have very bad side effects, and it will usually not compile.

Now let's look at a loop that's not overly useful, but that's interesting in a geeky way. Suppose you need to step through the set of numbers in the loop index by something other than one? PL/SQL doesn't allow this, at least not directly. You can, however, do it creatively from within the loop. If you want to perform actions only for even increments, you could use the MOD function as in this example:

```
FOR loop_index IN 1 .. 10
LOOP
    IF MOD (loop_index, 2) = 0
    THEN
        <Do your stuff>
    END IF;
END LOOP;
```

If you choose to do something like this, however, make sure that you document your code so that someone else can understand what you did and why, or even for you to remember six months or a year later. Documentation helps a lot down the line.

One additional note here. You need to make sure that you always have an exit condition that does not ever evaluate to null. Because null is not equal to anything, if your exit condition ever evaluates to something that is null, the loop will never end until it exhausts the resources or until it has decimated your data.

While Loop The WHILE loop is a conditional loop that continues to execute as long as the Boolean condition defined in the loop boundary evaluates to TRUE. It is very similar to the repeat-until version of the simple loop. However, it is the opposite of the repeat-until logic in the simple loop, in that the loop repeats until the condition becomes TRUE. Like the repeat-until loop, though, you don't specify how many times the loop will execute— you specify the condition that causes the loop to end. In this way, the loop is allowed to become as dynamic as the data requires that it be.

Here's the structure of the WHILE loop:

```
WHILE <condition>
LOOP
    <do stuff>
END LOOP;
```

The <condition> is a Boolean variable or an expression that evaluates to a Boolean value of TRUE, FALSE, or NULL. Each time through the loop, the condition is checked before the process begins. If it is TRUE, it is executed. If it is FALSE, it is bypassed. This means that there will be times when this loop logic is never executed. It also means that the information required for the first test of the loop's condition must exist in the program before the logic falls into the loop.

When programming the WHILE loop, you have to be certain that there will come a time when the condition will evaluate to FALSE. Otherwise your program will get stuck and continue to loop indefinitely. One way around this is to set logic within the program that will force the Boolean expression to FALSE so that the next time the iteration is attempted, it will fail the test.

Controlling Loops   Here are a few things to remember about controlling loops:

- You can associate a label with a loop and use that label to increase your control over loop execution. This is especially useful if you have loops within loops, or when you want real clarity in your code. By using labels, you can also use dot notation to refer to those variables that are located within the loop, such as the loop index. The following code shows how the label my_loop is associated with the loop structure.

```
<<my_loop>>
FOR my_record IN my_cur
LOOP
    <do stuff>
END LOOP my_loop;
```

NOTE
Dot notation is a way of appending a schema name to a table name to a column name (for example, SCOTT.EMP.FNAME). The same concept applies to loop variables. An example of dot notation in the previous loop construct would enable you to reference the my_record record as follows: my_loop.my_record.

- The loop boundary creates a scope similar to that of a PL/SQL block. Anything that you declare within the boundary of the loop lives only while the loop is executing and cannot be accessed either before or after the logic is in the loop. The loop scope for variables and other names takes precedence over other variables in your program that have the same name. This is true for the loop's label, should you choose to use it, as well. Using the lable.loop_variable means that you can name variables inside the loop the same thing (bad programming practice, but possible) as variables outside the loop and assure that anyone reading your code knows what variable is really being referenced. This is handy for very long loop logic, as well, so you can keep better track of what is really going on.

- There is only one way to enter a loop, but there are usually a number of ways you can exit your loop.

- Naming your loop indexes makes them easier to understand and later maintain:

```
FOR hire_date IN start_id .. end_id
LOOP
    <Give them another week's vacation>
END LOOP;
```

Cursors

A cursor is simply a named mechanism through which you can write a `SELECT` statement and then manipulate that data within a SQL statement. You can select information from the database tables for manipulation with a loop, but it is much more efficient to turn that loop into a cursor. You can also turn loop structures into implicit cursors to aid clarity in coding. You can use the ability to turn many loops into cursors when working with a developer to simplify code, or you can use cursor logic when you are saving your work as a stored procedure so that you don't have to recode it every time you want to use it. Data changes, there seems to be more and more of it all the time, and with cursors, you don't have to know how many times the iteration will occur or necessarily what the condition is that will cause the loop to exit; you can continue to process until there is no more data on which to work. While it is often enough that code works, making it efficient and its purpose apparent is better still.

Part of the benefit of using cursors is in the reuse of code. If you reuse the same code in different parts of the program, cursor processing enables the cursor to reexecute without the statement having to be reparsed. This performance savings can be improved further by opening several cursors with each cursor performing a single task.

The drawback to using cursors over using loop constructs is that the more open cursors you have, the more memory is consumed by your code. Each cursor requires virtual memory, which means that a session's total number of cursors is limited not only by the MAX_OPEN_CURSOR parameter, but by the maximum amount of memory that is available to the process. The same is not necessarily true when using a loop to accomplish the same purpose on simple record types.

In the following sections, we will look at different kinds of cursors and discuss their differences.

Implicit Cursors   Implicit cursors are used when you execute SQL statements directly in your PL/SQL code, and you haven't defined a formal cursor. Implicit cursors are more efficient, they are less prone to data errors, and they give you much more control than explicit cursors.

NOTE
Tom Kyte, in Effective Oracle by Design *(McGraw-Hill/Osborne Media; 2003), goes into great detail on this, and the whole book is a very good read.*

Explicit Cursors   An explicit cursor is a `SELECT` statement that is explicitly defined in the declaration section of your code. In the process of declaring it, it is assigned a name. While there is no such thing as an explicit cursor for UPDATE, DELETE, and INSERT statements, you can UPDATE or DELETE the current row of an explicit cursor.

With explicit cursors, you maintain complete control over exactly how data is accessed in the database. You decide when to OPEN, FETCH from, and CLOSE the cursor. Information about the cursor's current state is available by examining the cursor attributes. Of course, with control comes responsibility. You have to open the explicit cursor, fetch it, and then close it when you are done.

Explicit cursors are much less frequently used than implicit cursors, but are very frequently used by new developers who are getting their feet wet on cursor processing and therefore it would behoove you to have a basic understanding.

Cursor Processing   Once you have declared a cursor, you need to open it. The syntax for this is simple:

```
Open mycursor;
```

Now that the cursor is open, you can use it. The purpose of using a cursor is usually to retrieve the rows of one or more tables so that some type of operation can be performed on the data. After declaring and opening your cursor, the next step is to FETCH the rows from your cursor:

```
Fetch mycursor into
        <either a list of variables, or a record >;
```

Once you have finished using your cursor, you must close it. A cursor stays open until either the user program exits and implicitly closes it, or (if the program is an OCI program (Oracle Call Interface) or a precompiled application) the cursor can be explicitly closed during execution of the program. Termination (either planned or unplanned) implicitly closes any open cursors. And if you leave the scope of the cursor, it will close.

What follows is a list of those tests that you can do on a cursor to determine its state. You can determine this state by checking with an "IF" statement (as in IF %FOUND THEN...) and drive your cursor processing logic by the different states that the cursor can take.

■   %FOUND   Returns INVALID_CURSOR if the cursor is declared but not open, or if the cursor has been closed. Returns NULL if the cursor is open, but a fetch has not been executed. Returns TRUE if a successful fetch has been executed. Returns FALSE if no row was returned.

- %NOTFOUND   Returns INVALID_CURSOR if the cursor is declared but not open, or if the cursor has been closed. Returns NULL if the cursor is open, but a fetch has not been executed. Returns FALSE if a successful fetch has been executed. Returns TRUE if no row was returned.

- %ISOPEN   Returns TRUE if the cursor is open, and FALSE if the cursor is closed.

- %ROWCOUNT   Returns INVALID_CURSOR if the cursor is declared but not open, or if the cursor has been closed. Returns the number of rows fetched if a successful fetch has been executed.

SELECT FOR UPDATE   The SELECT FOR UPDATE statement of a cursor allows you to lock the records in the cursor result set. You are not required to make changes to the records in order to use this statement, but it puts row-level locks on the table. The record locks are released when the next COMMIT or ROLLBACK statement is issued.

Cursor FOR Loops   Cursor FOR loops are defined by explicit cursors or a SELECT statement incorporated directly within a loop boundary. These loops are used whenever you need to fetch and process each and every record from a cursor, regardless of what data is associated with the row. This is the case most of the time you work with cursors. Using cursor FOR loops reduces the volume of code needed to fetch data from a cursor, and it greatly reduces your chances of incurring LOOP errors in your programs.

The basic format of the cursor FOR loop is as follows:

```
FOR my_record_index IN my_cursor_name
LOOP
    <do stuff>
END LOOP;
```

Optimally, my_record_index is a record that is declared implicitly with the %ROWTYPE attribute, based on the cursor specified by my_cursor_name. The loop terminates, unconditionally, after every record returned by the cursor has been fetched and processed. Optionally, you can exit the loop with an EXIT statement, but this is not usually recommended. After each iteration of the loop, PL/SQL performs a FETCH and checks the %NOTFOUND attribute of the cursor. When %NOTFOUND evaluates to TRUE, you're done.

Error Checking and Reporting   When errors are encountered in PL/SQL processing, control of the block shifts to the exception-handling section. The section is optional, but including it is good programming practice. Whenever your code finds something that it doesn't know how to handle, either a user-defined or system-defined exception is raised.

Whenever PL/SQL encounters an exception, it scans the exception-handling section for the definition of the exception—the exception-handling section always begins with the keyword EXCEPTION and goes until its corresponding END command. If it can't find the particular exception listed, it uses the WHEN OTHERS clause to address the error. It is in your best interest to encourage your developers to use (or create a standard set of libraries to be used) robust exception-handling section so that all of your programs can take advantage of it and won't simply fail with no logical exceptions returned. It is very frustrating to try to help a user determine what is wrong with "your database," and the programming logic is not robust enough to provide clear and concise error messages.

It is important to note that using the WHEN OTHERS clause to catch the majority of the errors in the code is really pretty sloppy programming, and it usually implies that sufficient thought has not gone into considering exactly what the code is doing and what you expect it to do or not do. You can really only catch the exceptions that you plan on catching. A NO_DATA_FOUND error is something that you can usually anticipate by knowing the data and the code. When you catch something that you are not expecting, it is usually a case of bad data (never a good thing) or possibly inefficient programming.

PL/SQL Functions

A function is a subprogram that can take parameters and be invoked. Generally, you use a function to compute a value. Functions and procedures are structured alike, except that functions have a RETURN clause.

A function has two parts: the specification and the body. The specification (*spec* for short) begins with the keyword FUNCTION and ends with the RETURN clause, which specifies the data type of the return value. Parameter declarations are optional, and functions that take no parameters are written without parentheses.

The function body begins with the keyword IS (or AS) and ends with the keyword END, followed by an optional function name. The body has three parts: an optional declarative part, an executable part, and an optional exception-handling part. The declarative part contains declarations of types, cursors, constants, variables, exceptions, and subprograms. These items are local and cease to exist when you exit the function. The executable part contains statements that assign values, control execution, and manipulate Oracle data. The exception-handling part contains handlers that deal with exceptions raised during execution.

Using Packages in PL/SQL

Packages are a flexible and powerful programming construct that provide you with the ability to logically bundle related types, variables, cursors, and subprograms together. Each package, if well constructed, is easily understandable. Interfaces between packages should be elegant, simple, clear, and well defined. This is the way that developers create good code. It is also true that code is only as good as the programmer who develops it. Good constructs only provide good tools, not good code.

Packages usually have two parts, although only one is mandatory. The first part is the mandatory specification, and the second is the optional body. The specification is the interface to your applications. In it are declared the types, constants, variables, exceptions, cursors, and subprograms available for use. You can create a variable-only package specification to hold things like global variables, or variables that are defined the same way in every program.

NOTE
A variable-only package is something like ICOPIES in COBOL programming. ICOPIES (aka copybooks) are usually definitions of file layouts using variable definitions, or they include a set of common variables used in multiple programs. It is one of the earliest forms of the reuse of code or program units. There are also procedure division ICOPIES that contain commonly called code, such as sort routines, date-conversion routines, or other common processes.

The package body provides the meat of the matter. In it reside the definitions of the cursors, subprograms, and exception handling that are defined in the specification.

Only the declaration details in the package specification are visible to the outside world, and are therefore accessible to applications that are making use of the package's logic. The implementation details of the code in the package body are hidden and inaccessible. In this way, Oracle implements the principle of encapsulation.

Packages, as well as procedures and functions, have to be compiled and stored within an Oracle database. Unless you are dealing with Oracle Forms, forms are compiled and stored at the operating system level. When packages and procedures are stored in the database, the programs are called stored program units. In this way, you can allow the contents of program units to be shared by many applications. This allows you to create a library of stored procedures, which can assist with code reusability.

Packages enforce the hiding of information. This object-oriented type of construct allows you to predetermine which elements are public (those that allow the package to interact with the outside world) and which are private (those that are only available to the package itself). This is but one of the object-oriented principles that packages bring to PL/SQL and Oracle.

Probably the biggest benefit of using packages is the performance improvements they permit. When any object in a package is referenced, the entire package is loaded into memory. At this point, it is already compiled and validated and ready for use. This means that the package, and all of its components, are ready for use during any future call to the package's program units. No more calls to disk to retrieve the individual components. This is great for performance in any database, but it is particularly important in a distributed environment where one instance can reference a package that is loaded into the memory of another instance, minimizing the network traffic required to execute your code. You can even ensure that a package will be called into memory on database startup by creating an ON STARTUP trigger that calls an innocuous function or procedure in the package, thereby forcing it into memory.

Another very important benefit of using packages is the breaking of the dependency chain. If you compile a procedure, everything that calls it is invalid. When you compile a package body, nothing goes invalid, regardless of what that body contains.

Package Specifications

The package specification contains all of the definitions (or specifications) of all of the elements in the package that can be referenced from outside the package. These can include the program units, the variables, the global values—any object that you want people to be able to access by calling the package. These are called the *public* elements of the package, because they are available to anyone for the calling.

Public elements can be thought of as those defined in the specification that can be referenced from other programs and PL/SQL blocks.

Package Bodies

The body of the package contains all the code that lies behind the package specification: the implementation of the modules, all cursors, and other objects. It also contains those objects that you want to keep people from being able to access directly—the private constructs that only the objects defined in the specification have direct access to.

Private elements are those you define only in the body of the package; they do not appear in the specification. They can never be referenced from outside the package. However, private elements in a package still must be defined before they can be referenced by other elements of the package. This means that you have to think carefully when creating the package body. If a procedure that is defined in the specification calls a private function defined only in the body, the private program unit needs to be defined before (linearly above) the public program unit's definition in the body. This means that you have to understand how the code calls itself when creating the body.

Because you have to define the package's specification before you define its body, you can follow top-down design principles. That is to say, you can create the specifications for in-depth code before you actually implement the code itself. You can define, in the specification, what you want the code to do before you define, in the body, how you want it done. This means that you can modularize your code, implementing different pieces as you go.

One neat thing that I have done with packages is to create a specification-only package that defines global values that I know several different packages are going to need in different application code. This way I can provide those global variables or global constants to all of the programmers to use. This lets me control the variables that they use, to an extent, and it allows those values to be defined once. This is very useful when coding an Oracle Forms and

Reports application, where you need to have persistence of data between screens.

Wrapping PL/SQL Code

If code is written using PL/SQL, all of its procedures, functions, and triggers are stored in the data dictionary and are viewable in the USER_SOURCE data dictionary view. Any user who has direct access to the database can view and potentially edit the source code easily. Oracle provides a security utility PL/SQL Wrapper to assist with this problem.

Wrapping code is a way to obscure the code so that none of the implementation details are readily apparent to those looking at the code. When you wrap your PL/SQL source code, you convert your easily readable code into unreadable source code that can quickly and easily be distributed whenever and wherever necessary for inclusion in database instances. This means that if you are creating applications for sale or distribution to clients who have licensed your software or services, no one can cancel your contract and still make use of your code. It permits you to protect your intellectual property. The database into which this wrapped code is loaded maintains any and all dependencies for the encrypted code in exactly the same way it would for programs that were loaded from easily readable text, and the wrapped code is treated the same as any other PL/SQL programs are treated. The only material difference is that no one can query the USER_SOURCE data dictionary to extract your intellectual property or trade secrets.

When to Wrap Code

You will want to wrap code when you are creating program units that you don't want anyone to be able to pirate later. You can also wrap code if you are providing database applications via the Web or another hosted service (such as an Application Service Provider or ASP) and you want to maintain an added level of security so that no one will accidentally (or not so accidentally) gain access to the code.

You will probably want to wrap code that is sold with a software product that is either packaged with its own Oracle database (as is Oracle E-Business Suite) or that is to be installed to run on an Oracle database. It would be entirely too simple for someone with even a little bit of database experience to come in and reverse-engineer your application or just steal the logic and create their own application.

When Not to Wrap Code

You probably shouldn't wrap the code if you have been contracted by a company to provide them with the source code for a component. Sometimes it might be attractive to do this, particularly if you believe that they won't notice the difference right away, and that they will have to come back to you for any changes. This is not the way to get a good reputation in the industry, however. Just because you think you can get away with something isn't a reason to do it.

How to Wrap Code

The PL/SQL Wrapper utility is a standalone Oracle utility that converts plain text PL/SQL source code into a portable, secure, obscured object. It encodes the code by converting its ASCII text representation into hexadecimal digits, making it virtually unavailable for perusal or modification. The USER_SOURCE view will not display the wrapped objects in a readable format. This keeps the source hidden from view and protected from alteration or misuse. The wrapped code is portable and platform-independent, it can be imported and exported with Oracle's utilities, and it is dynamically loaded when re-interpretation needs to be done (no shutdown, and restart of the database is necessary, no relinking of the program units; just rewrap the code in question).

The WRAP utility executable is run at the operating system level. In most systems, the command is as follows:

```
WRAP INAME=input_filename [ONAME=output_filename]
```

The arguments are the input filename (mandatory) and output filename (optional). It is very important to remember that there are no spaces around the equal signs.

It is also important to remember that the input file must be a SQL or PL/SQL file that can contain any combination of SQL and PL/SQL program statements. PL/SQL Wrapper wraps only CREATE statements:

- `CREATE [OR REPLACE] PACKAGE`
- `CREATE [OR REPLACE] PACKAGE BODY`

- ```
  CREATE [OR REPLACE] FUNCTION
  ```

- ```
  CREATE [OR REPLACE] PROCEDURE
  ```

All other SQL statements are passed through to the output file intact.

The output file is typically larger than the input file, and the default extension for the wrapped code is .plb. However, you can define your own extension if you specify the output filename parameter. Once wrapped, the output file cannot be unwrapped, read, or edited.

Error Handling   One thing that people don't typically take into account is that the Wrapper utility will not check the details or semantics of the input file—its job is just to wrap the code as it is. Wrapper assumes that you have already checked to see if the program will compile. Any errors that the code contains won't be reported during wrapping. They will, however, be reported the first time the wrapped file is run.

This means that when the code is written, it should be loaded into a database somewhere to check for syntactical inaccuracies. It should also be run and tested for logical and programmatic errors, but, at the very least, you will want to be sure that it compiles, and then you can test it thoroughly after it has been wrapped.

Triggers

When I was a brand-new DBA the instructor was teaching us about triggers and was explaining that triggers are very effective and efficient tools for programmers and database administrators to use, but many of us are still reluctant to implement them at any level. The line that he gave us has stuck in my head (which was, after all, the purpose) and got smiles from virtually everyone in the class. When thinking about triggers, remember "Hoo Hoo, a trigger's a wonderful thing" (only slightly altered from Tigger's line in A.A. Milne's book). Despite their early reputation for being flaky and difficult to get working properly, a trigger really is a wonderful thing, now. With triggers, you have a very useful tool for managing and controlling data and data access, enforcing referential integrity, and enforcing business rules and logic. While it is true that much of this type of logic can be programmed at least as well in functions, procedures, or constraints, it is the trigger's feature of control on firing time and firing sequence that makes it an attractive mechanism for enforcing many of these rules. If the logic is programmed into stored procedures, the trigger can call that stored program unit, combining the best of both features.

> **NOTE**
> *Any trigger whose purpose is to enforce an integrity constraint, and that crosses rows in a table or crosses from one table to another, must contain LOCK TABLE as a part of the trigger code. In practice, this is rarely done, and it is almost never done correctly. It is much better to enforce integrity with integrity constraints.*

Triggers are most often used by DBAs to audit different aspects of database access and manipulation (or to limit the same), to enforce business rules, or to control many behind-the-scenes data manipulations.

Officially, a trigger is a stored program until that is implicitly run (or fired) when some event within the database occurs. The particular event depends on the version of Oracle you are using, and exactly when the trigger fires in response to the event is something that you can control to a great extent. A database trigger can fire after logon (firing before would be pointless), after database startup, before database shutdown, and before, after, or during an INSERT, UPDATE, or DELETE. You can use table-level or row-level triggers. Oracle Forms offers an even more robust set of triggers, and a vast number of events (since it is really event programming) on which you can trigger.

There was a time when triggers had a bigger impact, from a performance perspective, when they were called or included in a database, but with Oracle getting more and more robust, this drawback has been minimized. If you do something silly like compute statistics after every row is inserted into the database, there will be a significant performance impact, and, as with anything new that you add to a database, you will want to test to assess the real impact, but it is important that triggers not be ruled out just because they have historically had a bad reputation.

DML triggers are the best known of the Oracle trigger types, but there are some interesting types that have been added over the years. Instead-of triggers, database-level triggers, and DDL triggers are all handy tools from a DBA perspective.

Instead-of triggers help with updating views that cannot be modified directly using DML; they are good tools for avoiding the mutating-table-trigger type of error that used to be more common. "Instead-of" refers to the fact that Oracle fires the trigger instead of executing the underlying DML statement that caused the trigger to fire. When the trigger is fired, the underlying tables are updated directly and appropriately, rather than updating the view. Whenever deleting a view row could mean deleting the row from a base table, or whenever updating the row would mean that the given row would no longer be selectable by the view definition, an instead-of trigger is a good tool to use. Updating a view that involves a join might mean that rows and values are affected that are no longer projected by the view, and this can lead to issues with program logic and user's interpretations of what they have done. Care should be taken by programmers in these cases to rely on the instead-of logic to assist them in their efforts. Further, the addition, by Oracle, of new object types (like nested tables and varrays) can represent complex relationships that involve implicit joins but whose modification can be somewhat ambiguous. In all of these cases, where ambiguity is implicit, instead-of triggers can be used to manipulate the objects as well as those views that are otherwise unmodifiable.

Database event triggers can be attached to an entire database so that the trigger affects all users logging in to the database, or it can be attached to an individual schema and affect only those logging in to the schema.

DDL triggers are attached to data definition types of events, and they are designed to capture `CREATE`, `ALTER`, and `DROP` events. These are typically used to maintain an audit trail for events, or as a means of maintaining a history of object manipulation in the database.

There are, of course, limits on triggers. You can only store 32KB of code in a trigger (approximately 870 or 4,000 characters), but you can get around this limit by coding PL/SQL program units and using the triggers to call these program units to perform more complex manipulations than would otherwise be possible.

Summary

We have arrived at the end of the PL/SQL discussion, with a little bit of information on database connections and some encouraging words on triggers thrown in to help you in your dealings with program units of every kind and in how they operate. I hope you now have a better understanding of how you, as a DBA, can use and allow others to use this programming language to better control your database and your day-to-day operations.

CHAPTER
3

Saving It and
Bringing It Back

aving it and bringing it back. Sounds a bit like resurrecting the dead, doesn't it? In a way that's how I think about it sometimes—like it's witchcraft or voodoo. So, in this chapter we'll discuss various ways to prepare your system for the inevitable day when the music dies.

Perhaps it seems a bit morbid to put it in those terms, planning for the day when your system will die, but at some point your system will face just such a disaster, and you must be prepared to recover your system when that time comes. If you don't plan for the possibility of having to recover it, what will you do when it happens? The system failure, ironically, isn't the critical part. The recovery, or the ability to recover, is what is critical. After all, no matter how good your backup is, if your recovery plan isn't satisfactory, the rest won't matter.

The wise DBA knows it's important to back up early and often because database crashes can happen to anyone at any time for any reason, or sometimes for no reason at all. Backup and recovery is, arguably, one of the most important jobs of a DBA. Thus, it's important to understand that there's only one thing that you, as a DBA, will likely not be forgiven for, and that is failure when it comes to recovery. Nearly anything else can be fixed, but if you can't recover your system, nothing else said here will be of much help. Whether you're a permanent DBA or a contracted employee, if you (actively or passively) allow your company's data to be lost, you could quickly find yourself out of a job. Data is irreplaceable. A DBA is not.

This chapter offers you practical information on just how to proceed with backup and recovery, but more importantly, it should help guide you in what decisions to make regarding recovery options. Don't think that once you have some kind of backup in place you can automatically recover (or restore) your system, or that if you've performed a recovery once, you're now completely prepared. You must continually plan and test and practice, to be sure you can actually can recover your databases should the inevitable occur. Plus, raising the dead isn't all that's necessarily needed.

Now is not the time to be laying out detailed recovery and backup plans though. Those kinds of plans and decisions not only depend on your databases' requirements, but also on your company's tolerance for data loss, the expected downtime, the backup window you're provided with, and the recovery window you anticipate. This chapter provides you with information on the different methods commonly used to back up the database, and recover from each failure. With information like this under your belt, you can make informed recommendations and decisions when designing your own plan.

Oracle's 9.2 *Backup and Recovery Concepts* manual defines a backup as:

"A copy of data—that is, a database, tablespace, table, datafile, control file, or archived redo log. You can make a backup by:

■ *Making a copy of one or more tables with the Export utility*

■ *Using Recovery Manager to back up one or more datafiles, control files, or archived redo logs*

■ *Making a copy either to disk or to tape using operating system utilities (such as cp, tar, dd)"*

If you lose the primary copy of your data, use the backup to reconstruct it.

Backups are typically of two types: physical backups and logical backups. Physical backups (what we're primarily concerned with here) deal with copying physical database files to an alternative location. Logical backups, on the other hand, deal with the data at the data (or object) level. These are extracts of parts and pieces of the database (the stored procedures, a table here or there) and are usually extracted with the Export utility and stored as a binary file on whatever media you choose as your backup location. The manual goes on to define backup and recovery as:

"The set of concepts, procedures, and strategies involved in protecting the database against data loss due to media failure or users' errors. In a wider sense, backup and recovery also involves performing maintenance on backups as well as keeping records."

To restore a database, you copy a datafile, a control file, or other file as a means of reconstructing it and then making it available to the database. Simply restoring a file (unless it was deleted when the database was down and you just happen to notice that it is gone before you try to start the database the next time) isn't terribly useful. If what is deleted, however, isn't a datafile, but is instead an index tablespace file, you can always simply drop the index(es) that would have been in the tablespace, offline drop the tablespace, re-create the tablespace (but you can do that with a new file instead of restoring the old one), and re-create the index. Unfortunately, it doesn't do you much good to just put back a file you might have dropped accidentally.

Also, did you know that if you're using the tried and not-so-true method of mousing in Unix to delete files at the OS level while the database is up, and you aren't extremely careful, you can accidentally delete more files than expected with a simple right mouse click? There's no way to undo it once it's done, nor is there any "Are you sure you want to do this?" window that pops up before the mistake is made. Not that I, or you, or any of us would ever have done anything like this, but if you are using a mouse to select/copy/paste the file names to be deleted, you have to be very careful and pay attention to what you are selecting. Getting into too big of a hurry can mean that you select more files than you intended, and one wrong click can delete several critical files, and you are sunk. It is a sinking feeling to know that there is no simple "undo" for the rm command.

You must be able to recover the database from any event. Recovery takes this a step further by taking the restored file and updating it. This is done by applying redo logs or archived redo logs and thus restoring any changes made after the backup was created. In this way, you reinstitute any changes made to the database within that time period.

Before going any further, there's some information you should know. First is the concept of a redundancy set. A redundancy set contains a backup of the control file and all datafiles, all archived redo logs since the last backup was taken, a duplicate of the online redo logs, a duplicate of the online control file, and a copy of all configuration files as they were at the time of the backup (for example, the tnsnames.ora and listner.ora files, and the PFILE or SPFILE). It's the most complete set of information available and is the best you can hope to have available when recovering the database. From this set, you can recover, restore, or re-create the database. The second concept to note is that the redundancy set should *always* be kept separate from the primary files they represent. This way, if you lose the original due to media failure, you *won't* lose the backup.

Let's start with what's generally considered the most reliable backup solution (cold backups) and work our way up to the least intrusive but often less reliable method (hot backups). We'll then look at the alternative provided by Oracle called Recovery Manager, or RMAN.

Some Concept Definitions

Before getting too ahead of ourselves, let's first go over some basic vocabulary.

- **Restore**   The replacement of a lost or damaged file with a backup of the same file.

- **Recover**   The application of redo data, archived redo data, or incremental backups to database files (either original or restored) in order to reconstruct lost changes.

- **Redundancy Set**   A set of files that contains a backup of the control file and all datafiles, all archived redo logs since the last backup was taken, a duplicate of the online redo logs, a duplicate of the online control file, and a copy of all configuration files as they were at the time of the backup (for example, the tnsnames.ora and listner.ora files, and the PFILE or SPFILE). It is the most complete set of information available and is the best you can hope to have available when recovering the database. From this set, you can recover, restore, or re-create a database.

- **Backups**   Backing up the database means essentially taking a picture of it. Three types exist.

  - **Logical Backup**   This is a copy of the data in the database but not a copy of the physical files. Typically, you would do a logical backup of the database when you want to get an exact copy of the defined structure of the database without any data or when you want to mothball a database, or right before you delete a table or schema from an existing database (just in case). Usually, DBAs won't perform a major recovery using a logical backup.

  - **Physical Backup**   A copy of the data in the database as stored in the physical files. This backup is usually what IT professionals use in recovery operations.

  - **Application Backup**   A copy of the data in the database (either logical or more often physical) as well as the application logic and any associated programs. Typically, application backups are done as a precaution when faced with running an errant batch program that could cause broad destruction or disruption to a system, or when recovering from user error. Often, application backups are performed prior to installing a new release of the application, or applying patches to an existing release of the application (as in Oracle E-Business Suite).

■ **Recovery** This includes many ways of reviving the system after a crash, such as the following:

■ **Media Recovery** This is often referred to as datafile media recovery and is used as a means of recovering from a lost or corrupt datafile, SPFILE (in the absence of an accurate PFILE), or control file. In order for this to work, the database must be closed or the datafile in question must be offline. Fortunately, any database which needs to be recovered, and that has an online datafile, cannot be opened. Oracle won't even attempt media recovery on its own; it requires a DBA (you) to intervene and make use of both the archived and online redo logs for the given database.

■ **Block Media Recovery** Corruption happens in the datablocks of the database files. They can be logically corrupt or media corrupt. Logically corrupt infers that the block was corrupted by an incorrect block type. Media corrupt implies incorrect checksums, wrong datablock addresses, or an impossible block type. Block media recovery is the means by which you can restore or recover an individual data block or set of data blocks even while the file is online. This can lower the mean time to recovery (MTTR) and reduces I/O overhead because the minimum amount of writing is done.

■ **Crash Recovery** A crash recovery occurs when Oracle attempts to recover a datafile that was left inconsistent after a crash. It requires only the online redo logs and usually doesn't need any intervention from the DBA. Oracle performs automatic crash recovery whenever the database is started after a shutdown abort or after a crash. It uses the online redo log files to recover the online datafiles.

■ **Instance Recovery** A recovery in a Real Application Cluster (RAC) environment of one of the instances involved in the cluster by another member of the cluster. The instance that detects the crash of another instance applies the online redo logs as a means to recover the crashed instance.

■ **Disaster Recovery** Regardless of the definition of "disaster," in this instance, this is the kind of recovery you'll likely be involved in. The disaster does not have to be an extremely intrusive kind (Denial-of-Service attacks, hurricanes, floods), it can simply be a careless user or developer who makes a mistake that adversely affects the database and causes you to take actions to restore it (and perhaps the applications surrounding it) in order to get your users back to being productive. In these kinds of events, the longer the period of time between when the users notice the problem and when they alert you (perhaps they think they've just made a mistake, because the database can't possibly be wrong), the longer it will take you to figure out what restoration method to use.

ARCHIVELOG MODE

Redo logs are circular. This means that once you get to the end of your redo logs, Oracle automatically wraps back to the beginning, overwriting the changes housed in the first. So if you want to recover any changes in the first log, you must recover the system to some previous point in time (no one ever tells you until long after they've made a mess of things that you need to recover something like 32,500 deleted rows in a production table). To accomplish this, Oracle provides a means of copying filled redo logs to an alternative location where they can safely reside until needed or until copied to an alternative media. These copied files are known as ARCHIVED REDO LOGS (or ARCHIVE LOGS). These archived logs can be used to recover a database, update a standby database, or provide an additional location where you can run log miner to determine the history of the database.

■ **NOARCHIVE MODE** Protects the database from instance failure, so if the loss of your database history isn't due to media failure, you can reliably recover your database to your last full backup. Remember that only the most recent changes to the database can be found in the redo log files. You cannot perform online backups of the database or of a tablespace because online backups require changes to be written to the redo logs and then out to the archive logs if sufficient transactions occur to force a log switch. Oracle is smart enough to know that most of the time at least one log switch will occur while the backups are in process and you can't reliably be sure you haven't lost information; it won't let you do something damaging if it can stop you.

■ **ARCHIVELOG MODE** Allows Oracle to automatically write the redo log files out to archive destinations. While this does mean some additional overhead and I/O associated with the overall database, it also means that you can recover a database to any point in time where you have a combination of backup and archived redo logs. You can back up the database while it's still open to users, allowing you to make backups more often, and do so invisibly to end users. Conceptually, you could use the backup you made the day you created your database and, if you have every single archive log that has ever been created, you can recover the database to any point within its history.

Now that we have our definitions, we must first decide on what's to be done prior to implementing a strategy—that is, we must determine how to choose our strategy.

Many organizations choose a blanket backup and recovery strategy for their entire company. If this is the case for your firm (perhaps they shut down every system from Saturday at 6 a.m. until 4 a.m. Monday morning to enable a good backup of all data in the system), then your decision is easy. But if you play any part in determining your backup and recovery strategy, the following section is for you.

User-Managed Backup vs. RMAN-Managed Backup and Recovery

The best place to start is by exploring the differences between what is referred to as user-managed backup and recovery and RMAN (Recovery Manager)-managed backup and recovery. There are times when each is appropriate, given that both have their advantages and disadvantages.

User-Managed Backup and Recovery

User-managed backup and recovery is any backup and recovery strategy where the user uses some facility other than RMAN to drive the backup and recovery effort. Traditionally, user-managed backup entails using operating system commands to make backup copies (either on disk or on alternative media) of all relevant datafiles, control files and archive logs, initialization parameter files (either PFILE or SPFILE), and any password file that you may be using. It is important, too, if possible, to include a BACKUP CONTROLFILE TO TRACE trace file, just in case.

A restore from a user-managed backup starts with a restore of the database files that have operating system commands. The database is recovered from these restored files with the SQL*Plus RECOVER statement. At this point, if the database is closed, then open it for normal use. If it is open, then make sure the tablespaces are online.

This backup type is usually only suggested by Oracle support under special circumstances—for example, if you're upgrading from one version of Oracle to another and don't want to update the scripts you've been using with the older database version. If you maintain a network that includes an Oracle 7 database as well as later databases and want to employ a single backup and recovery method, then user-managed backups are the method to be used because RMAN is only supported in Oracle 8 and later. In more recent releases, RMAN is the supported and recommended means of backup and recovery. Ironically, given that the only suggested means of backup and recovery is RMAN, it's recommended that if all of your RMAN backups have been lost or destroyed and you need to recover the database, you should recover using your user-managed backup.

Methodology

The basic methodology for taking user-managed backups is to first determine what files need to be included by querying the V$ views that are relevant. To find out the datafiles, use

```
SELECT NAME FROM V$DATAFILE;
```

Or, if you want to be able to see to what tablespaces each datafile belongs, use

```
SELECT t.name, d.name
FROM V$TABLESPACE t, V$DATAFILE d
```

```
WHERE t.ts# = d.ts#
ORDER BY t.name;
```

To find out the redo log files, use

```
SELECT member from V$LOGFILE;
```

And to find the current control file, use

```
SELECT name FROM V$CONTROLFILE;
```

Then, simply type

```
BACKUP CONTROLFILE TO TRACE;
```

And start your backup using the operating system commands relevant to the OS on which your database resides.

Need to find out if a given datafile is part of the current online backup of a tablespace? The following script can be run during the time when a tablespace is in backup mode and provides you with a list of all tablespaces, the files associated with each tablespace, and the status of the tablespace in the backup.

```
SELECT t.name, d.file#, d.name, b.status
FROM V$DATAFILE d, V$TABLESPACE t, V$BACKUP b
WEHRE d.ts#=t.ts#
AND b.file#=d.file#
AND b.status='ACTIVE';
```

A status of INACTIVE means that a file is not currently in backup mode.

New Features for User-Managed Backups

While user-managed backups are not the optimal backup methodology since the advent of RMAN, Oracle has introduced several new features in recent releases that enable an easier recovery (and one that performs better) from this type of backup.

Redo log parallelism allows server processes to generate redo in parallel. This is meant to allow update-intensive workloads to leverage improved throughput, meaning that logs that use this new feature write logs in a different format (this is only applicable to databases version 9.2 and later).

Since Oracle 9.0.1, users have been able to end a backup immediately for the entire database by issuing one command: ALTER DATABASE END BACKUP. This command takes all tablespaces currently in backup mode and moves them out of backup mode. The purpose of this feature is to allow a crash recovery script to restart a database that was shut down or crashed when all or part of it was in backup mode. Previously, the entire database could not be affected with one command. Instead, every tablespace that was affected had to be worked on separately or media recovery had to be done on the database.

Another handy feature that came with 9.0.1 is the ability to open the database after a media recovery encounters a problem. A new command allows you to open the database in a state with the RESETLOGS option. This feature allows you to make a backup of one database while it was open and then clone that database to another location, under another name, using the backup and any relevant archive logs. In this cloned database, you can perform testing that mimics the production system, or use it as an Oracle 11*i* database so users can access production data for training or testing.

```
ALTER DATABASE OPEN RESETLOGS;
```

Trial recovery allows you to see what would happen if you tried to actually recover the database. It's accomplished entirely in memory and so doesn't affect the actual physical database. This allows you to test backup and recovery strategies without actually having to apply changes to the files on disk. You can use it to uncover and troubleshoot problems with media recovery that you wouldn't otherwise uncover until an actual recovery effort.

RMAN-Managed Backups

Recovery Manager (RMAN) is the Oracle-provided free utility that backs up, restores, and recovers database files. It uses server sessions to perform backup and recovery, stores the metadata associated with all of its operations in either the control file of the target database (the one you are backing up) or in the optional recovery catalog.

Because backing up and recovering databases is becoming more complex with every new application and each incremental jump in size, creating a greater chance for human error, RMAN is Oracle's suggested means of backing up and recovering the database. With RMAN, it's easy to scale reliable backups as your database, backup, and recovery needs grow.

Perhaps more important is the ability of RMAN to allow you to back up incrementally only that database data that changed since the last RMAN backup. This isn't possible with user-managed backup and recovery. It means you can back up the minimal data necessary to recover the database and thus both minimize the time spent backing up the database and recovering it as well.

Finally, RMAN is much less prone to error than user-managed backup and recovery because you can almost completely take the human element out of the management. You don't have to worry about the location of every datafile, because it's all handled for you. There are times, especially when file systems are running low on space, when using operating system commands to restore a datafile from a backup is difficult, to say the least, and prone to error since entire files don't quite recover or restore completely. With RMAN, this is less of an issue. Also, because RMAN has a published API, it can work seamlessly with many third-party media management products. This means that even less user management must be part of the equation (limiting the variables in any equation means it's easier all the way around).

Now, let's look at setting the strategy for what our backups need to accomplish.

Strategy

The word "strategy" implies planning, critical thinking, and determining the best plan of action for whatever endeavor you're considering. This is no less true when planning the backup recovery strategy of an organization.

Requirements

The first thing that needs to be done when determining your backup strategy is figuring out your requirements. Not only do system requirements need to be taken into account, you must determine operational and business requirements as well as technical requirements. If the business concludes it can survive for 72 hours without its systems, and can afford the 36 hours of downtime weekly it takes to do a full backup, then its backup strategy will be different than it would be if the organization decides it needs 24/7, or nearly 24/7, uptime, but can afford a 60-hour downtime in the event of a disaster. However, what happens if it turns out that no downtime for backups or disaster recovery is tolerable to the organization or its customer base? If this is the case, then an even more stringent backup and failover strategy is needed.

Plenty of questions need to be answered first though. From what will you be recovering? Are you planning *only* a disaster recovery backup strategy? If so, what's your definition of a disaster? What about a Denial-of-Service attack? Will your users be able to get to the database data? With more and more of today's applications being web-based, this is a very real concern. What happens if a virus infects the network and by extension your data and database? What happens if a single disk in your RAID array fails? What happens if two fail? Or three? What happens if a controller fails, or if the whole server on which your database is running falls through the data center floor? Can you recover from key personnel leaving the organization? What about deliberate sabotage? What happens if a disgruntled employee systematically goes through the database (through the interface or through SQL*Plus or some other tool) and alters or removes data, doing it a little at a time over a lengthy period? Or what happens if a system administrator manipulates the files at the operating system level, or if the files are tampered with directly? These are all situations where some form of backup strategy needs to be followed.

In the case of key personnel leaving the organization, the backup strategy should involve cross training. Think there just isn't enough time for this, given the current number of employees in a department? These are just the departments that need it most. A DBA group with 15 DBAs supporting 30 or 40 databases could survive the loss of a single DBA far better than an organization with 10 or 15 databases that are administered by two or three DBAs.

Failures

Start out by listing the types of failures that are likely to occur in your particular circumstances. It is less difficult to hit a stationary target, so if you can accumulate even a mostly accurate listing of potential failure points in a database system, you can plan better for how to recover from these failures.

User Process Failure

When an Oracle user process ends abnormally, the PMON process takes care of the failure as well as the cleanup and recovery from it. Usually, when only a single process fails, the DBA need not do anything to maintain the database's integrity.

Instance Failure

When the Oracle instance fails, typically the SMON background process performs the instance recovery the next time the database is started. It does this by using the online redo log files to return to a stable state. But what made the instance fail? Memory is cheaper now than ever, and typically there is sufficient physical memory on a server to allow all instances to remain running. But what happens when memory goes bad? You need to take into account what may have caused the failure when you are looking at your backup and recovery strategy. Simply recovering the database doesn't mean it will run if the underlying cause still exists.

Media Failure

Media failure occurs when files (any of the files) needed by the database become unavailable due to a hardware failure (disk crash, controller failures, and so on). Typically, these are the types of failures that determine the backup and recovery strategies of most organizations.

Other Considerations

Will the recovery following the failure be a complete recovery (one that applies all available redo and archived redo logs and recovers to the last committed transaction) or incomplete (recovery to a point in time that is some time previous to the last committed transaction)? Business rules help determine this, as do user requirements. Again, the most important consideration associated with backup and recovery isn't which type of backup strategy you prefer, it's meeting the needs of the organization.

How much information can you afford to be without? If you're running in NOARCHIVELOG mode, you'll lose any changes that occurred after your last full backup. If that's fine given your business, great. After all, there are times when a reporting instance can be re-created nearly as fast as it can be recovered. Data warehouses may change slowly enough that recovery from the last full backup is okay. Transactional systems, however, are not likely to have the same requirements. Finally, where are you going to store your backups? The fastest media to write your backup files to is disk. It's also the fastest media from which to recover your files. But if you suffer media failure, can you get to those files? Tapes are accessible from anywhere given a functional tape drive, but where will you store the tapes, and who's responsible for getting the tape backups to wherever they're being stored? Whoever it is needs to be extremely responsible. It would be a bad idea to put the tape backups in the trunk of a car and then drive them around Austin, Texas in July and August, before remembering to take them to the climate-controlled vaults.

Now that you've determined your organization's requirements for backup and recovery, you're ready to consider what kind of backups should be implemented in order to meet those requirements.

Cold Backups

Arguably, the most reliable backups are what are known as cold backups, or closed database backups. With this procedure, the database is shut down cleanly and the backups are done at the operating system level. Since they're consistent backups, you can simply restore the files to their proper location and open the database. Not very exciting.

Cold backups do have their place, however, even in today's 24/7 global society. They can be performed whenever there's sufficient downtime to allow for the complete copying of datafiles from the database to the backup media. Even with the wonderful advances in RMAN and other backup utilities and strategies, it's always good, particularly right before an upgrade or right after a fresh install, to have a place to fall back on. If you have lived through an E-Business Suite implementation, complete with multiple patches and inline upgrades, you know that a good cold backup right before a really big run of patches can save you time in the long run (and provide you with a couple hours of well-needed sleep at key moments).

It's important to note that once a database is in ARCHIVELOG mode, there's no reason to ever do a cold backup, other than to comply with Oracle's installation or upgrade instructions.

Shutdown

The first thing you need to do before performing a cold backup is to shut down the database. Using SHUTDOWN TRANSACTIONAL, SHUTDOWN IMMEDIATE, or SHUTDOWN NORMAL are all good ways to shut down the database to get a good, consistent cold backup that can be recovered from.

SHUTDOWN ABORT, while a valid way of shutting down the database, is not optimal when you're looking at shutting it down as a beginning to a cold backup.

SHUTDOWN TRANSACTIONAL

Shutting down the database transactionally means that no more new connections are permitted to the database, no new transactions can be started after the currently running statements complete, and no new transactions can begin. After all running transactions have completed, any client that is still connected to the database is disconnected and the instance shuts down. The next time the database starts up, instance recovery procedures will be necessary. A transactional shutdown prevents users from losing any work and does not require them to deliberately log off.

SHUTDOWN IMMEDIATE

SHUTDOWN IMMEDIATE is typically used when you need to start a scripted and unattended cold backup. It can also be used when you know that a power shutdown is going to occur, or when one has already occurred and you're running on a UPS, or when one of your database applications is acting weird and you can't get all of your users logged off.

When you issue the SHUTDOWN IMMEDIATE command no new connections will be permitted and no new transactions can be started. Uncommitted transactions are rolled back (and if they were long running transactions, this can take a while despite the IMMEDIATE keyword) and Oracle disconnects all connected users. The next time the database is started, there won't be a need for any manual or automatic instance recovery.

SHUTDOWN NORMAL

SHUTDOWN NORMAL is the most polite way to shut down the database. While no new connections are allowed, those who are connected can continue working until they're finished, regardless of when that is, and then disconnect themselves from the database. This manner of shutdown, if you don't have rules in place governing inactive connections, could take days or may never happen (which is actually more often the case).

But the next time that you start the database, there won't be any need for recovery, and every transaction will be committed unless deliberately rolled back, keeping users from losing any information.

SHUTDOWN ABORT

SHUTDOWN ABORT shuts down the database as soon as the command is entered. While Oracle Support assures me that SHUTDOWN ABORT is a perfectly valid way of shutting down the database, you should really only use this option as a last resort. Employ it only when no other method of shutdown is working, when your applications or the database is acting abnormally, or when you know you have to shut down the database immediately. SHUTDOWN ABORT is also useful when you're having problems starting the instance and you need to bring it down immediately.

When using SHUTDOWN ABORT, all current and user transactions are terminated. No commits or rollbacks are done at this point, and the database is left in an inconsistent state.

The next startup of the database will require instance recovery procedures, which Oracle handles automatically as a part of the restart after SHUTDOWN ABORT.

Now, in an ideal world, this is all true … SHUTDOWN ABORT will shut down the database immediately, without question. However … it's also true that there are occasions when SHUTDOWN ABORT fails. Recently, I was witness to one such occurrence in which two people were working on the same database, a test database, debugging scripts. One person brought up the database with the PFILE and the other person was doing file system maintenance. The one doing the file system maintenance renamed the udump directory that the database was using to something else. When the SHUTDOWN ABORT command was issued, it failed because the database couldn't find the udump destination directory. It took a while to figure out what the issue was, and it took killing off the background processes (sometimes pkill can be your friend) to get the database down. It was determined that had the udump directory simply been put back, the database could probably have been brought down with SHUTDOWN ABORT. So sometimes having access to the operating system utilities *is* a good thing.

Now that the database is down, you can continue with the cold backup, copying off the files to another location, tape, or disk of your choice. If you shut down your database with SHUTDOWN ABORT and the database is currently in NOARCHIVELOG mode, you will need to copy the online redo log files. While they're often included in a backup, this is really the only time these files are ever used. And it's yet another justification for being in ARCHIVELOG mode.

Copying Files

Copying files off is not usually an Oracle function in a cold backup situation.

You can manually run copy commands or script the process to run automatically. Often this is accomplished by tar-ing off the files in Unix or zipping the files in Windows.

You can use backup software (Veritas, Legato, or others) or simply write your own scripts to copy off, or tar-off, the files to tape.

Often, this step is done by the system administrators, so you can just sit back and relax and believe they've done everything the way they should have and that not only are your backups good, but that you can recover from any one of them. Of course, something unexpected always happens— that's a given—but in a perfect world this is all you need to do. Oh, and of course, testing testing testing that the backup can be used for recovery. Unless you can recover from it, your backup plan is useless.

No matter who performs this step, it won't necessarily be the SA that recovers the database from a backup. It will be you. According to Tom Kyte (of *Ask Tom* fame), "The only thing that a DBA is not allowed to mess up is recovery."

Double-check the backups. Look at the logs. Try to recover or restore from the backups. Make sure they were complete and that you don't spy anything that might have gone wrong. More than one set of eyes means you can be surer you'll recover from whatever you need to.

Startup

Now that you've completed the cold backup, you can restart your database (before or after the server is restarted). No extra steps need be taken. Just type in STARTUP.

Unattended Startup and Shutdown

While it is a very comforting way to perform a cold backup, script the database to shut itself down, run an OS utility to back up the datafiles, and then script the database to start itself back up, it is very often the case that these shutdowns take a very long time to finish. Plus, many times an unattended shutdown will take far too long for it to fit into the backup window (if it actually finishes at all without human intervention). Other times, values have mysteriously gotten changed in the initialization file to something Oracle can't process and the database fails to restart at all. This is particularly true if you're using the init.ora file.

It is frustrating to you, your users, and management when everyone arrives in the morning and the database either hasn't completely restarted (if it restarted at all) or that it's still trying to shut down from the night before. Not only does it mean that your users are losing valuable work time, but it makes you and your database look bad, and that's never good.

Not only is a cold backup less certain than a hot backup or a supervised shutdown and restart, it is much more difficult on Windows to perform backups to tape, and scripting the shutdown startup cycle is more difficult than it is in Unix or Linux.

Therefore, you're far better off never using an unattended or scripted startup or shutdown, because something will inevitably break, and you'll be called on the carpet to explain.

Restoring from Cold Backups

Restoring from cold backups is simply undoing backups. You take the backups from whatever media they reside on, and copy the files back to their original location. It's important that every file that was associated with the database at the point in time that the backup was done be restored simultaneously. There's no way to recover to any other point in time, and there's no way to perform a partial recovery. Everything done in the database after the cold backup, if this is the only backup strategy you have, has been lost. This is, of course, only true if you aren't running in ARCHIVELOG mode. A cold backup in ARCHIVELOG mode is little different from a hot backup under the same conditions.

Disadvantages

So, with this method, you can actually restore your whole database successfully (usually) with zero data loss when backing up or restoring and the database comes up fast from the restoration. While a hot backup with archive logs available can also mean you have zero data loss, the only time you're positively sure you can restore to a given point is where the database is backed up. If all this is true, what can possibly be the downside?

Well, the downside is that the database has to be shut down and unavailable to users for the entire time when the backups are taking place. If you're backing up even a moderate amount of data, this can mean a significant period of time. The caches need to be loaded and repopulated, adding additional time.

This is the only option for consistent backups if ARCHIVELOG mode is not enabled in the database. You'll lose all changes made after the database backup was completed and the database restarted.

Warm Backups

What I'm calling warm backups is what DBAs typically think of when they describe hot backups. You put the tablespaces into backup mode and copy the associated datafiles off to another location (either on disk or on tape). Users never actually have to know what is going on, and work can, ordinarily, proceed as usual (maybe with some minor noticeable slowdowns, but nothing overly significant). It is a little more complex than a cold backup, but oftentimes the differences are worth it in the long run.

Differences

The difference between cold and warm backups is that warm backups allow you to back up the database at the same time your users access the database. This means your database has to be in ARCHIVELOG mode, at least for the duration of the backups. The other major difference between cold and warm backups is that warm backups need to be done as a user with SYSDBA or SYSOPER privileges, not just as a user with ROOT access to the server. This means you either have to implicitly trust whoever does the backups, or you have to carefully script the backups so they can run without any human intervention.

Putting Tablespaces into Backup Mode

You're likely well aware that when you perform a hot backup, you have to put your database, or at least a tablespace (or 20), into hot backup mode. This has the effect of allowing the tablespace to be backed up inconsistently, but when redo logs and archive logs are applied it can be restored consistently and users can continue with their applications or query or update information without missing an update. This also means you'll be seeing an inordinate number of log switches, and as an extension, a considerable amount of archive logs generated during the period of time it takes to back up the database. Why the inordinate number of log switches? Because when your database is in backup mode, the information that would ordinarily be being written to the tablespaces (the ones that are in backup mode and are therefore not being written to directly) has to go somewhere so it can be applied after the tablespaces are taken out of hot backup mode. It goes to the redo logs, and by extension (depending on how long you're in backup mode) your archived redo logs. This is why you have to be in ARCHIVELOG mode to do this.

This all means two things to you as a DBA. First, you want to limit the amount of time that any given tablespace, or your database as a whole, is in backup mode in order to minimize the amount of space required for the extra logs—and second, you'll need to build enough room into your archive log directory to account for the additional space.

Minimizing Backup Time

Minimizing the time the database is in backup mode means you both limit the time added to the overhead of the backup mode and the extra space required.

You can minimize this time in a number of ways. One way that is particularly effective is to make use of Oracle features like read-only tablespaces.

Make tablespaces read-only if the data in the objects in those tablespaces really don't ever change (like lookup tables ... state tables, city state tables, or date lookup tables). Many times we leave these tables in regular tablespaces out of habit.

You can put tablespaces into backup mode one at a time, copy the files off, and then take that tablespace out of backup mode. Afterward, you progress through the database one tablespace at a time putting each into backup mode.

Estimating Space

Typically, you must estimate how much space you believe archive logs will require for storage on disk for an interim period of time (the time between when they are written to disk and when they have been moved off to tape and deleted from disk). To do this, look at your alert log and determine how often, on average, your database log switches (actually, I use the peak load time as a metric just to be on the safe side). Next, look at how often you'll be backing up your archive logs. This will give you the total number of log switches in the given period.

```
Log switches * time between backups = total log switches
```

If your database switches logs every two minutes and you will be backing up every 24 hours, that's 720 log switches between backups.

Now, how big are your redo logs? 2MB? Okay, you have 720 log switches, where each log is 2MB, meaning you will have 1440MB necessary for the redo logs between backups.

```
Total log switches * size of log = size needed on disk
```

Keep in mind that you'll have to allocate more, because the minute you allocate 1500MB, you'll find your database activity picks up and you run out of space (and you come to a dead stop when you run out of archive log destination space).

This will tell you, typically, how much space needs to be allocated for archive logs for day-to-day business. Keep in mind, however, that during the time the database is being backed up, every change is being written to the log files. Log switches occur much more often during the backups. Whenever the tablespace is in backup mode, the full block is written to the log file, rather than just the change vector information. The log thus contains more information during this time than it typically does.

You need to determine how long your backups will take given the current amount of data in the database. Perform a backup of your database and find out how long that backup takes, and how many times the database log switches in that time. And make it realistic. Don't take metrics on a backup at midnight if you know you'll be doing the actual backup at 2 p.m. This will only give you bad statistics on which to base your decisions. The opposite scenario would be less harmful. Taking metrics at the busiest times and sizing your efforts based on those metrics will serve you well.

Scripting

Keep in mind, this can all be scripted. Remember, if you know of something you'll be doing more than once, script it. Chances are, you'll want to back up your database more than once, so script it. Backing up the database in warm backup mode means it will be open, thus you can store your warm backup scripts in the database. You can also back up your backup script because of this.

Example Script

A working example of a warm backup script follows:

```ksh
#!/bin/ksh
#
#       Generic Hot Backup Script
#
# uncomment for debugging
# set -x
# error files to be text of email message
export arch_errfile=/scripts/errfile.arch_err
export dbf_errfile=/scripts/errfile.dbf_err
export ctrl_errfile=/scripts/errfile.ctrl_err
export init_errfile=/scripts/errfile.init_err
export redo_errfile=/scripts/errfile.redo_err
export eject_tapes=/scripts/eject_tapes
export done_message=/scripts/done_message
# email addresses to use to email errors to those who need to know
export U1=awells@myemail.com
export SID=PROD
export DATE=`date +%m%d%y-%H%M`
export SWITCHES='-cvf'
export BACKUPARCH=/oracle/archives_tarred
#
#       Tape device needs to be a no-rewind device...
#
export HOTDEV=/dev/rmt1.1
export ARCHDEVICE=/dev/rmt1.1
export HOTBCK=/hotbackups
#
#       Where should I put my backups of my control files?
#       Where are my database create scripts?
#
export CTRL_BCK=${HOTBCK}/control_backup
export CREATEDB_BKUP=/mydev/create
export HOTLOG=${HOTBCK}/hotbackup-${SID}.${DATE}.log
export HOTARCH=${HOTBCK}/hotbackup-${SID}.${DATE}.arch.log
#
#       Where are my redo logs?
#
export REDO_LOC=/oradata/proddata/data01
#
#       This script must be run by the 'oracle' logon!
#
```

```
if [[ `id -un` != "oracle" ]]; then
    print "You must be Oracle to execute this!"
    exit 1
fi
echo "*************************************" >> ${HOTLOG}
date
echo "Log Switch... `date`" >> ${HOTLOG}
sqlplus -s '/ as sysdba' << SQLEND
            alter system switch logfile;
SQLEND
echo "backup of ctrl file in process. `date`" >> ${HOTLOG}
#
#     Backup Control File
#
sqlplus -s '/ as sysdba' << SQLEND
  alter database backup controlfile to '${CTRL_BCK}' reuse;
SQLEND
mv ${CTRL_BCK} ${CTRL_BCK}.${DATE}.1
#
#     Create list of Tablespaces that can be backed up...
#
echo "Hot backup started... `date`" >> ${HOTLOG}
sqlplus  -s '/ as sysdba' << SQLEND
            set heading off
            set pages 0
            set feedback off
            spool ${HOTBCK}/hot_tablespaces
            select tablespace_name from dba_tablespaces
            where status = 'ONLINE';
            spool off
SQLEND
#
#  Build a list of datafiles to be backed up for this tablespace...
#
for TS in `cat ${HOTBCK}/hot_tablespaces.lst`
do
sqlplus  -s '/ as sysdba' << SQLEND
            spool ${HOTBCK}/dfile
            set heading off
            set pages 0
            set feedback off
            select file_name from dba_data_files
            where tablespace_name = '${TS}';
            spool off;
```

```
SQLEND
cp ${HOTBCK}/dfile.lst ${HOTBCK}/dfile.lst.${TS}.${DATE}
echo "Backup of tblspc ${TS} in process. `date`" >> ${HOTLOG}
sqlplus  -s '/ as sysdba' << SQLEND
            set heading off
            set pages 0
        set feedback off
        alter tablespace ${TS} begin backup;
SQLEND
for FNAME in `cat ${HOTBCK}/dfile.lst`
        do
            cd /
            echo "Backing up ${FNAME} to ${HOTDEV}" >> ${HOTLOG}
            tar ${SWITCHES} ${HOTDEV} .${FNAME}
        done
sqlplus -s  '/ as sysdba' << SQLEND
        set heading off
        set pages 0
        set feedback off
        alter tablespace ${TS} end backup;
SQLEND
echo "Backup of tblspc ${TS} complete. `date`" >>${HOTLOG}
done
echo "Backup of datafiles complete. `date" >> ${HOTLOG}
#
#      Force a log file switch prior to end of backup
#
echo "Log switch... `date`" >> ${HOTLOG}
sqlplus -s  '/ as sysdba' << SQLEND
        alter system switch logfile;
SQLEND
#
#      Make a second disk backup of a control file
#      add it to the tape with the first backup of a control file
#
echo "backup of ctrl file in process. `date`" >> ${HOTLOG}
sqlplus -s '/ as sysdba' << SQLEND
    alter database backup controlfile to '${CTRL_BCK}' reuse;
SQLEND
mv ${CTRL_BCK} ${CTRL_BCK}.${DATE}.2
tar ${SWITCHES} ${HOTDEV} ${CTRL_BCK}.${DATE}.[1-2] ||
  mail -s " Tar of $CTRL_BCK  to $HOTDEV on $DATE failed $U1
      > /dev/null < $ctrl_errfile
echo "Backup of initdev.ora.... `date`" >> ${HOTLOG}
#
```

```
#      Backup init.ora File
#
cp ${ORACLE_HOME}/dbs/initPROD.ora ${HOTBCK}/initPROD.bu
tar ${SWITCHES} ${HOTDEV} ${HOTBCK}/initPROD.bu ||
      mail -s " Tar of init file  to $HOTDEV on $DATE failed
      $U1 > /dev/null < $init_errfile
#      Backup redo logs in case of full database restore
#
tar ${SWITCHES} ${HOTDEV} $REDO_LOC/log*.dbf ||
      mail -s " Tar of redo logs to $HOTDEV on
      $DATE failed " $U1 > /dev/null < $redo_errfile
#
#   Database MUST USE ARCHIVING for Hot Backups to be successful!!!
#
#
#      Backup archive logs
#
tar ${SWITCHES} ${ARCHDEVICE} ${HOTLOG}
tar ${SWITCHES} ${ARCHDEVICE} /archives/prodfin/*.*
   if [ $? -eq 0 ]
      then
          mv /archives/prodfin/*.dbf /archivesback
      else
   mail -s " Tar of archive logs to $ARCHDEVICE on $DATE failed.
   Clean the tape drive " $U1 > /dev/null < $arch_errfile
   fi
#      Cleanup stuff
#
mv ${HOTBCK}/hot_tablespaces.lst ${HOTBCK}/hot_tablespaces.${DATE}
#
#      Rewind and Eject Tapes
#
echo "Tape rewinding  at `date`" >> ${HOTARCH}
echo "*********************************" >> ${HOTARCH}
mt -f ${ARCHDEVICE} rewind
date
echo "Hot backup completed at `date`" >> ${HOTLOG}
echo "*********************************" >> ${HOTLOG}
#**************************************************#
mail -s "Eject Tapes" $U1   > /dev/null < $eject_tapes
mail -s "Backup $DATE finished " $U1 > /dev/null < $done_message
exit 0
```

While this script should be customized for your environment, and will only run on a system that either is Unix or Linux or pretends to be Unix (cygwin, for example, in Windows; available from www.cygwin.com), it is still a functional script.

One word of caution, however. Because the warm backup script can be run by anyone with SYSDBA access, it's important you protect the script you use to run the backups.

Recovering from Warm Backups

How do you recover from a warm backup? It depends on the calamity from which you're recovering. The following will provide you with some detail.

Total Loss

Recovery from a total loss of data is probably one of the easiest scenarios from which to recover. You simply have to lay down the backup of the datafiles (untar them if they were tarred to tape) and apply the archive logs using the point in time to which you want to recover. For some reason, with Windows, it is a little less simple and elegant. It can often mean that you have to reinstall the operating system. If this is done, you have to not only unzip the backup back to disk, but you have to use oradmin to create and register the service and get it ready to be accessed *before* recovering the database.

Loss of Data

Losing data, unlike losing your keys, does not happen simply because you've mislaid your tables or because you forgot where you inserted the data. Loss of data means that someone (either accidentally or deliberately) deleted or altered data that they shouldn't have. Sometimes this is malicious, while sometimes it happens just because someone made a mistake. Whatever the reason or cause, you often have to recover from it. The only way to be sure you aren't going to have to recover from it is to make all of your data read-only, and if that's the case, then what use is the database other than running reports?

Recovering from a loss of data means you probably have to determine at roughly what time the alteration or deletion occurred. You have to go to the user (if there is a user involved and it wasn't malicious deletion) and determine at about what time they altered the data. Users are notoriously bad at remembering exactly what time they did something, so you should view their response as a rough estimate.

And before everyone gets too comfortable with the idea that you can magically restore your system after anything and everything, make sure they understand that you may or may not be able to simply restore the one little thing that happened. In the case of Oracle E-Business Suite, you may have to restore dozens of interrelated tables in order to recover that one tuple that was altered or deleted. Make it known that this kind of "undo" is something that probably should be done only as a last resort. Miss one thing and you'll end up having to restore from much further back.

What you're doing, in this case, is a point-in-time recovery, which means restoring one or more files to a backup prior to when the data was altered (if that can be determined) or to the last time that the data was known to be good. The latter is often the case when someone maliciously alters data. Once you've restored the file to the operating system, you can then reapply any changes that may have occurred since the time of that backup to a point in time just prior (or as prior as possible) to when the loss occurred.

In a point-in-time or, more precisely, a database point-in-time recovery (DBPITR), not all of the redo that's generated since the last backup is applied to the database. The Oracle 10*g* alternative to a DBPITR is Flashback Database.

You'll need to march through all archive logs that were created between the time of the applied backup and the time to which you want to recover. It's often wise to recover to a time slightly before the time the user cites as when the alteration occurred (in case their estimate is slightly off). That will, of course, mean the users have to re-enter or re-alter the data that would have been affected in the interim, but it also means you won't end up restoring to a point in time a few minutes *after* the alteration occurred and then have to restore it all over again. The time trade-off is often worth the extra work.

An Aside

An interesting slant on performing warm backups is when a company has a storage solution that allows for putting the entire database into backup mode, and creating a snapshot of what the files or file systems looked like at that time and then, within minutes, putting the database back into regular operation. Pictures of this sort can then be written out to tape and used for recovery later. When using this kind of technology, the database has to be in backup mode for a minimal amount of time, saving overhead, and the picture is as reliable as any warm backup for a backup and recovery solution. The bonus for the system is that the database has to be in backup mode a much shorter amount of time than in a typical warm backup.

The trade-offs? You have to invest in the Business Continuity Volumes that will allow you to do this. The technology isn't inexpensive, but the trade-offs can be well worth it depending on your situation.

Real-Time Backups

Since we've covered both cold and warm backups, let's now talk about real-time backups. The real-time backup we're talking about here is what is more commonly referred to as an automatic failover. But before discussing it in depth, the following are a few terms you should become familiar with.

- **Standby Database**   A replica of the production database that's ready to take over as the production database within minutes.

- **Quick Recovery**   With tape-based recovery, it can take a minimum of six to eight hours (more depending on how much data needs to be restored and the throughput on your tape device) to restore a database. Standby databases allow you to fail over to an active database in minutes.

- **High Availability**   High availability used to be an optional selling point of databases. Today, having data available whenever and wherever a user needs it is a requirement. Standby databases offer organizations the ability to guarantee uninterrupted service.

- **Reporting or Query-Only Picture**   Standby databases can be freely accessed in read-only fashion and allow users to do more resource-intensive querying without affecting the primary database. With the addition of a logical standby, additional schemas not included in the primary database can be introduced to allow for different levels of querying not available in the primary database.

- **Failover**   Database failure is unplanned, while database maintenance is usually planned. Ordinarily, either activity means that the database is unavailable for access for the duration of the event. With a standby database, business can continue as usual while the recovery due to a failure of maintenance is underway.

The standby database, like many things in Oracle, has gone by many different names as it's evolved over the years. In Oracle 7, some functionality for standby databases existed, but the process of creating and running the database was a complex and labor-intensive undertaking. In Oracle 8*i*, it acquired the name standby database. In Oracle 8*i* and Oracle 9*i*, the process of creation and maintenance became more automated; however, it still required a considerable amount of skill.

- **Copying Files**   The database itself takes care of copying most things for you but there's a little bit of setup still required.

- **Scripting**   There really isn't much to do with a hot backup. Oracle really does take care of most of this itself.

- **Restoring from Real-Time Hot Backups**   Restoring from a hot backup, a true hot backup, is simple. All you have to do is fail over the database and allow users to access it that way.

Suspended Backup

It's important to note, and here's as good a place as any, that some third-party tools (particularly disk maintenance software) allow you to do something interesting that doesn't quite fall in to any of these backup categories. If you have software that allows you to mirror sets of disks, or mirror logical devices for that matter, and maintain an exact duplicate of the files on one set or the other set, you can then, depending on the vendor and the software, split the disks, thereby separating the different copies and be able to access them independently. You can then re-marry the different copies after you're done, allowing the software to re-sync them back together.

Using Oracle's SUSPEND/RESUME functionality you can suspend all I/O to the database and then split the mirror, and make a backup of the split mirror. It's necessary to make sure your database is free of dirty buffers whenever you do this. ALTER SYSTEM SUSPEND does not initiate a CHECKPOINT. You can only use SHUTDOWN ABORT if you need to shut down the database while it's in this suspended state, and if you do have to shut down this way, it automatically reactivates the database. By reactivating the database in this fashion, it allows media or crash recovery to proceed without hanging.

Because simply issuing the ALTER SYSTEM SUSPEND command does not mean I/O activity is immediately stopped, Oracle suggests (okay, they strongly suggest) that you precede the SUSPEND command with the BEGIN BACKUP command so all tablespaces are placed in backup mode.

RMAN

Every DBA has written backup scripts. Many of these scripts are the basis of the backup strategy for an organization. You've probably written some of your own. But have you tested them? Have you had to rely on your backup scripts being right and your recovery scripts (you do have recovery scripts, right?) being exactly what you need when you needed them? Do you know exactly where they are? Are they backed up successfully so that in the event of an actual emergency they'll be where you need them when the time comes?

Database recovery is too important to the organization for you to rely on ad-libbing backup and recovery for long. Being extemporaneous may be all well and good when it comes to a dinner toast, but it's a bad idea when your company's data is at risk.

Oracle's tool to help you not rely on your extemporaneous scripts is Recovery MANager (or RMAN). I understand that the early releases of RMAN were less elegant to work with, and when you're dealing with people who are set in their ways, changing is a difficult thing. But with each release of RMAN, additional features were added and each change built on earlier ones, until today more people have taken it on themselves to try out its powerful new features.

RMAN is the free backup and recovery utility, provided by Oracle with every database engine. You don't have to worry about getting the Enterprise Edition or enabling any features. RMAN comes standard. And it has become more and more powerful and stable with every release since its inception. RMAN provides you with a means of backing up and restoring the database without affecting its availability, and to do so by employing just a handful of predefined commands.

With Oracle 8*i* came the additional feature of being able to duplicate a database. This meant that RMAN could be used as a mechanism for cloning databases in order to provide as production-like an environment as possible for the purpose of testing and development, should you choose to utilize its features. The ability to do cumulative incremental backups was added in Oracle 8*i*, which meant even more flexibility for your backup strategy. And the best part: fewer commands made it more robust.

In Oracle 9*i*, there have been some very interesting advancements. While there's absolutely nothing better than being able to field test a recovery or restore, and you should test as many scenarios as possible in a test environment, RMAN provides you with some very interesting (and almost as good) features for testing different situations.

One of the most useful is that you can now perform trial recoveries without ever affecting the database. This has the net effect of proving that your backup is valid without having to go through the actual act of recovery. This doesn't take the place of performing an actual recovery, but it does prove you should be able to recover the database should you need to.

The commands for this are

- RESTORE CONTROLFILE VALIDATE

- RESTORE DATABASE VALIDATE

- RESTORE TABLESPACE *tablespacename* VALIDATE

- RESTORE DATAFILE *datafilename* VALIDATE

- RESTORE ARCHIVELOG *archivelogfile* VALIDATE

- VALIDATE BACKUPSET *backupsetname*

There are, however, still some things that are less than optimal about using RMAN. It still requires that you link it with whatever media management software you're using to communicate with your tape system since it doesn't come with tape manipulation software of its own. If you choose to back up to disk and manage your tapes on your own, it does that without having to use any further steps. Plus, in Oracle 10*g* Release 2 you get packaged media managers for tape. In fact, Oracle 10*g* offers tremendous changes compared to how things were previously done and how the software was packaged.

Vocabulary

Now it's time for a little more vocabulary. You didn't realize there were so many new words to learn, did you?

- **Recovery Catalog**   An optional catalog database that's used to store backup and recovery information performed on any given target database. Consists of the recovery database (database separate from the target database, but not necessarily dedicated solely to RMAN), the RMAN schema within the database, and within that schema a set of tables that contain the information relevant to RMAN operations, such as details concerning the physical structure of the target database, logs of backups performed on target databases, and stored scripts relevant to RMAN backups and recoveries.

- **Target Database**   The database against which RMAN takes backups and to which RMAN runs restorations and recoveries. This is the database that owns the datafiles, control files, archive logs, and all other structures that RMAN is backing up. There can be many target databases associated with an RMAN recovery catalog.

- **Channels**   The RMAN server process that gets started when RMAN needs to communicate with any I/O devices (tape or disk). Channels are responsible for reading and writing RMAN backup files.

- **The RMAN Server Process**   The processes responsible for the work that RMAN does in connection with backups and recoveries. All RMAN server processes are background processes. They are allocated in order to allow RMAN to communicate between RMAN and the target database, between RMAN and the I/O devices via channels, to allow RMAN to connect to a target database, or to allow RMAN to connect to its recovery catalog database.

- **RMAN Executable**   A program (usually named rman) that is responsible for managing the RMAN backup and recovery operations. It interacts with the target database, starts all necessary background processes, and performs all operations that you request (provided that you ask nicely). It is also responsible for maintaining the information (either in the control file of the target database or in its own recovery catalog) that pertains to backups and recoveries.

■ **Media Management Layer** Typically, a third-party piece of software that manages reading and writing RMAN files to and from tape. Further, it keeps track of which files it wrote to which tapes. This layer isn't necessary if you want to write your files directly to disk and then manage their relocation to other media manually.

■ **RMAN Backups** The backups performed by RMAN. Consists of one or more backup sets, where each backup set consists of one or more backup pieces.

■ **Backup Sets** Logical groupings of backup files (known as backup pieces). These sets are created when you issue the backup commands to RMAN.

■ **Backup Pieces** Physical binary files created by RMAN during a backup. These pieces are written to your backup media (disk or tape) and contain blocks from the target database's datafiles, its archived redo log files, and its control files, depending on the command you issued.

NOTE
A few rules to keep in mind about backup pieces and sets:

■ *A datafile can't span backup sets, but it can span backup pieces.*

■ *Datafiles and control files can coexist in the same backup sets, but archived redo logs can never be in the same backup set as either datafiles or control files.*

■ *RMAN is the only tool that can operate on backup pieces and backup sets, so if you need to restore a file from RMAN backups, you must use RMAN to do it.*

■ **Retention Policy** Defines which backup is no longer needed. You can use either redundancy (how many redundant copies of a backup to keep) or window (how many days you want to keep the oldest backup). This parameter is only applicable to datafiles and control files... there's still no retention policy for archived redo logs since

RMAN prefers to remove the archive logs after it has backed them up successfully. This may or may not be a bad thing. If you keep them around too long, you can run out of space, and you don't have to delete one subset of archive logs at a time.

- **Duplicate Target**   Cloning. Another one of the handy-dandy Oracle 9*i* enhancements to RMAN is that it allows you to duplicate the entire source database or a subset of the database. You can clone a portion of the database (skipping some tablespaces in the given duplication; this way, unskipped tablespaces can be recovered to a previous point in time if so desired). This is particularly useful when you want to recover tablespaces or even individual tables.

To Catalog or Not to Catalog

There are two ways to use RMAN. You can configure it to run with a catalog, or make use of RMAN's capability to retain (in the control file of the database itself) the information necessary for it to function.

There are different schools of thought with regard to these decisions, and I'll provide you with a quick set of pros and cons here. Some of these thoughts are based on historical perceptions, others on feelings, and still others on hard cold facts.

It's important to note that, regardless of whether or not you make use of an official recovery catalog, the control file for each database is the actual catalog of all backup, restoration, or recovery actions taken against the given database, as well as all of the structural information about that database. Optimally, recovery of the database in any situation should be done with the assistance of the control file.

We'll look at the easiest and least-invasive option first (the no catalog option), followed by the repository catalog option.

No Catalog

The no recovery catalog option makes use of the control file as the media in which to store the RMAN backup and recovery information.

When you opt to make use of the control file as the catalog for recovery manager, RMAN stores not only information about the database's configuration, and the backups and recoveries that have been done to that database, but also key configuration information relevant to the running of RMAN itself.

The default device type for your backups that you have chosen is stored there (CONFIGURE DEFAULT DEVICE TYPE DISK or CONFIGURE DEFAULT DEVICE TYPE SBT) as is information regarding the default channel allocation for those devices (CONFIGURE DEVICE TYPE DISK PARALLELISM 3 or CONFIGURE DEVICE TYPE SBT 6 for an example of configuration of parallelism).

By running RMAN without a recovery catalog, you can limit your choices and disable your ability to use some features.

Primarily you can't store your scripts centrally anywhere except at the operating system level (meaning that you are at the mercy of the operating system backups should you need to recover those scripts).

Catalog

The official recovery catalog along with its resident database is an optional piece of your RMAN puzzle, but one that is often handy. The recovery catalog maintains data that is replicated out of the target database's control files as a means to keep a second copy of that information in another location. Further, it's used as a repository for all of the backup and recovery RMAN scripts so that a database backup of the repository-containing database will back those pieces up as well. While having a recovery catalog for a single Oracle database is pretty much overkill, when you're backing up multiple databases (dozens or hundreds or even thousands of them), having a single place where you can determine the overall state of your system is very helpful.

It's important to remember that none of RMAN's core functionality relies on the recovery catalog; only the advanced features (some of which are very useful, to be honest) rely on its use.

One of these features is the ability to cross-check RMAN's contents (and what it remembers that it has) against the Media Management Layer's catalog (and what it remembers that it has). RMAN can also, with the use of the catalog, remove expired or obsolete entries from both catalogs because of the way the two are integrated.

Another nifty thing you can do when you using a catalog is to centrally report on all databases, the redundancy of all backups, and the need for backups on any part of a database.

It's usually recommended by Oracle and those who've used RMAN in the past that you use a separate database as the RMAN repository, and that you keep your central catalog in this repository database. Keeping the information in a central catalog (that itself is backed up) means you're more likely to successfully recover your database should you use RMAN. Creating more than one recovery catalog, each housed in a different database—one used to back up the primary databases and the other used to back up the RMAN repository–containing database—gives you an even better chance.

Catalog Commands
And now—ta da!—more vocabulary!

- **DELETE OBSOLETE**   Deletes the catalog entries and backup set files according to the given configured retention policies.

- **DELETE EXPIRED CROSSCHECK**   Detects expired backup set files if those files are missing from backup media.

- **DELETED EXPIRED**   Deletes the entries from the recovery catalog and target database control files.

Creating a Catalog
In order to create a catalog, the first step is to generate a database to use for the RMAN user. Afterward, you can issue the following commands to then create the RMAN user and grant recovery_catalog_owner to the RMAN user.

```
$Sqlplus '/ as sysdba'
SQL> Create user rman identified by rman;
SQL> Alter user rman default tablespace rman_tbs temporary tablespace temp;
SQL> Alter user rman quota unlimited on rman_tbs;
SQL> Grant connect, resource, recovery_catalog_owner to rman
SQL> exit
```

Once you've created the rman user, you can create the recovery catalog (should you choose to use one).

```
$ rman
$rman CATALOG rman/rman@catalog_database
Rman> create catalog;
```

This will create the tables, indexes, views, and procedures for the RMAN catalog in the RMAN user's schema. It can then be used to store scripts as well as backup and recovery information.

Connecting

Connecting with rman uses the following syntax, where catalog_database is the catalog database and mytargetdb is the target database:

```
$rman catalog rman/rman@catalog_database target system/
manager@mytargetdb
```

This command should be issued from the mytargetdb server and will result (all things willing) in the following prompt:

```
rman>
```

At this point, you can issue rman commands to perform any backup or recovery tasks you need to.

It's important to remember that the catalog database (should you choose to utilize it) needs to be in the tnsnames.ora file with the target database, while the target needs to be in the tnsnames.ora file of the catalog database.

REGISTER DATABASE

The REGISTER DATABASE command will register your target database in the catalog database. The command is irrelevant if you're using the control file to maintain the RMAN information. REGISTER DATABASE will, in the process, create all of the entries needed to manage the backing up and restoration of the target database.

Once a database is registered, you can report on it, maintain scripts for it, and automate backups and recoveries via the RECOVERY CATALOG.

Allocating Channels

Before doing anything else, we need to tell rman where we'll put the backup files, and where to get the recovery files from. We do that by allocating a channel using commands that resemble the following:

ALLOCATE CHANNEL disk1 DEVICE TYPE DISK FORMAT '/disk1/backups/%U';

This command allocates or assigns a channel to the rman process that is of type disk (in this case, but could be of type tape) with the files of the format that shows the full Unix path, while the %U formats the names of the files that rman creates. A number of other things can be specified with the

ALLOCATE command, you can see them on page 2-8 of the Rman manual from Oracle.

It's important to note that, while you can allocate several channels of one kind (several going to disk, or several going to tape), you cannot, as yet, configure RMAN to send to disk and to tape at the same time. This feature would be most useful, but it hasn't been created yet.

Creating Backup Sets

The easiest way to create a backup set is to issue the following after the ALLOCATE command.

```
Rman> backup database
```

Yes, it really is that simple. The preceding command will create a backup set, consisting of several backup pieces in the location you specified in the ALLOCATE command, which will contain all the datafiles, the SPFILE (if there is one), and the current control file. You might want to add "plus archivelog" to the command to include all the archive files.

It will also register the backup set with the catalog so you can use it to restore later.

Now don't get me wrong, you can make the BACKUP command as complex and convoluted as you want. Options exist to do a full database backup, incremental backups at various levels (only back up what's changed since the last higher-level backup), copy datafiles, make image copies, make tablespaces, make tables, create users, and lots of other options. These are all covered in the Oracle documentation.

Restoring and Recovering from Backup Sets

Need to restore the database? With the database backed up, you can now bring it back. Again, the easiest way is to use the RECOVER DATABASE command.

Yes, again it really is that simple. This will take the latest backup set registered with the catalog and look for it at the location you specify with the ALLOCATE command. It then applies all the datafiles, control files, the SPFILE (if it's used), and the archive files if they were included.

Once again you can make the RECOVER command as complex and convoluted as you want. All the options available for the BACKUP command have their counterparts in the RECOVER command.

There are, however, alternatives to this simple phrase, one of which is block level media recovery, the first topic of the next section.

Recovery

Instead of restoring and recovering the entire database, you can perform a block level media recovery (in this case, blocks to be recovered must already be identified by RMAN as corrupt). This allows the database to stay up and available during the restoration and recovery; however, attempts to access the blocks that are being recovered will result in error messages that the block is marked as corrupt.

Another option is to use BLOCKRECOVER DATAFILE n BLOCK nnn;.

Remember, this can only be performed as part of a full backup, however. In comparison, you can use an incremental or a cumulative incremental backup for block level media recovery (one of the drawbacks of not performing a full backup every time).

Other alternatives include

- **RESTORE DATABASE**   Restores datafiles.

- **RECOVER DATABASE**   Restores archive logs and performs database recovery. This used to have to be done in two steps, but as of Oracle 9*i* it can be done in one. It's easy to run out of space during a recovery.

- **RECOVER *whatever* DELETE ARCHIVELOG *whichever* MAXSIZE *nnn***   Restores the nnn number of megabytes or gigabytes of archivelogs at a time, uses them for the recovery, and then deletes them once the recovery is complete.

- **V$BACKUP_CORRUPTION**   View that shows information about corrupt block ranges in datafile backups from the control file.

- **V$COPY_CORRUPTION**   View that shows information about control file copies on disk.

- **V$DATABASE_BLOCK_CORRUPTION**   View that shows information about database block corruption that has occurred since the last backup.

Reporting

Reporting in Oracle 9*i* still leaves a lot of room for improvement. It's come a long way since its beginnings, but it still has a long way to go. What follows are some useful reporting commands that you might want to make note of. They're pretty much self-explanatory.

- **REPORT NEEDS BACKUP**

- **REPORT OBSOLETE**

- **REPORT UNRECOVERABLE** (There's no positive to this negative— no REPORT RECOVERABLE—so you still have to figure out what's recoverable by determining what is unrecoverable.)

Scripting

One of the best things about creating a RECOVERY CATALOG is the ability to score scripts within the catalog, back up those scripts, and maintain them. The first script allocates a single tape channel, while the second allocates two.

```
Allocate channel td1 type 'SBT_TAPE';
```

Okay, that allocates the single channel. Now, to allocate two, use the following:

```
allocate channel td1 type 'SBT_TAPE';
allocate channel td2 type 'SBT_TAPE';
```

To release the channels, the following command can be used.

```
release channel td1;
release channel td2;
```

To back up all archive logs, use

```
sql 'alter system archive log current';
@@alloc_3_tape_devices.sh
backup archivelog all
  filesperset 20
  format '%d_s%s_p%p_t%t_arc'
  delete input;
@@rel_3_tape_devices.sh
```

or for Windows

```
sql 'alter system archive log current';
@@alloc_3_tape_devices.cmd
backup archivelog all
  filesperset 20
  format '%d_s%s_p%p_t%t_arc'
  delete input;
@@rel_3_tape_devices.cmd
```

The following full script can be used to back up the archive logs:

```
connect target /
connect catalog rman/rman@rmancat
run {
sql 'alter system archive log current';
@@alloc_3_tape_devices.cmd
backup archivelog all
  filesperset 20
  format '%d_s%s_p%p_t%t_arc'
  delete input;
@@rel_3_tape_devices.cmd
}
```

To back up the entire database, the following script can be run:

```
connect target /
connect catalog rman/rmanp@rmancat
run {
@@alloc_3_tape_devices.sh
backup full database format '%d_s%s_p%p_t%t_dbf';
@@rel_3_tape_devices.sh
}
```

Need to run an incremental backup? Use the following:

```
connect target /
connect catalog rman/rman@rmantest
run {
@@alloc_4_tape_devices.cmd
backup incremental level = 0
database
include current controlfile
format 'full_level0_%d_s%s_p%p_t%t_dbf';
```

```
@@rel_4_tape_devices.cmd
@@backup_arc_all.cmd
}
```

So, as you can see, the scripts are simple. You can store them either in the catalog or at the OS level in a file system or directory.

Want to store them in the database? Simply add the command CREATE SCRIPT <script name>. Thus, a script to back up the whole database would be

```
CREATE SCRIPT BACKUP_WHOLE
{
BACKUP INCREMENTAL LEVEL 0 TAG backup_whole
DATABASE PLUS ARCHIVELOG
}
```

And to run it…

```
RUN {EXECUTE SCRIPT BACKUP_WHOLE;}
```

Yes, it's that simple.

Extras

The following are some nifty new parameters you should be aware of for RMAN today. While the choice to use them is yours, you should at least be familiar with each and know what they can do for you.

- ■ **CONFIGURE CONTROLFILE AUTOBACKUP [ON or OFF]**
  Automatically backs up the control file and SPFILE after ordinary RMAN commands (like BACKUP and COPY), and after any structural changes to the database are detected. It's highly recommended by both Oracle and DBAs alike that you turn this on. There's little overhead associated with it (no more than deliberate backup control-file commands), but it can mean the difference between having a control file that's accurate and not having one to recover from.

- ■ **BACKUP CURRENT CONTROLFILE**   Backs up the current control file.

- ■ **BACKUP DATABASE (or BACKUP TABLESPACE *tablespacename* or BACKUP DATAFILE *datafilename*) INCLUDE CURRENT**

CONTROLFILE Backs up the current control file along with the other pieces of the database you're backing up.

- **RESTORE CONTROLFILE** Restores the control file if all control files are lost or damaged.

- **CONFIGURE RETENTION POLICY TO REDUNDANCY *nn*** Retains the nn number of complete backups specified.

- **CONFIGURE RETENTION POLICY TO RECOVERY WINDOW OF *nn* DAYS** Retains the backups and archive redo logs to allow for any point-in-time recovery within the specified (nn) day recovery window.

- **BACKUP SPFILE** Backs up the server parameter file (SPFILE) that's currently being used by the database. RMAN can back up SPFILEs, but can't back up the server parameter file if the instance was started with an initialization parameter file (PFILE), nor can it make incremental backups of the SPFILE. The latter, however, is not really that big of a deal since the SPFILE isn't that large.

- **RESTORE SPFILE TO "*xxx*" or RESTORE SPFILE TO PFILE "*yyy*"** Since you can use RMAN to back up the SPFILE, you can also use it to recover the SPFILE it backed up. In order to recover the SPFILE, you need to STARTUP NOMOUNT the database, thereby starting it up using a dummy parameter file. Once up in the NOMOUNT state, you can restore the SPFILE from the backup and then restart the database so it can use the restored SPFILE.

```
RMAN> restore spfile from 'd:\db_backups\SP_BAK_C-1234567890-
20050423-00';
```

- **BACKUP ... PLUS ARCHIVELOGS** Allows the database to automatically log switch immediately prior to backups of archive logs. This is convenient because you don't have to remember that you have to switch log files before and after backing up the database. A really interesting feature of it is that there are no error messages if the backup of the archive logs doesn't find any new files. This means one past annoyance has been eradicated. It also means there's automatic failover between log file members if a sequence happens to be missing. This can be good and bad. It's good to know this is happening, and to have the ability to determine that you are or aren't doing this. It's bad because you're missing information.

Backing Up Parts and Pieces

Don't need to back up the whole database, or maybe you want more fine-grained control over the backups you plan? This section offers some ideas on ways to back up just a part of the database so that section is available elsewhere, or to select a piece of it that can be used in case you're worried about decommissioning a schema only to later find that someone was using it. Or what about when someone wants to do some file system cleanup and knows they shouldn't delete anything ending in .dbf, but unfortunately your control files have .log or .ctl extensions?

Backing Up Your Control File

Whether or not you are doing a warm backup, an export, or even if you're just doing invasive things to the database (adding tablespaces, removing tablespaces, adding or changing log files) you can, and should, back up your control file. You can back up the control file in such a way that you can re-create it later if necessary, or you can back it up to an alternate location so you don't have to re-create it, simply using the backup control file instead.

Backing up the control file to trace is also one of the steps needed when cloning a database to an alternate location.

Backing Up Your Control File to a Location

You can create a backup of the current control file to a backup location. This backup can be used to recover a database should the active control file be lost. You can recover from this by copying the control file from the backup location to the "regular" location and then recovering from the loss by using the RECOVER DATABASE USING BACKUP CONTROLFILE command.

The command used to back up the control file is as follows:

```
alter database backup control file to 'd:\backups\backup_
controlfile.ctl'
```

Backing Up Your Control File to Trace

To create a SQL script that will re-create the control file at the SQL prompt, use

```
Alter database backup control file to trace;
```

This creates the script as a .trc file in the udump directory. It's highly recommended you create a backup of the control file whenever you alter the structure of the database. Any time you create or remove tablespaces and datafiles, you should create (before and after) a backup of the control file so you can recover to either point in time, should you need to.

One auxiliary benefit to backing up the control file to trace is that you can use this create control file script to rename the database or to clone a copy of one database to another database name (production database cloned down to test or development) so you have an adequate test environment, a representative system on which users can learn, or a test environment in which developers can test their code

Backing Up with Exports

A backup can be done utilizing Oracle's Export utility. These backups are logical rather than physical in nature. This means that the data is extracted along with the definition that goes with the data. This can be a definite advantage when you're looking to export just the definition of the underlying structure (rows=no) or when trying to determine if there is underlying block corruption (file=/dev/null).

Exports can be scripted so the exact same export can be run over and over, whether it's the full database, a single table, a single tablespace, or one schema at a time. You can also export just the definition of any or all of them.

The difficulty with an export-based backup strategy is that it's limited to the recovery of exactly what is backed up. It requires that at least the database structure exists and that there is sufficient space allocated into which to recover the database.

You can, however, recover at a finer level than usual, or you can use export to get data from one database to another.

Don't want to take the chance that your export will end up in one massively huge file, or that you won't be able to export the whole database because of operating system file size limitations? You can limit the size of the export file and make the export switch from file to file after it reaches a certain size limit.

```
exp system/manager full=y FILE=/backup/F1.dmp,/backup/F2.dmp
FILESIZE=2000m LOG=scott.log
```

Considering using exports, but you know that exports take forever and you don't have much time to dedicate to them? You can (using the EXPORT command) set the buffer value to a higher-than-standard value (for example, 2MB), set the record length to higher than normal (64KB), run multiple export sessions (each exporting a different part of the database and have each session write to a different location on disk), and if at all possible have exports write to direct-mount file systems, not file systems that are mounted with an NFS mount. To do this, you must add the DIRECT=Y command to your export script, however.

Summary

And so here we are … at the end of the chapter on backing up and restoring your database. We've seen several different ways to back up and recover your data, and we now have the ammunition to make intelligent decisions on how to plan a company's strategy. From here on out, it's all a matter of putting that strategy into place.

CHAPTER
4

Database Tuning:
Making It Sing

f backup and recovery are the most important things a DBA does, then tuning is the runner-up. Oracle's database engine is a highly tunable creature and, metaphorically speaking, you *can* make it sing by monitoring how Oracle performs as it runs, and then adjusting different parameters, increasing (hopefully) its performance.

It's often the case that the time spent waiting for various computing functions to finish adversely impacts both a company's expenses and its man hours. Time is wasted when users have to wait (sometimes for extended periods of time) for queries to be returned. Sometimes it's imperative your system keeps pace with the speed and ever-increasing needs of the business community, or perhaps you need to optimize use of your existing hardware infrastructure particularly at a time when organizations insist on doing more work, even with less capital invested in hardware. In the words of Gaja Krishna Vaidyanatha (co-author of *Oracle Performance Tuning 101* and owner of DB Performance Management Consulting), you may be one of the unfortunate souls suffering from "compulsive tuning disorder," who spends an inordinate amount of time tuning the database by looking at irrelevant things.

Whatever your reason for tuning, however, and regardless of the approach you take, the fact is you'll often be called upon to spend time in the tuning arena.

While there are widely differing schools of thought concerning tuning methodology, what to tune typically falls into six major categories.

Database Design

Optimally, if you can (that is to say if you're lucky enough to have a say in the design process), the biggest bang for the tuning buck is typically at database design time. Knowing the design, being able to put structures in place from the get-go, and normalizing the design to the extent it is practical (even third normal form is too normal for some databases) will go a long way when it comes to tuning. Understanding how users will use the data also helps, and not being afraid of employing a lot of Oracle's new features (new as of Oracle 8, Oracle 8*i*, Oracle 9*i*, or even Oracle 10*g*) even if they are scary new features like materialized views, dimensions, and partitioning can also benefit a design, either from the planning stage or even later, after the database is in place. Also, a word to the wise: work with your system administrators to lay the files out on disk as optimally as possible. They know the disks that will perform better, if your organization segregates job responsibilities between system administration and database administration, and you know the tables and tablespaces that are likely to be more active. Many that don't know end up putting the most active data on the least well performing disks.

Application Tuning

If you can't tune the database design, the next best option is to tune the application and the application code. In many cases, the 80-20 rule applies. Eighty percent of all performance problems can be resolved with coding more optimal SQL or appropriately scheduling batch jobs during off-peak hours. Of course, if you're in a global organization, finding an off-peak time may be next to impossible, but it's still worth a try. The majority of this chapter will cover this kind of tuning.

Memory Tuning

Properly sizing the SGA, your database buffers, and pools can go a long way towards maintaining an efficiently running database. Having sufficient space to allow you to pin objects into memory, in particular those frequently used on large objects, can limit the amount of disk access needed. Of course, it's difficult by any stretch of the imagination to justify pinning a few billion-row tables into memory, even if it were possible, but in this, as with all things, moderation is the key.

Disk I/O Tuning

The proper placing of datafiles and aptly sizing them to provide the maximum throughput of data from disk to the application can be an important step in tuning. Again, placing active files on controllers with the best throughput can mean your users won't notice the application slowing down. The best throughput possible can mean your application won't be noticeably slowed down.

Database Contention

To really tune a database and make it sing well, it is important to have the best understanding possible of not only all of the components of the database, but of the way they operate together and interact. Two, often misunderstood, components are locks and latches.

In order for different users to share and access resources concurrently (and remember, as far as the database is concerned, a process is nothing more than a user) and serialize access to the SGA, and in order to protect the contents of the database while they are being modified and accessed by users and processes, Oracle employs the use of locks and latches.

Latches provide exclusive access to protect the data structures. With latches, requests are not queued; if a request fails, it fails, but it may try again later. They are simple, very efficient data structures whose purpose is to protect resources that are briefly needed. Latches can be requested in one of two modes: the patient, willing-to-wait mode that says "It's okay if you aren't available right now, I will just sit around out here waiting for whatever resource to become available and then try again" or the immediate or no-wait mode (ever have to deal with a toddler or a teenager?) that says "NOW! I want it now! Give it to me now!" Sometimes, when more than one latch is requested on a resource latch, contention can occur and this can affect performance significantly if enough latches are not available or when a latch is being held for a relatively long time. Latch contention can be resolved by upping the init.ora parameters.

Locks provide serialized access to some resources. Requests that fail are queued and are processed and serviced in order. These are more complex and less efficient data structures that are often protected themselves by latches and which protect resources (like tables) that are needed for a longer time. Locks allow sessions to join a queue for resources that are not readily available and are used to achieve consistency and data integrity. Locks are either invoked automatically by Oracle or can be invoked manually by users.

When it comes to database contention, watch locks and latches. Pay attention to wait events—look at them closely and eliminate as many of those that are avoidable as you can.

V$SESSION_WAIT dynamic view can be monitored for latch-free waits (P1 parameters tell you the SGA address and correspond to the V$LATCH_PARENT and V$LATCH_CHILDREN views, P2 parameters tell you the type of latch, and P3 parameters tell you the number of times that the process that is trying to acquire the latch has had to sleep).

V$RESOURCE provides you a view into locked resources that are causing lock queues to form. V$ENQUUEU_LOCK tells you the enqueue state caused by the locks. All locks that are held by Oracle or that are outstanding requests for locks can be found in the V$LOCK view.

Excessive numbers in any of these V$ views can indicate that you may have a problem in your system with people having to wait, sometimes unnecessarily.

Operating System Tuning

Monitor and tune the overall operating system, checking CPU usage, I/O, and memory utilization. Many tools are available to help you with this. Several depend on the operating system on which they run, while some are fairly OS-transparent.

Finding the Trouble

It is difficult, at best, to fix the trouble if you don't know what's wrong with the application or code. Oracle thankfully provides many tools useful to a DBA in trouble. The majority of this chapter is thus dedicated to these tools, their use, and how to determine exactly what it is that's broken.

EXPLAIN Please

The first procedure you should develop when tuning is running (and demanding that others show you proof of running) an EXPLAIN PLAN for every non–ad hoc SQL query. While you can't actually get most of the end users to provide them, it is always helpful if you can acquire the explains for those ad hoc and often horribly created queries as well.

Traces

Traces are one of the most useful tools Oracle provides. They're the base on which many other tools ride. Oracle background processes, such as log writer, pmon, smon, or database writer, create many trace files automatically whenever they encounter an exception. These trace files (often the exception as well as the trace name) are recorded in the alert log and are created to provide a dump of the information surrounding the exception. They're also frequently used for diagnostic purposes. I'll discuss them in greater detail in Chapter 5.

In this chapter, I'll cover the trace files that are deliberately created when attempting to fine-tune information.

AUTOTRACE

AUTOTRACE causes Oracle to print out the execution plan for the SQL statement following the AUTOTRACE command, and details the number of disk and buffer reads that occurred during the execution. It offers instant feedback on the execution plan for any successful SELECT, INSERT, UPDATE, or DELETE statement based on information that it stores in a plan table (which has to be present) under the user's schema. It also requires that the plustrace ($ORACLE_HOME/sqlplus/admin/plustrce.sql) or DBA role be granted to the user executing the trace. These reports are particularly useful in monitoring, and are an excellent tool for tuning the performance of any given statement.

Controlling the report is a simple matter, accomplished by setting the AUTOTRACE system variable. Table 4-1 shows the different AUTOTRACE commands along with their descriptions.

It's important to remember that you can only use AUTOTRACE if you've been granted the PLUSTRACE role and a PLAN_TABLE has been created in your schema. It's often not a bad idea to grant the PLUSTRACE role to public so that anyone wishing to have a better understanding about what his or her SQL is doing can use the trace function. Couple this with the creation of a PLAN_TABLE as SYSTEM and creating a public synonym and granting SELECT, INSERT, UPDATE, and DELETE on the PLAN_TABLE to public to complete the ability for everyone to do an EXPLAIN or an AUTOTRACE. But you knew that.

Before you can grant the PLUSTRACE role, however, you must first create it. To create the PLUSTRACE role, use the following commands:

```
CONNECT / AS SYSDBA
@$ORACLE_HOME/SQLPLUS/ADMIN/PLUSTRCE.SQL
```

Now, grant it to public.

```
SQL>GRANT PLUSTRACE to PUBLIC;
```

Then:

```
SQL>@$ORACLE_HOME/rdbms/admin/utlxplan
```

AUTOTRACE Command	Description
SET AUTOTRACE OFF	No AUTOTRACE report is generated (default).
SET AUTOTRACE ON EXPLAIN	The AUTOTRACE report shows the optimizer execution path with executed statements and output.
SET AUTOTRACE ON STATISTICS	The AUTOTRACE report shows only the SQL statement execution statistics.
SET AUTOTRACE ON	The AUTOTRACE report includes both the optimizer execution path and the SQL statement execution statistics.
SET AUTOTRACE TRACEONLY	Like SET AUTOTRACE ON, except that it suppresses the printing of the user's query output, if there is any.

TABLE 4-1.   *AUTOTRACE Commands*

EXPLAIN PLAN

If AUTOTRACE creates a report of what execution path and statistics (and the statement was successful) did, an EXPLAIN PLAN is what you should create first (or what would be best for developers to provide you with when they submit a script for you to install) when you create a SQL statement or when you embed SQL in a package or procedure. The EXPLAIN PLAN shows you what Oracle's optimizer intends to do whenever it tries to run the statement.

The EXPLAIN PLAN output report is generated using the EXPLAIN PLAN command.

An EXPLAIN PLAN tells you how Oracle and the Cost-Based Optimizer (CBO) plan to execute your query. This information is particularly useful in tuning SQL queries that run against the database (whether stored in the database or in a third-party tool or as scripts in a file system) in order to structure either the queries or the data and database objects in order to get the queries to perform better. Once you have some idea how Oracle thinks it will execute your query, you can change your environment or the structure of the query so you can make it run faster.

What are some of the red flags that can be brought to light in an EXPLAIN PLAN? While the list is not exhaustive, and by no means should constitute your entire attention when studying the EXPLAIN output, the following list tells you what you should be searching for.

- Cartesian products when they aren't anticipated

- Table scans, particularly on larger tables

- Unnecessary sorts

- Nonselective index scans

The EXPLAIN PLAN can give you the leverage to help convince developers to look at the code they're submitting and address inefficiencies. While this may bring a smile to many DBAs' lips, it can also point out those places in the database, design, and inner workings where it is inefficient as well. So don't get too puffed up if their code isn't always optimal. It may come back to bite you.

Before you can make use of the EXPLAIN PLAN command, you need to make sure you have a PLAN_TABLE installed and available to everyone who'll be running an EXPLAIN PLAN for insert update and delete. You can build the plan table by running the utlxplan.sql script that's located in the $ORACLE_HOME/rdbms/admin/ directory (%ORACLE_HOME%\rdbms\admin\). After you have the PLAN_TABLE created, issuing the EXPLAIN PLAN command for the query you are interested in can be accomplished as follows:

```
EXPLAIN PLAN SET STATEMENT_ID='somevalue' FOR <your SQL statement>;
```

You need to provide a STATEMENT_ID so you can retrieve the information associated with just the given SQL statement. Then, you need a SQL statement that you're interested in looking at from a tuning perspective.

Once the explain is finished, you need to find out what Oracle is planning to do. This can be done by getting the information back out of the plan table.

```
SELECT LPAD(' ',2*(level-1)) || operation
     || ' ' || options ||' ' || object_name || ' ' ||
```

```
DECODE(id,0,'Cost = ' || position) QUERY_OUTPUT
FROM plan_table
START WITH id = 0
AND statement_id = 'my_statement'
CONNECT BY PRIOR id = parent_id
AND statement_id = 'my_statement';
```

Now, want to look at the information a little more elegantly, and understand what's going on more easily? Try using DBMS_XPLAN. Starting in Oracle 9*i*, provided in the package was something that could not only make things easier to run, but easier to read as well. The format of the command follows:

```
DBMS_XPLAN.DISPLAY(
table_name    IN VARCHAR2,
statement_id IN VARCHAR2,
format        IN VARCHAR2);
```

The table name is the name of the table you're using to store your EXPLAIN PLAN. By default, it looks for a table called PLAN_TABLE if you don't pass it this parameter. statement_id is what you named the statement when you explained it to make it unique, and if not passed, it will assume you want to see everything. Format is how you want the output formatted, and assumes typical is the way you want it formatted. Yes, you do have choices in the way your output is formatted. The following is an explained list of formatting choices:

- **BASIC**   Displays the minimum information

- **TYPICAL**   Displays what is considered to be the most relevant information

- **SERIAL**   Provides the same information as TYPICAL but without parallel information

- **ALL**   Displays all available information

You can use DBMS_XPLAN in a variety of ways. It's best to set your line and page size up early when you're running your queries. This will save you aggravation later if you find you have to set them again after running a couple queries and discovering you're having trouble reading things.

```
SET LINESIZE 130
SET PAGESIZE 0
```

If you just want to display the last plan explained, the following will accomplish this:

```
SELECT * FROM table(DBMS_XPLAN.DISPLAY);
```

If you've named your plan something relevant (as is good practice), you can retrieve information on the named plan:

```
SELECT * FROM table
(DBMS_XPLAN.DISPLAY('PLAN_TABLE','my_plan','TYPICAL'));
```

Another handy way to use DBMS_XPLAN is to set up a view that shows the last plan created. You can then simply query this view whenever you want to format the output of a plan. This is handy, too, when you don't want to give everyone access to the plan table, but you want everyone to be able to quickly see what's going on with their statement. Someone trusted can create the plan and then give select rights to that view to everyone.

```
CREATE OR REPLACE VIEW plan_view AS
SELECT * FROM table(DBMS_XPLAN.DISPLAY);
SELECT * FROM plan_view;
```

To read the output of either method, look at the indention caused by the query. The further indented the statement, the earlier in the process it's executed. Equally indented statements under the same parent are executed at the same time or one following the other, and then the combined total of the indented statement (or statements) is fed to the parent operation.

Keep in mind that full table scans can mean missing or inefficient indexes, statistics that are particularly outdated, or data used in unanticipated ways. They can also mean that the code is doing exactly what it should do. You need to understand the code and data to truly conclude whether the code is as inefficient as it may appear. A lot of what comes back from an explain may reflect badly on you, too, so cut everyone a little slack.

If you're lucky, you'll have your own developers and designers who are willing to embrace the idea of running EXPLAIN PLANs before they run their complex queries against a production database, or who are willing to wait to move up new code until the anticipated performance of the code is examined. This is *not* a replacement for testing and retesting against realistically sized data, but it does give you a place to start looking at what might happen with the data and the code.

Granted, it's often because of management pushing that you don't have the time to address code inefficiencies upfront, but if you can show them that procedures like these are frequently a case of "pay me now or pay me later," and that paying later often is much more expensive in terms of time, effort, and lost efficiency, many of them may come around.

Running an explain is an inexpensive way to determine what the anticipated performance is of the new code and what effect the design of the database will have on it.

Want to go a step further? Let's look at the bigger picture. You can gather a set of baseline statistics (or what we'll call baseline statistics even if you don't take them at the beginning when the code first goes into the system) in an application, regardless of whether it's done at design time (although this would be the ideal) or when you start your tuning efforts, and you can amass the information and use it as a guide to measure changes against. Whenever there are any changes to the code, the structure of the data, database objects, or anything associated with the application, you can re-explain the changes and, based on the baseline, show how the code will affect the application, or how overall performance is likely to increase or decrease (yes, explains can point out good things as well as bad) as a result of the changes. By showing management how you can use this information to proactively tune both SQL and the database, you can prove your worth as a tuning DBA and provide convenient proof that may help you justify asking for training or books to help in further endeavors.

Keep in mind, however, that an EXPLAIN PLAN's results alone cannot unequivocally tell you which statements will perform well, and which will perform badly. An explain may show that a statement will do a full table scan. But this does not really mean anything by itself. A full table scan on a 100-row table (or other small table) may be far more efficient than using an index. The results of an explain may, on the other hand, show that a statement may be using an index, but if it's a pathetically inefficient index, then the fact it's actually being used is a trifle misleading. It may not run as quickly as it may appear. An EXPLAIN PLAN is only a tool. Use it to determine where to look and where to make changes. Use it to find out what a statement is doing before you make any changes, and then compare it with an EXPLAIN PLAN taken after any changes to see what those changes have done. It's nothing magic—no silver bullet for the database werewolf—it's just a tool to use.

NOTE
The EXPLAIN PLAN simply tells you what execution plan the optimizer would choose under the specific set of initialization parameters. It is not necessarily what would be used if the statement were actually executed. It may be interesting to see an explain of what Oracle chooses to do with a real execution of the statement.

V$SQL_PLAN

An advance in DBA tools came with Oracle 9.2. Now, Oracle gives you the following newer views to help you identify spots where your users' SQL is performing below par, information which is available simply by running queries at the SQL prompt. You should keep an eye on these views, and check them periodically to see statistics associated with the SQL or to uncover full table scans that aren't expected in the database. They can be a very useful tool for gathering information required in planning corrective actions. Freely use the tools Oracle gives you. They're a wonderful place to start.

- **V$SQL_PLAN**   Shows the same kind of information seen in an EXPLAIN PLAN. The only difference? EXPLAIN PLAN shows the predicted execution plan, while V$SQL_PLAN shows the one that was actually executed.

- **V$SQL_PLAN_STATISTICS**   Contains the execution statistics for each step in the V$SQL_PLAN. Check this view to find poorly performing SQL operations. In order for this view to be populated, the initialization parameter STATISTICS_LEVEL must be set to ALL.

- **V$SQL_PLAN_STATISTICS_ALL**   Combines the information from VSQL_PLAN, VSQL_PLAN_STATISTICS, and V$SQL_WORK_AREA. In order for this view to be populated, you must set the initialization parameter STATISTICS_LEVEL to ALL.

It is sometimes an interesting exercise to compare the EXPLAIN PLAN of a SQL statement with the real execution plan for the same statement from

V$SQL_PLAN and see if what the CBO thought it might do is actually what happened when the statement executed.

Personally, I like to request an EXPLAIN PLAN from my developers to see if they have thought about what the statement should do and what the new code is likely to do. Then, after the code is run in the target environment, I query the V$SQL_PLAN view to see if that's really what happened.

You yourself can look to the V$SQL_PLAN view to see those pieces of code that are run by the users, either through a tool like Business Objects or freehand through SQL*Plus or Toad. Not that user-created SQL is ever anything but terribly efficient, but sometimes it's worth the effort to see if they really are running as well as they can. Plus, it can open up avenues of discussion with users and may give you the opportunity to educate some of them on how to better construct some of the statements—things like an IN list with two values may be more efficient than a NOT IN list with 50 values, or that EQUALS usually performs better than LIKE if you can use it. Again, it isn't necessary to try and remove all the things we think of as "bad" SQL (like those performing full table scans), just look at the statement, think through the logic of what it's really trying to do, and decide if it should be reworked or not.

10046 Trace

One of the most popular trace events is the 10046 trace, which can tell you where a session is spending most of its time waiting and (depending on the settings you use) the bind variables and values employed in each instance. Enabling a 10046 event trace in a session creates a file that includes the details of all of the SQL statements and optionally the wait events and bind variables that occur in a session while the event trace is enabled (depending on the trace level you choose). It's one of the best tools to find out why a session is experiencing performance problems, and exactly what the session is spending its time waiting on.

So just what is a wait event (or timed event, depending on the version of Oracle you're using and the information you're viewing)? Well, at any given CPU cycle, Oracle is either busy doing something productive that serves a request, or it's waiting for something, some resource, that allows it to continue doing something productive. Often it is simply waiting for something to do, while occasionally it's waiting on database resources. Sometimes it's waiting for the I/O subsystem to be available in order to provide Oracle with information.

Using these wait events lets you see what Oracle is spending its time on. Is it wasting many cycles waiting for disk reads? Is it performing an inordinate number of full table scans just so it can get the information? Or, shudder, is it doing Cartesian joins to provide everything but the information the user ought to be getting?

You get data that touches upon so many different areas of your database, such as disk I/O, latches, parallel processing, network traffic, checkpoints, and blocking. Using this method, you can easily get at data showing you many different areas of your database, areas you might not otherwise have access to. Through the resulting trace, you can see information on disk I/Os, latches and locks, parallel processing, network traffic, and checkpoints. Furthermore, you'll get detailed information on such things as the file number and block number of a block being read from disk, or the name of a latch being waited on along with the number of retries.

In Oracle 8.1 and later, enabling tracing for the session can be accomplished as follows:

```
execute dbms_system.set_ev(sid, serial#, 10046, 8, '');
```

It's important to note, however, that you need to replace the "sid" and "serial#" in the preceding command with the real sid (or session ID) and serial number of the session you want to trace.

The "8" in the statement tells you the level of information you're gathering about the event. There are several different, and useful, levels of information you can gather. Table 4-2 displays what the useful levels are, and the meaning of each. The higher numbers include all the information of the lower numbers, and add their own details to those lower levels.

Level	Description
1	SQL statements
4	Includes details of bind variables as well as information from level 1
8	Includes wait events as well as information from level 4
12	Includes both bind variables and wait events as well as all lower levels

TABLE 4-2. *10046 Trace Levels*

This provides you with a trace file. Looking at the trace file, you can see that reading the raw trace is not for the faint of heart. It takes real dedication to wade through the trace file to get at what's really going on. Fortunately, running TKPROF on the file allows you to easily see in English (instead of computerese) what's going on.

One of the things a 10046 trace can't show you, however, is the time Oracle spends waiting on the CPU to become available or the time it spends waiting on requested memory that may have been swapped out to then later be swapped back in. This means that, if you're working on trying to figure out why a SELECT statement is taking so long to process, you may find your 10046 trace shows you nothing in the way of wait events. This may lull you into a false sense of well-being that the SELECT is as efficient as it can possibly be. But if memory is an issue on the server, and the query is doing a very large number of logical reads, you may well be able to reduce the time the query takes by reducing the number of buffer gets through a rewrite of the query.

Do you see a large disparity between ela (elapsed time) and cpu (CPU time) without any apparent waits associated with those disparities? These disparities can be caused by waiting on the CPU, so indirectly you can infer waits associated to these as well. This takes inference, however. It isn't provided directly.

But this information is typically only used for SQL statements, or for tracing the path of a PL/SQL package to see what it's doing. Ever want to know the same kind of information from an export? While import and export aren't really the kinds of things people tend to trace, you can find some interesting information if you run a 10046 trace on an export or import "session."

You start out, naturally, by running the export session.

```
Exp system/manager full=y file=myfile.dmp
```

Keep in mind this is just an example. You can use whatever parameters you would ordinarily use in your export.

Once you've started your export running, log in to the database as a user with dba privileges and run the following statement.

```
Select sid, program from v$session where username = 'SYSTEM'
```

A list of all the sessions running as the SYSTEM user is then returned. The one that has the program exp@mydatabase.com associated with it is the export session you're looking for. Make note of the sid connected with this session and run the following statement:

```
Select s.sid, p.pid, p.spid
from v$session s, v$process p
Where s.paddr = p.addr
and s.sid = <the sid from the above statement>;
```

The sid and the pid from this command are used to generate the trace file for the process. spid is equivalent to the operating system ID of the export running.

```
Sqlplus '/ as sysdba'
oradebug setospid  <p.spid>
oradebug event 10046 trace name context forever, level 12;
...
oradebug event 10046 trace name context off;
```

This will generate the trace file in the udump directory with the operating system process ID appended to the name.

10053 Trace

If you want to know why the Cost-Based Optimizer makes the decisions it does, use a 10053 trace. While the output of setting the trace to look at this is rather cryptic and difficult to wade through, you can make it less tortuous by searching in the output file (with find or grep or some other string-locating tool) for either the phrase "Join order" or "Best so far" to see why it made the choice it did.

The text associated with "Join order" can tell you the tables by name and the order the optimizer chose to join them. This may not be of much help to you if you've deliberately tried to get Oracle to join in an order that you would like to see, but you can at least view what order it's decided on as the most efficient. You can then check if there's anything you can do to influence the optimizer's decision.

"Best so far" is associated with what the optimizer has decided should be the most optimal plan and join order. By looking for this phrase in the trace file, you can start to see what the optimizer is thinking would be best, even if you have other thoughts on the matter.

10032 Trace

10032 trace checks what happens during sorts. This can be useful for many ad hoc queries seen in your system, particularly those that you may notice are doing several different sorts, or which seem to be spending a poor amount of time in any given sort.

```
alter session set events '10032 trace name context forever, level 1';
```

So why is this in any way useful?

While we all know it isn't possible to eliminate every single disk sort, it is possible to minimize these. You can tinker with the SORT_AREA_SIZE parameter and the SORT_MULTIBLOCK_READ_COUNT parameter to make a big difference in the way these sorts perform.

Understand that a great part of the performance of a disk sort has to do with the number of merge passes required for the sort to occur (this dictates the amount of temporary tablespace I/O that occurs in the sort).

You may be running a SELECT statement that retrieves rows from several different tables. The results are retrieved separately, but are then merged. The number of these sets you can merge simultaneously is called the merge width. This merge width is directly related to the combination of SORT_AREA_SIZE and SORT_MULTIBLOCK_READ_COUNT. If the number of sets of rows returned by the statement is larger than the merge width, then multiple passes will be needed for the merge to complete.

The SORT_AREA_SIZE is made up of read buffers and write buffers. The size of each buffer is SORT_MULTIBLOCK_READ_COUNT * DB_BLOCK_SIZE, and two read buffers are needed for each set of returned rows. The same write buffer configuration is used all the time during the sort. Consider a query that returns ten sets of rows—that's 20 read buffers. This means that up to 90 percent of the SORT_AREA_SIZE is allocated to read buffers.

If there are too many sets to be run through the merge width, then secondary passes will have to be made and more I/Os will occur. These secondary passes are what make the disk sorts particularly inefficient from a performance perspective. That's why the information retrieved from the 10032 trace can be particularly important in tuning, allowing you to more effectively set the SORT_AREA_SIZE so that secondary passes don't occur.

If you know you have a batch process (your most robust and data-intensive batch process, so you size for the biggest knowing that everything else will comfortably fit) that processes and sorts 12GB of data and you currently have your SORT_MULTIBLOCK_READ_COUNT using eight blocks (with each block being 8KB), this means that the number of initial sets that can be run through your SORT_AREA_SIZE will need to be

12GB/.9 * SORT_AREA_SIZE

Thus, your merge width is

round(.9 * SORT_AREA_SIZE / (8KB * 8)/2

Therefore, to ensure that the sets that fit are no greater than the merge width, you have to have a SORT_AREA_SIZE of at least

SQRT(12GB * 64KB * 2/.81)

This is 43.6MB.

There is virtually no benefit to having a SORT_AREA_SIZE of greater than 45MB.

So you see, you can use the output of this trace to help you determine if you have sufficient space allocated to SORT_AREA_SIZE, and thus limit the disk sorts that occur in your system. Every trace fill provides you with information on your system's SORT_AREA_SIZE, SORT_AREA_RETAINED_ SIZE, SORT_MULTIBLOCK_READ_COUNT, and the MAX INTERMEDIATE MERGE WIDTH. There are three additional pieces of information you can get from the resulting trace file: initial runs, intermediate runs, and number of merges.

10033 Trace

If you want to see the same kind of information found in a 10032 trace generated for particularly large sorts, you can get that information by setting the event trace to 10033.

```
alter session set events '10033 trace name context forever level 4';
```

While most intensive sorts occur with batch processing, every once in a while a truly huge sort is needed. Setting the parameters to allow for these unusual sorts of circumstances can be assisted with the 10033 trace. Particularly with the combination of a 10032 and 10033 trace.

In a 10033 trace, Oracle lists each section of sorted data it's writing to disc. Then it describes, in database-ese, how it's re-reading each of these sections back so it can merge them into sorted order. Whenever a sort gets very large, the time it takes to perform the sort is to a very great extent based on the number of merge passes that have to take place. So taking the information from a 10033 trace combined with the 10032 trace may give you the information you need to add that extra oomph, allowing as much sorting to occur in memory as possible.

10104 Trace

While it's often true that hash joins are more efficient than sort merges, it's sometimes difficult to get statistics on hash joins to tell you if they're as efficient as they can be. While this won't tell you overall what's going on with all hash joins in your system, you can look at what's going on with any given query, and the hash joins that are occurring within it. To look at what's going on during a hash join, use the 10104 event trace.

In the resulting trace file, look for the line that provides you with the line Memory After Hash Table Overhead and the line with the information on Estimated Input Size. If the Estimated Input Size is larger than the value associated with Memory After Hash Table Overhead, then Oracle estimates your hash area is likely too small. It's as true here as anywhere that poor statistics will result in poor estimates on the required sizes because Oracle won't be sure how many rows it should expect.

You can also find in the trace file the total number of partitions and the number of partitions that fit in memory. If the number of partitions that will fit in memory is smaller than the total number of partitions, then your hash area will likely be too small and should at least be multiplied by the ratio of

Total number of partitions/number of partitions that will fit in memory

Now that you've created a bunch of trace files, how do you find them so you can do your analysis?

Finding Your Trace File

Looking at these last several ways of gathering tuning information, you can see that the trace events all produce trace files, which are all written to the udump directory (since they're associated with user processes). The trace files end up in the udump directory and, unless you make some minor adjustments, will look disturbingly like any other trace files that might be in the directory. How on earth can you distinguish your trace file from all of the other trace files in the directories? The best way is to use the following code as an example to set your file apart by linking it to something of significance.

```
Alter session set tracefile_identifier = 'something significant to you';
```

Now you should be able to find the files associated with your trace session.

> **NOTE**
> *It's important to remember that when you're tracing statements you need to make sure you've informed the database that you want to see as much information that it will generate as possible. To this end, you must make sure you've set the maximum dump file size (which is really what these trace files are: dump files) to a size sufficient to hold all that information. The parameter you're concerned with is MAX_DUMP_FILE_SIZE and you must make it large enough to hold what you need. Valid settings are simply numbers (indicating the number of physical operating system blocks), a number followed by an M or a K (indicating megabytes or kilobytes), and unlimited. For the duration of the information gathering session, it would be wise to alter the session or alter the database so that MAX_DUMP_FILE_SIZE is set to unlimited. However, make sure that when you're done you turn the feature off or else you'll find your user dump destination filling up with huge trace files for things you didn't realize were being generated.*

TKPROF

The TKPROF program converts your trace files (both those you create deliberately and those created by the background processes if you like) into a more readable form. You can use TKPROF to see the contents of the trace file created in order to view what a problem query is doing.

It's important to note, however, that in order to get the most out of either the trace file you create or the TKPROF utility, you must have enabled timed statistics either by setting the initialization parameter in the init.ora or the spfile, or by running the following command:

```
ALTER SYSTEM SET TIMED_STATISTICS = TRUE;
```

A plan table can be used with TKPROF. If you do use it, the plan table must already be present for it to run successfully. If one isn't present, it can be created by the SYSTEM user and granted access and synonyms to public.

```
@ORACLE_HOME\rdbms\admin\utlxplan.sql
CREATE PUBLIC SYNONYM PLAN_TABLE FOR SYSTEM.PLAN_TABLE;
GRANT SELECT, INSERT, UPDATE, DELETE ON SYSTEM.PLAN_TABLE TO PUBLIC;
```

Including the explain is particularly helpful when the SQL statement you're examining has a cursor that isn't closed by the end of the trace file. In this case, the TKPROF output does not automatically include the plan of the SQL statement. TKPROF also doesn't report on commits and rollbacks that might be in the trace file.

Now, you can create a trace file either by setting SQL_TRACE to true in a session or by setting the event you want to analyze and running the queries of interest. Remember that the resulting file will be in the UDUMP directory for your instance (USER_DUMP_DEST from either the PFILE or the SPFILE) and you can now run TKPROF at the command prompt with the following:

```
TKPROF <your trace file> <your output file> explain=query_user/pass@db
```

It will assume you want to use the table you created called plan_table unless you tell it otherwise (this is one of the benefits of creating the public synonym for the table). If the table doesn't exist, it creates its own table and then drops it when it's done. The resulting sorted and explained file contains the following kinds of information for all SQL statements executed and found within the trace file (this includes the ALTER SESSION commands used to get the trace file). See Table 4-3.

Command	Description
COUNT	The number of times something occurs during the run of the statement (fetches, parses, executions, and so on)
CPU	The CPU time in seconds that elapsed during the statement's execution
Elapsed	The elapsed time in seconds that occurred during the execution of the statement
Disk	The number of physical reads from the disk
Query	The number of buffers acquired for a consistent read
Current	The number of buffers acquired in the current mode (usually found in update, insert, or delete statements)
Rows	The number of rows processed by the fetch in the statement (implicit or explicit fetches) or the execute call

TABLE 4-3. *Types of Information Obtained from SQL Statements*

Things to watch for in the trace include

- When tracing lots of statements at once, such as batch processes, you can quickly discard those statements which have unacceptable CPU times. It's often better to focus on those statements that take most of the CPU's time.

- Inefficient statements are mostly associated with a high number of block visits.

- High CPU values or high elapsed-time values may indicate you have latching problems and inefficient PL/SQL loops. Multiple parse calls for a single statement imply you may have an issue with your library cache

- Highly inefficient coding

- *Always* check the execution plan to see why the statement is performing badly.

■ Also, you should compare the autotrace traceonly explain to a TKPROF output so you can compare what the autotrace's explain thought would happen with what actually occurred. The TKPROF with its counts should be very similar to the autotrace's explain. If there are significant differences, then the optimizer is making bad assumptions likely based on stale, missing, or invalid statistics. Step one in correcting this is to figure out why the optimizer is making bad assumptions.

Trace Analyzer

Trace Analyzer is a lesser-known tool (available for download from Oracle) that acts as a substitute for the TKPROF utility, which is used in analyzing trace files.

The latest version of Trace Analyzer can be acquired from Metalink by clicking the link in text note number 224270.1 on the Oracle web site. It also includes excellent information on the utility itself.

Trace Analyzer goes TKPROF a step further, however. It provides information on more wait events than TKPROF does, offers actual values of bind variables used when each included SQL statement was executed, and shows information on the hottest blocks, CBO stats for tables, and indexes included in the statements and execution order (things that TKPROF isn't always able to provide).

Trace Analyzer can be used on any database (OLTP, DSS, or Oracle E-Business Suite), but it does require that a one-time configuration be performed. This installation puts into place many database objects that are used as a tracing repository.

Once the utility has been downloaded from Metalink and the setup steps have been followed, you can execute a SQL statement and then the name of the resulting trace file can be passed to Trace Analyzer, which then provides you with the tuning information. The scripts involved in the installation are as follows:

■ **TRCACREA.sql**   Creates all of the objects needed by Trace Analyzer. It calls the following scripts:

■ **TRCADROP.sql**   Drops all schema objects

■ **TRCAPKGB.sql**   Creates the package body

- **TRCAPKGS.sql** Creates the package specification

- **TRCAREPO.sql** Creates the staging repository

- **TRCADIRA.sql** Creates the directory object that points to the place where the given trace file lives. This is really only useful when using a destination other than that pointed to by user_dump_dest.

- **TRCAGRNT.sql** Grants privileges needed to use Trace Analyzer

- **TRCAREVK.sql** Revokes privileges granted by TRCAGRNT (this runs first to remove the privileges before the grants coming from TRCAGRNT.sql)

- **TRCAPURG.sql** Purges old SQL traces from the repository

- **TRCATRNC.sql** Truncates the staging repository

- **TRCANLZR.sql** Script that generates the report

- **TRCACRSR.sql** Generates report for one cursor

- **TRCAEXEC.sql** Generates report for one cursor execution

TRCSESS

What, there's more? Hey, Oracle is nothing if not prolific when it comes to providing tuning tools. For those of you who are using, or who are considering using, Oracle 10g, this one's for you! Though available for use, it doesn't work with earlier releases.

Need to find out what's going on in the database across several different trace files, and you know you generated these trace files for a given user on a given database? Don't want to struggle with figuring out how to analyze each trace file individually and then try to pull together the information from each file into a whole application situation analysis? The answer: TRCSESS.

If you know which trace files you're dealing with (the set of trace files containing the right combination of SID, CLIENT_IDENTIFIER, SERVICE_NAME, ACTION_NAM, and/or MODULE_NAME variables) in order to pull all the information together for a given analysis, you can use TRCSESS to do it for you. This can be very beneficial if you're trying to tune out the bottlenecks in the database or in an application that's consuming large amounts of resources. TRCSESS is particularly useful in shared server environments where several processes are each running and writing trace files.

TRCSESS is a Java application executed from the command line that consolidates trace information from multiple trace files. Oracle provides a shell script which you can execute rather than call Java directly. The output of the TRCSESS utility can then be used as the input to TKPROF or Trace Analyzer.

Statspack

There are some very good books out there about the care and feeding of your database using Statspack, but no tuning chapter would be worth its salt if it didn't cover the use of Statspack as a way to determine where performance is an issue.

Before you rely too heavily on Ststspack reports, make sure they provide you with database-wide information and aren't looked at as a tool simply for tuning individual SQL statements.

One of the most useful things you can do with Statspack is find out your top five wait events and determine which ones you can actually do something about. To this end, Statspack provides a report called "Top 5 Timed Events." While this report can be minimally useful even if TIMED_STATISTICS is set to false, setting it to true can provide you with a list ordered by time waited rather than just the number of times waited. This can be more valuable because you may not care that the event that waited the longest was SQLNET Message From Client, but you indeed might care that you waited 874 seconds for a DB file scattered read.

Table 4-4 provides you with a general overview of what the most common "Top 5 Timed Events" mean to you and what you can do to fix them.

Event	Meaning	Potential Fix
DB File Scattered Read	Generally indicates waits related to full table scans.	Find where you may be missing indexes or where indexes may be advantageous.

TABLE 4-4.   *Wait Events Prevalent in Statspack Reports*

Event	Meaning	Potential Fix
DB File Sequential Read	Generally means you're doing an index read. A lot of waits attributed to this can mean that join orders are less than optimal or that you have unselective indexing.	Check joins on tables to see if you can make them more efficient.
Free Buffer	Your system is probably waiting for a free buffer in memory. There probably aren't any currently available. This is usually indicative of a need to increase the DB_BUFFER_CACHE or to tune your SQL statements to be as efficient as possible (do this first, before changing database parameters).	To fix this (remember, one at a time), tune the SQL, increase DB_BUFFER_CACHE, increase the amount of checkpointing you're doing, use more Database Writer processes, or increase the number of physical disks over which your data is spread.
Buffer Busy	You are waiting for a buffer that is already being used and is currently unsharable, or that is currently being read into cache. Waits for this are expected, but should not be excessive.	If you're seeing an excessive amount of waits for this, you may want to increase DB_CACHE_SIZE, or migrate to ASSM.
Latch Free	Latches protect shared memory structures and are usually very rapidly obtained and released. They prevent the concurrent alteration of shared memory structures. Concurrent select is not only okay, it is often a way of life in a busy database, but Oracle protects data from concurrent updates. Typically, when you see many of these, it indicates that you aren't using bind variables, buffer cache contention, or hot blocks in the buffer cache... or that you may be running into a latch-related bug (remember, Metalink can be your friend).	Further investigation is usually needed. Because there are so many causes, you can look at Statspack reports to see if the top latch waits, allowing you to start working through the issues with your database.

TABLE 4-4. *Wait Events Prevalent in Statspack Reports* (continued)

Event	Meaning	Potential Fix
Enqueue	Enqueue is a lock that protects shared resources. It takes care of queuing (first in, first out) requests so that resources are allocated equitably. Common events that cause these waits are space management and the allocation of dictionary-managed tablespaces, attempts to duplicate unique indexes, multiple concurrent attempts to update the same bitmap index fragment, and multiple users updating the same row.	Setting Inittrans or Maxtrans to a higher number, thereby allowing more concurrent access to any given block is one place you can look to get around this problem in pre-Oracle 10g versions. With the advent of Oracle 10g, maxtrans became 255 regardless. You can also make sure you have indexes on foreign keys as a means to avoid enqueue waits. It's important to note, however, that one of the major problems that contributes to this being an issue is poor application design.
Log Buffer Space	You are filling log buffers faster than log writer can write them out to redo.	Putting your redo logs on faster disks so that writes to them can occur as quickly as possible will ease this problem. You need to empty the log buffers as quickly as possible.
Log File Switch	Caused by commits waiting for a log file switch (particularly if archiving is needed or checkpointing is incomplete).	Make sure your disk isn't full. Look for I/O contention. Add more or increase the size of the redo logs. As a last resort, try adding more database writers.
Log File Sync	Log writer isn't flushing the session redo information from the buffer to the redo logs rapidly enough.	Commit more records simultaneously (50 or 100 at a time rather than one at a time). You could try to move your redo log files to faster disks, but if it comes at the expense of hot data files, you may end up robbing Peter to pay Paul, as they say. Avoiding RAID 5 may help, but then you probably already knew that.

TABLE 4-4.   *Wait Events Prevalent in Statspack Reports* (continued)

Event	Meaning	Potential Fix
Idle Event	The ever-popular System Idle Events. While it's typically okay to ignore most of these, you may want to note if they suddenly start happening. It could indicate you've moved your bottleneck and may need to revisit some of your other tuning tools.	

TABLE 4-4. *Wait Events Prevalent in Statspack Reports* (continued)

So you see, Statspack can be very useful when looking at tuning the overall database. It can give you yet another useful tool, a means to come at the problem from another avenue, and some extra ideas on why your applications aren't performing the way users anticipate.

Since users typically have preconceived notions about how a database should perform, let's look at them next.

Users

While it's true that without users the database would absolutely fly, it's also true that without users you'd probably be out of a job (after all, what good is a database—and by extension a DBA—if there aren't users using the data?). Given that users happen, what is the best thing we can do to tune the users?

It may not be high on your list, but teaching users, training them, and/or creating a series of presentations or conversations to help them learn is your best asset from a database tuning perspective.

Training doesn't always have to be formal. Lunch with the DBA in a meeting room where you just sit around and talk about SQL and PL/SQL and the wonders of Triggers is a great idea. One of the best Oracle University classes I ever attended was the PL/SQL class in Minneapolis where I learned that a *Trigger's a Wonderful Thing* (thank you very much, Winnie the Pooh). It may be a somewhat long process, but it will be well worth the effort in the long run, and you might just find out that developers, and users, are real people, too. Plus, it will impress everyone that you're trying to foster a team atmosphere.

I don't know about you, but I've never been all that much of a people person; it is, after all, mostly why I got into computers. You don't have to deal with people all that much. But if you can get an idea of what the users (the developers, the designers, the end users) are trying to do, you can do a better job at tuning the database from the outside, and you can give the users information that will help make your life a whole lot easier. It really is a win-win situation.

Fixing the Trouble

Once you've gathered the information needed using your arsenal of tools, you can set about fixing the trouble, or at least addressing the issues that were uncovered as a result of the tuning efforts to this point.

There is something of an art to tuning SQL statements. It's important to remember (and I can't stress this enough) that you should only change one thing at a time and then see what effect that change has on the performance of a statement.

Tuning Database Parameters

You can make some inferences on database parameters that need to be tuned based on a lot of the V$ views (the dynamic performance views, wink wink) available in the database. These views are built with you in mind. Make use of them wisely and you can have your database humming in no time.

V$FILESTAT

V$FILESTAT provides you with information on activity relating to each file in the database. Interesting columns include PHYRDS (physical reads), PHYWRTS (physical writes), SINGLEBLKRDS (random I/O that's occurred with the file), AVGIOTIM (the average time, to the hundredth of a second, that has been spent on I/O), READTIM (the time spent, in hundredths of seconds, doing reads), WRITETIM (the time spent, in hundredths of seconds, doing writes), and LSTIOTIM (the time spent, in hundredths of seconds, doing the last I/O operation). This view is typically joined to V$DATAFILE and V$TABLESPACE to provide really relevant information. It is important to note, however, that if you are using async io, you should not set too much store in the write time. In fact, in that particular circumstance WRITETIM is meaningless.

```
select d.name as file, t.name as tablespace,
       f.phyblkrd, f.phyblkwrt, f.readtim, f.writetim
from v$filestat f, v$datafile d, v$tablespace t
where f.file# = d.file#
and   d.ts# = t.ts#
NAME
```

```
---------------------------------------------------------------
```

NAME	PHYBLKRD	PHYBLKWRT	READTIM	WRITETIM
------- -------------	----------	----------	----------	----------
D:\ORACLE\ORADATA\10G\TEST10\SYSTEM01.DBF				
SYSTEM	5308	351	2409	457
D:\ORACLE\PRODUCT\10.1.0\ORADATA\TEST10\SYSTEM02.DBF				
SYSTEM	4241	132	1788	194
D:\ORACLE\ORADATA\10G\TEST10\UNDOTBS01.DBF				
UNDOTBS1	36	3989	253	6472
D:\ORACLE\ORADATA\10G\TEST10\SYSAUX01.DBF				
SYSAUX	2573	1473	897	2879
D:\ORACLE\PRODUCT\10.1.0\ORADATA\TEST10\SYSAUX02.DBF				
SYSAUX	1488	1190	1713	2206
D:\ORACLE\ORADATA\10G\TEST10\USERS01.DBF				
USERS	13	7	26	8

It's important to note that V$ views are cumulative. They are virtually empty when you start up the instance and they accumulate data while your database is open. Though this means you don't see what's happening at exactly the time when the query is run, the way you would with, say, a 10046 trace, it does mean you can run a query now, run it again in 15 minutes (or set it to run every 15 minutes for a couple of hours), and then write the results out to a file. Look at the files when you're done (diff them in Unix… heck, download and run CYGWIN on Windows and diff the files) and see what I/Os have been happening during the time. Yeah, yeah, I know, Statspack will give you the same thing, but sometimes I like to have ultimate control of what I'm looking at. Frequently I know that my developers are testing and yet I want to be able to granularly run the queries on that environment every five or ten minutes. Though I already have Statspack set up to run every hour, I may just want to do something quick and dirty. I have this scripted so I can simply run it whenever I want and spool the output to flat files. The same information will end up aggregated in Statspack, but I can send the files to the project manager who just doesn't get that whole SQL stuff but who does really understand file processing (or just feels more comfortable with files that he/she can touch and feel), and it gives them a warm fuzzy feeling without changing my Statspack reporting. Sometimes it's as important to be flexible and to know your users (know your audience) as it is to know your database, the data, and the application. Have as many tools as you can in your toolbox so you can meet any need.

V$LATCH

When I was growing up, there was an interesting latch on my bedroom door. It was metal and ornate and had a lever that swung across and clasped another metal piece on the other side of the door. This latch was designed to keep people out and protect the privacy of the people in the bedroom. There was no way to swing the latch to lock the door from the outside, or to unlock it from the outside. Its purpose was to temporarily block access to the room.

Database latches are pretty much the same, although way less decorative. They temporarily prevent access to the inside of Oracle (its memory structures primarily) while the inside process is already accessing them. When that process completes, it opens the latch and leaves, allowing the next process to make use of the memory. Some processes (like your parents) are willing to wait outside the door for you to come and open the latch. Others, like your little brother, will stay there until they get tired of waiting, and then finally give up.

V$LATCH tells you about the latches, the address of the latch object, its level and name, the number of times it obtained a wait (GETS) and the number of times it obtained a wait but failed on the first try (MISSES), the number of times it got tired and decided to nap while waiting (SLEEPS), the number of times it was obtained without a wait (IMMEDIATE_GETS), and the number of times it failed to be obtained without a wait (IMMEDIATE_ MISSES). If you're seeing an inordinate number of latches in your wait events, this view may be one you'll want to investigate further.

V$LIBRARYCACHE

Just like when you go to the library (you DO go to the library, right?), the first time you try to find a book, you usually have to go look it up in the online catalog or the card catalog (yes, there are still libraries that use them). Once you find the call number, you then search the stacks till you find the book (if it's not checked out or misshelved, that is). If you find you like the book, or similar books, or books by the same author, you may not have to go back to the card catalog to find the books. You may just decide to return to the stacks where you found this book and dig up others that are similar.

Oracle kind of works the same way. Once a SQL statement is presented to Oracle for processing, Oracle goes to its card catalog to find where the information can be found and gets it for you. The first time the information has to be read into memory (like reading the Dewey Decimal number of the book into your own memory). Every time after that (well, okay, every time after that until you shut down the database or until it gets aged out of memory) that you want to find the same piece of information (as long as you want the same information the same way), Oracle will remember the statement and won't need to look up the information again. If Oracle can use something stored in active memory (like you using what's in your short-term memory rather than having to dredge it up from your long-term memory banks), it will be much faster. That's why cursor sharing, set correctly, can be critical—so that the more Oracle can use what it knows and make as many inferences (okay, you want blue sneakers and then next time the only difference is that the bind variable says you want red sneakers) as it can and reuse as much of what it has in its memory, the faster the queries will run. And that's what we're after here, right? So let's talk about that next.

Cursor Sharing

So what is cursor sharing exactly? Well, sometimes you may have SQL statements that you run over and over again where the only difference between them is what kind of information you want to bring back. This is often particularly true when using forms to allow input from the user into the statement. But if you let Oracle make some inferences, and set cursor sharing up so it can leverage those inferences, your queries will run faster.

CURSOR_SHARING is a parameter that Oracle 8*i* brought with it that allows developers to make liberal use of bind variables and then let Oracle use those bind variables (rather than their literal values) to imply how to predict selectivity of the statement. In Oracle 8*i*, you could set the initialization parameter up so that Oracle would re-use the bind variable–laden cursor (cursor_sharing = force) for subsequent runs. Historically, it's proven difficult for the optimizer to guess accurately on the selectivity of what might be coming in buried in the bind variables. Originally, the functionality was limited. In Oracle 8*i*, it meant that if the first time the statement was parsed it used an index, every time it was rerun it used an index even if other times it might have been more efficient to use a full table scan and vice versa.

Oracle 9*i* brought added functionality (cursor_sharing = similar) that allowed the optimizer to examine histograms associated with the columns connected with the bind variables every time the statement was run, and then determine if a full table scan or an index scan would be more efficient when reusing the same statement. This means that code in memory is reused (pinned maybe) and that the optimizer can creatively change its mind based on the values in the bind variables, making cursor sharing the best of both worlds.

Unlike the inferences you can make about book topics or authors, Oracle can't make inferences about similar information possibly being in similar locations. It has to rely on what it really knows for sure.

If you see waits associated with the library cache, you can use the V$LIBRARYCACHE view to see what might be going on. GETHITS means that the object was in memory when Oracle tried to find it. GETS is the number of times Oracle tried to find the objects it needed in memory. GETHITRATIO is the number of GETHITS compared to the number of GETS. PINS is the number of times a PIN was requested for objects in memory (pinning an object in memory means you can usually rely on it being there the next time that you want it). PINHITS is the number of times all the pieces for a request were found already in memory. RELOADS happens the first time a pinned object is requested, and is the effort it takes Oracle to read that piece of data into short-term memory (like when you look up a phone number the first time, 555-1212... 555-1212... 555-1212; after that, when you have it all nice and recalled, it's just a matter of hitting redial).

V$LOCK

As you go through your day, take notice of how many locks you see or use. Think back to when you were a kid and try to figure out how many locks you use now as compared to back then.

Looking around me right now, I can see the lock on my office door, the lock on the roll top of my roll top desk, the one on the drawers of the desk, the one on the door of the desk, the two on the window, the one on each file cabinet, the lock on the administrator account of the computer, and the one on my PDA. I can infer that, across the street, there's one or more locks on the front door of the house opposite me, one on the garage door, one on the gate of the fence, one on the car parked under the street light, one on the electric meter, one on the gas meter, one on the telephone junction box, and a lock on the utility box on the corner. I have a lock on my desk at work, one connecting my laptop to my desk, I have to go through two to enter the gate at work, and navigate at least four (and as many as seven) just to get to my desk in the office. There is a lock on the doors at the grocery store, at the drug store, and on the construction machinery lining the highway on my drive to work.

There are locks everywhere.

Just like how latches and locks in real life serve different purposes (latches usually keep you from accidentally getting into somewhere unless you really mean to, and locks keep honest people out of places where they might stray), they serve different purposes in Oracle, too. Latches are constructs that control accesses to memory structures, while locks protect storage structures and the data residing within them.

Oracle is a lot like your daily life. There are locks, or the potential for locks, almost everywhere. There are different kinds of locks, too. Oracle may use one kind of lock on a structure when you just want to go poking around looking at data but don't want the data to change while you're looking at it. If you want to change the data, however, Oracle will use a different lock so you, and only you, can change that data at a given time.

If you're seeing excessive waits associated with locks, there may not be anything you can do directly, but you *can* go and look at what's being locked, and why. With this information, you can then possibly make alterations to the application or the structures. V$LOCK view gives you some vital information on the locks currently held in your database. The view provides you with the following columns:

- **SID** The session ID of the locking session

- **TYPE** The type of lock being held (TM for table level, TX for row transactions, ST for space transaction locks)

- **LMODE** The lock mode in which the session holds the lock

- **BLOCK** Here, a value of 0 means this given lock isn't locking another transaction's lock. A value of 1 means it's blocking another lock.

You can use V$LOCK to find out what session is holding the lock, V$SESSION to find out what SQL statement is being executed by the sessions holding the lock and waiting on the locked resource, and the program and user holding the lock. You can also use V$SESSION_WAIT to find out what the session holding the lock is being blocked on.

```
SELECT LPAD('', DECODE(REQUEST, 0, 0, 1)))||SID,
     id1, id2, lmode, request, type
FROM V$LOCK
WHERE id1 IN (SELECT id1 FROM V$LOCK WHERE lmode = 0));
```

This leads to the following SQL hash:

```
SELECT sid, sql_hash_value
FROM V$SESSION
WHERE SID IN (<the sid list from the previous query>);
```

And now the SQL statement:

```
SELECT sql_text
FROM V$SQL_TEXT
WHERE hash_value in (<hash value from the last query>);
```

Okay, so now we've looked at the internals that can be used to fix the performance of the overall database, but isn't there something more that can be done?

Tuning the Database Structure

This is where I think being a DBA becomes fun... where you get to play with the art, not just the math. Even in the art, there is math, like the art of nature and the relationship of the spirals in a pinecone or the arrangements of leaves on a plant or Fibonacci numbers. But tuning the structure can bring out the creativity of a DBA.

While I've done some formal design study, and I know there's a time and place for a third normal form (although anything over that is questionable to me), there's also a time and place for a denormalized model, and not just in a decision support system. I've made some very unpopular suggestions that have met with much resistance because they're different than the way things are normally done. But it doesn't mean that the current way is the best one, or that it's particularly efficient.

Look at the data you're storing. If you have a date field, which is broken into month and year, ask yourself why. Advanced ideas in database design can mean you can build function-based indexes to do date manipulation more efficiently. So, you can get the month out of a date that contains day, month, and year. You can also get the year out of that same date. Thus, you've saved 15 bytes on every row, meaning there's less chance for row chaining, and less chance for error. While this is not (in the grand scheme of Oracle) really considered to be one of the more advanced concepts, if you work at an organization that balks at using stored procedures or changing the way an index is constructed because they've always done it a certain way, advanced design can take on an entirely new meaning.

Row chaining occurs when the process of updating a row makes it long enough that it no longer fits within the block in which it started. Why is there less chance of row chaining in this instance? Well, the smaller your row size, the less chance there is it will be forced into another block. Planning will also help you design block and row sizes that make optimal use of data blocks and which likely won't end up chained to other blocks.

Do you have a string of characters you're storing in a VARCHAR2(60), but you always use the first 15 bytes to mean one thing and the next ten to mean something else, and the next 25 to mean something else, while the last ten are always blank? And every query you run substrings out those chunks into their real meaning? The substringing probably means you aren't using the index you've built on the column. Instead, it means you may be performing the same function repeatedly on the same column so you can get each different chunk into its own variable in your code.

Do you have a primary key on the first and second column of a table? If so, do you have a unique index on the first, second, and 15th column on that same table? Why? If the primary key is unique, anything you put with it will be unique. Why not? The definition can allow the optimizer to make some intelligent inferences on the uniqueness of the combination that our "logic" tells us but that can only be built into the optimizer with enough information. The more information you can give the optimizer, the better. And as long as the index is used, the trade-off of space for speed will likely be to your advantage.

Are you storing a set of lookup values on every record of a hundred million–row table (for example, city, state, and ZIP code) just because you don't want to have to join by ZIP code to another table (everyone knows that if you can avoid a join, the queries will be performed faster), yet you only actually go after the details (city and state) 1 percent of the time a query is run on the table? The chances of data error are far greater than the price of a well-created join (a join, I might add, that could be precomputed with a materialized view).

And, no, there is no earthly reason to ask Oracle to come up with a database model that allows you to have a table with 2500 columns in it. No one will ever remember what is in half of those columns. Plus, joins are becoming more and more efficient over time.

Think through your ideas. Present them logically (maybe even hide a small database somewhere and do a small proof of concept using production statistics to bear out your ideas) and then see how it goes. Even a re-design of a database may be optimal in some cases.

What, More?

Want to see Import/Export run a little faster? Typically, Import/Export runs in two_task mode. To make it run faster, you can relink the programs in single-task mode. This can display significant speed improvements, but it does come with a cost. It can require significantly more memory to run these relinked programs. You may need to weigh the trade-offs when using this speed before you wholeheartedly give your faith to the added speed.

The following code can be used to perform this relinking.

```
cd $ORACLE_HOME/rdbms/lib
make -f ins_rdbms.mk singletask
make -f ins_rdbms.mk expst
make -f ins_rdbms.mk impst
make -f ins_rdbms.mk sqlldrst
mv expst $ORACLE_HOME/bin/
mv impst $ORACLE_HOME/bin/
mv sqlldrst $ORACLE_HOME/bin/
```

Now you can use expst (export_singletask) and impst (import_singletask) instead of imp or exp.

Want Import/Export to run even faster? Why not try using Data Pump? In Oracle 10g, Oracle redesigned Import/Export as Oracle Data Pump. While Import/Export are still included with the shipment of Oracle 10g, Data Pump is usually more efficient. Where Import/Export can both run as client server applications, Data Pump acts as a job inside the database, using command-line syntax very much like its client server predecessors. Anyone who's ever run and needed to monitor an Export/Import operation knows that, unless you're actually watching from the machine where the operation started, the best you can do is send the output to a log file so you can watch the process indirectly. With Data Pump, it doesn't matter where you start the job. Because it's running in the database, you can log on and check the process from any other computer that has access to the database.

But think about it. Client server architecture is inherently less efficient than something that runs directly within the database without having to make external connections in any way except for the connection that has to exist to the DIRECTORY housing the output files. Another reason it runs faster is because it can be run in a parallel fashion. If you specify the Parallel option, you allow Oracle to dump data into four different parallel threads, which is much faster than single threading.

As for the directory, since the job runs inside the database, if you want the export to go to the file system, the first thing you have to do is create a database DIRECTORY object into which you can output the file, afterward granting access to the user or whomever will be doing these exports and imports.

```
CREATE OR REPLACE DIRECTORY myexport  'd:\';
GRANT READ, WRITE ON DIRECTORY myexport to larry;
```

Once you've created the directory and granted read and write privileges to it to the export user, you can use the following export commands:

```
expdp larry/angel directory=myexport dumpfile=larry.dmp
```

As you can see, it's very similar to an export command.

You don't have to write the export out to a file, however, and honestly Data Pump is just as happy to export the database objects directly into a remote database over a SQL Net connection. Simply specify the option REMOTE with the connection string to the remote database and the process ends up like a once-and-it's-done replication job.

You can force the running Data Pump Export job into the background, and the messages will stop being sent to the screen, but the job will remain running inside the database. If you want to reattach to a job you forced into the background, you can do so with the command:

```
Expdpattac=<jobname>
```

As if using a stored procedure over a client server application isn't enough to get your performance appetite sated, you can make this run even better. While Data Pump leverages parallelism (inter table, and both intra- and inter-partition) to run load and unload processes, and also build and load package bodies, fully utilizing all available resources to maximize the throughput and thereby minimize the elapsed time of a job, for all of this to take place efficiently the system must be well balanced with respect to CPU, memory, and I/O distribution. Any tuning you can do to the overall system, database, and server will help Data Pump perform more efficiently.

Want to make Data Pump as efficient as possible? Allow it to create multiple dump files when it exports or reads from multiple dump files, and when it imports and distributes those files over separate disks, letting the I/O be distributed. This allows the parallelism to occur in as rapid a manner as possible. The disks on which these files are located should also not be the same disks on which the target tablespaces for the import, nor the source tablespaces for the export, reside.

Setting the degree of parallelism at the database level to no more than 2X the CPU count will allow you to maximize the way that Data Pump spawns its jobs to distribute them across the system. Keep in mind, though, that as you increase the degree of parallelism that a job is allowed to make use of, you also increase the CPU usage memory consumption and I/O bandwidth necessary for the jobs to run. It's important when setting up jobs that whoever is setting the parameters on the import and export jobs not only makes sure there are sufficient resources available for the job but that regular operations be allowed to occur on the database. One caveat here though: the PARALLEL parameter is only available in the Enterprise Edition of Oracle 10g.

You can set the following initialization parameters to help the performance of your Data Pump export and import processes:

- DISK_ASYNCH_IO = TRUE

- DB_BLOCK_CHECKING = FALSE

- DB_BLOCK_CHECKSUM = FALSE

- PROCESSES (high enough for maximum parallelism)

- SESSIONS (high enough for maximum parallelism)

- PARALLEL_MAX_SERVERS (high enough for maximum parallelism)

Keep in mind that setting these parameters will have ramifications on the overall system. Also remember that you'll get different results when setting these parameters on different operating systems.

All Operating Systems

- Use proper file placement so I/O is spread evenly across disks. If possible, use RAID devices.

- A good design is key. Index appropriately and watch row chaining. Row chaining occurs whenever a user updates a row in a table in such a way that it can no longer completely fit in the original data block. The migration of part of the row from the original block to another block is called row chaining, and it can, if allowed to become excessive, cause a great deal of additional I/O (first, Oracle has to find the block where the row starts, then it has to find and retrieve the block where the chain continues).

- Monitor V$SESSION_WAIT regularly to identify wait conditions. If the SEQ# column stops changing, the event is stuck.

- Monitor locking and latching (V$LOCK, V$LATCH, V$LATCHHOLDER, and so on).

- If you're trying to implement distributed or federated databases, keep in mind that two phase commits are slower than a single instance commit.

Need to Speed Up Oracle on Windows?

When Windows is the operating system on which both the database and application are running, it's often necessary to speed up the way Oracle and Windows play together. Possible steps to achieve this include the following:

- If you have the authority, remove any protocols you know you don't use from the installed network software list, and then move those used most frequently to the top.

- Stop all unnecessary services on your machine. Do this one at a time and make sure you test so you're sure they're really unnecessary.

- Windows NT and Windows 2000 support asynchronous I/O, so use it. This not only optimizes your I/O operations, it spares you having to configure multiple database writers.

- In Windows, it's important to note that the default DB_BLOCK_SIZE is still 2K. Rarely does an application perform optimally with this setting. Fortunately, if you use the Database Configuration Assistant, Oracle will help you choose more optimal block sizes. If you don't use DBCA, check before you create your database and increase this setting to 4K or 8K (or even 16K) if required.

- If you have to use a screensaver, choose something simple. While the really cool high-resolution ones are neat, and the 3-D ones are entertaining to watch, it makes your database very uncomfortable if it has to share this much of the resources with something so unproductive.

Oracle 10*g*

The highly-touted Oracle 10*g* database that tunes itself brings with it some truly impressive tuning enhancements. I'm not sure this means that DBAs are irrelevant, but it does mean we have yet more impressive tools to help us be more effective and efficient.

Tracing Enhancements

One interesting enhancement to tracing that was brought to the table with Oracle 10*g* is less of a revolution than it is an evolution in tracing. It's now possible to turn on tracing for one or more sessions at a time, and simultaneously watch sessions as they are connected in order to help you follow their progress through the database.

This means you can more accurately pinpoint exactly where the session is at any given time and during any process, the amount of resources being consumed at that specific point in time (and by extension what the process in question is consuming), and where the session is having difficulty and needs tuning. This feature is particularly important if you're trying to tune in a multitier and/or multiuser environment (and honestly, a single-user database isn't much more useful than one without users... plus, a single-user database may not be a good application for Oracle) with an application where connection pooling is taking place. In these instances, depending on the application, it might be difficult, if not impossible, to find some of this information.

Automatic Performance Diagnostic and Tuning Features

While in the past it's been possible to automatically schedule statistics collection in Oracle 8*i* and Oracle 9*i* (this was true even when using CRON, AT, or DBMS_JOB), Oracle 10*g* brings with it not only the ability to automatically gather statistics but also its recommendation that you let Oracle automatically gather and maintain them for you. Oracle thus gathers statistics on all database objects in a maintenance job that you schedule to have run automatically. This "frees" you from having to worry about gathering these statistics on your own. In theory, this allows you the assurance of always having a reliable execution plan because you will never again have stale or missing statistics.

GATHER_STATS_JOB is the job that runs in order to automatically gather statistics on all objects in the database, which have either missing or stale statistics. The job is created automatically at database creation time and is managed by Scheduler. Scheduler (the free new Oracle 10*g* feature that enables you to schedule jobs from inside the database) runs GATHER_STATS_JOB during the maintenance window, which by default it assumes to be between 10 p.m. and 6 a.m. every day and all day on the weekends. These defaults, fortunately, can be changed.

While you can't change the schedule of GATHER_STATS_JOB by passing the job a parameter of when to run, you can change the window in which the job runs either by altering the Scheduler window, or by defining your own custom window in which you want it to run.

Scheduler comes with its own predefined windows (one for weeknights, and one for weekends). If these windows don't fit your needs, you can create your own windows instead. Windows have three attributes. Schedules controls when the window is in effect. Durations controls how long the window is open. Resource plans control the resource priorities among different job classes.

NOTE
It's important to remember that only one window can be used at any given time.

You can manipulate maintenance windows, adjusting their timing and attributes, as detailed in Table 4-5.

Task	Procedure
Create a Window	CREATE_WINDOW
Open the Window	OPEN_WINDOW
Close the Window	CLOSE_WINDOW
Alter the Window	SET_ATTRIBUTE
Drop the Window	DROP_WINDOW
Disable the Window	DISABLE
Enable the Window	ENABLE

TABLE 4-5. *DBMS_SCHEDULER Procedures*

When you create a new window, you can specify the schedule for that window or you can create a window that points to a schedule that has been predefined and saved. The following code defines a window that is enabled at midnight, runs for five hours, and repeats every day. You can use your own defined resource plan with this window to handle the resource distribution during the maintenance window duration. Not specifying the resource plan means that the default plan will be used.

```
BEGIN
DBMS_SCHEDULE.CREATE_WINDOW (
WINDOW_NAME   => 'nightly_window',
START_DATE => '01-JAN-05 12:00:00 AM',
REPEATE_INTERVAL => 'FREQ=DAILY',
RESOURCE_PLAN =>  'my_maint_plan',
DURATION => interval '300' minute,
COMMENTS => 'nightly maintenance window');
END;
/
```

NOTE
Windows are created in the SYS schema. Scheduler doesn't check to see if there is something already defined for the given period of time. If it results in windows that overlap, the situation must be rectified.

You can disable the default windows, but it would be better not to drop them, because if there are maintenance jobs that rely on that window, you will disable those jobs as well, and it's never a good idea to delete or alter the default operators provided by Oracle. Plus, it's far quicker to re-enable any default windows than it is to re-create them.

Once the window is created, it has to be opened to be used. It can be opened automatically using the schedule that was defined when it was created, or it can be opened manually using DBMS_SCHEDULE.OPEN_ WINDOW.

NOTE
Only an enabled window can be opened.

GATHER_STATS_JOB, once started, runs till completion even if it overruns the maintenance window. Stale statistics are those on objects which have had more than 10 percent of their rows modified.

GATHER_STATS_JOB calls the GATHER_DATABASE_STATS_JOB_PROC of the DBMS_STATS package, which operates the same way as the DBMS_ STATS.GATHER_DATABASE_STATS procedure if you use the GATHER AUTO option. The primary difference between the two jobs is that the GATHER_DATABASE_STATS_JOB_PROC procedure can prioritize rather than serialize, so those objects that will benefit most from the procedure (in its opinion) will have their stats gathered first before the maintenance window closes. I haven't yet noticed places where its assumptions are wrong, thereby impacting the performance of queries against very large tables (that it's analyzing), so for now I'll assume its assumptions are valid.

In order to verify that automatic statistics gathering has been enabled, you can query the DBA_SCHEDULER_JOBS view as follows:

```
SELECT *
FROM DBA_SCHEDULER_JOBS
WHERE JOB_NAME = GATHER_STATS_JOB;
```

In order to disable automatic statistics gathering, simply run the Scheduler package as follows:

```
BEGIN
DMBS_SCHEDULER.DISABLE('GATHER_STATS_JOB');
END;
/
```

While it may be that automatic statistics gathering is the next best thing since sliced bread, there are cases where automatic statistics gathering routinely overruns the overnight-defined batch window and thus highly volatile tables become stale during the day. This is most applicable to tables that are truncated and repopulated or that are deleted and then rebuilt during the course of the day or to objects which are the target of large bulk loads that add upwards of 10 percent or more of the object's total size in a given day.

You can, of course, still gather statistics for these and other kinds of objects using either the GATHER_SCHEMA_STATS or the GATHER_DATABASE_STATS procedures in the DBMS_STATS package.

It's important to note here, however, that none of these methods, GATHER_SCHEMA_STATS, GATHER_DATABASE_STATS, or automatic statistics gathering, collects statistics on external tables. To get statistics on these objects, you need to manually run or manually schedule GATHER_TABLE_STATS with the ESTIMATE_PERCENT option set explicitly to NULL (since sampling on external tables is not supported). Because data manipulation on external tables also isn't supported, it's sufficient to analyze external tables whenever the underlying OS file changes.

Need to find a way to restore previous versions of statistics? It's simpler now than ever before. Whenever statistics in a dictionary are modified, the older version is now automatically saved for the purpose of future restoring. Do you get the impression that automatic stats generation is sometimes not as optimal as it could be? These older versions of the statistics can be restored using RESTORE procedures from the DBMS_STATS package.

Want to prevent any new statistics from being gathered on a given object or set of objects but still want the ability to run automatic statistics gathering? You can lock the statistics on a table or schema using the DBMS_STATS package, too.

The DBMS_STATS package in Oracle 10g lets you lock your statistics on tables or on indexes, even if the data in the table changes. If you discover you have an efficient set of statistics that allows your application to perform well, you can use these packages to lock the statistics. It's important to note, however, that if you lock the statistics you cannot recalculate them until they're unlocked. DBMS_STATS employs four commands that allow it to lock and unlock statistics at a table or schema level: LOCK_TABLE_STATS, LOCK_SCHEMA_STATS, UNLOCK_TABLE_STATS, and UNLOCK_SCHEMA_STATS. Passing these procedures, the parameters that allow you to set and unset locking at the level desired can ease a great deal of headaches caused when a set of statistics that allows an application to perform its best is overwritten by automatic statistics gathering.

Automatic SQL Tuning   Automatic SQL tuning? Simply wave a magic wand and developers and end users don't have to think, the SQL just tunes itself? Now that *would* be an awesome new feature. Unfortunately, this feature is really just an advisor (the SQL Tuning Advisor) that takes one or more SQL statements as input parameters and then turns them around, telling you how it would create changes to make the SQL more optimal. Its output is simply advice and recommendations along with the rationale it used for each suggestion. It also tells you what it expects the benefit of its recommended changes to be. It may recommend collecting statistics on objects, creating new indexes, or even creating a new SQL Profile to be used when running the given statement or statements. The user can then choose to use the recommendations or not. While it isn't likely to tell you to gather better statistics or use a materialized view, it can tell you whether you should restructure your SQL statement.

A new database object called a SQL Tuning Set (STS) comes with the SQL Tuning Advisor. These new structures can be created manually at the command line or by using OEM. An STS stores the SQL statement along with the execution context surrounding that SQL statement.

The inputs for the SQL Tuning Advisor can come from the Automatic Database Diagnostic Monitor (ADDM), which is often its primary source. ADDM is the Oracle-provided (for an extra license fee) utility that analyzes the data in the Automatic Workload Repository (AWR, also available for the same additional license fee). AWR is a repository for raw system statistics and object data. ADDM runs, by default, once every hour to search through the repository to find particularly high resource-intensive SQL. If it finds one, it will recommend you run the SQL Tuning Advisor. This is, however, a somewhat less proactive approach since it has to wait till the statement has already been run before it can suggest tuning.

Alternatively, you can provide it with your own SQL statements. If you choose this proactive approach, you can include any not-yet-implemented statements, but you also have to manually create an STS so the SQL Tuning Advisor has input on which to work. This is, honestly, the option that I prefer to use. Proactive rather than reactive. Tuning before users have a chance to get angry over poorly running code.

You can control the scope and durations of any given SQL Tuning Advisor task. If you choose the limited option, the advisor provides recommendations based on statistics checks, access path analysis, and SQL structure analysis, and no SQL Profile recommendations are generated. If you choose the comprehensive option, the advisor carries out all of the analysis available to it under the limited option, adding any SQL Profile recommendations. You can limit the duration of the advisor run by giving it a set time. The default time limit is 30 minutes.

The output of the advisor is advice on optimizing the execution plan, the advisor's rationale for the proposed optimization, the estimated performance benefit, and the command to implement the advice given. When it's finished, all you have to do is decide whether or not to implement the recommendations.

End to End Application Tracing   End to End Application Tracing is a tool that helps simplify the inherently complex process of performance problem diagnosis, particularly in multitier environments. When user requests are routed to different database sessions by a middle-tier environment, it can mean that you lose the ability to directly attribute a session, definitively, to a given user. This can make using tools like 10046 trace difficult to use. End to End Application Tracing makes use of a unique client identifier to help trace a specific end-client's session and show what it's doing through all of the tiers to the database server.

Just like the other tools in your toolbox, this feature can help you determine where there is excessive workload, where SQL statements are performing less than optimally, and can provide you with information you can then use to contact the appropriate user to help determine what issues he or she is having. This can mean proactive tuning rather than reactive, and thus turn you in the eyes of users from a troll into a wizard. Even if you don't have time to sit around poking about your database checking if there's anything less than optimal happening, you can still use this feature as a means to troubleshoot an end user's issue when that user calls with a problem.

Issues can be identified by client identifier (the end user's ID), service (a group of applications with common attributes or a single application), module (a functional block of application programs within an application), or even the action being performed (INSERT, UPDATE, or DELETE within a module).

After tracing information is written to the trace files by End to End Application Tracing, you can use TRCSESS to help you diagnose the problem, and then hand off that file to TKPROF.

When I wear the hat of an APPS DBA, I can see many uses for End to End Application Tracing. While Oracle's E-Business Suite 11*i* actually has its own 10046 trace interface built in (which can become a pain when users "forget" to turn it off after they've traced what they're having issues with), it can sometimes be more bothersome than trying to enable tracing on a session-by-session basis because it's often the case that users will turn on tracing with binds and waits and then forget to turn them off. If this happens, you can find yourself overrun with trace files for sessions you have no need or desire to trace.

Automatic SGA Memory Management   Automatic SGA Memory Management (ASMM) was created as a means to help simplify configuration of the database's System Global Area (SGA) and its parameters. It does this through the use of self-tuning algorithms. It's a really interesting concept that works the majority of the time, but somehow it still makes me feel like maybe my database is starting to think it knows more than I do. This utility helps you simplify most database configurations by helping you make the most efficient utilization decisions regarding the available memory on your system. It goes a step further than a lot of the advisors from Oracle 9*i* and allows them to dynamically make many of the decisions on their own. In order for ASMM to work correctly, you have to have some initialization parameters set correctly. SGA_TARGET must be changed to a nonzero value and should be set to the amount of memory you want to have dedicated to the SGA (see, you still have a say in the matter). STATISTICS_LEVEL has to be set to either TYPICAL or ALL. Once these are set up, the automatic SGA management makes decisions on how best to allocate that memory across the following pools (yeah, you guessed it, the ones we tinker with the most anyway):

- DATABASE BUFFER CACHE (the default cache, not the nondefault sized caches, the recycle, or the keep caches)
- SHARED POOL
- LARGE POOL
- JAVA POOL

If you've already tinkered with any of these, and they were set to non-zero values, those values are used as the minimum levels on which the

ASMM bases its decisions (again, you still have a say in the matter). It's important to keep in mind with this utility that if you know you have an application that has a minimum requirement for any of these parameters in order for it to function properly, set them upfront so ASMM doesn't make decisions that will end up shooting you in the foot.

The SGA_TARGET parameter is dynamic and can be changed with the ALTER SYSTEM command, while appropriate values are less than or equal to the value set for the SGA_MAX_SIZE parameter. Changes to SGA_TARGET automatically filter down to the appropriate tuned memory pools. Setting SGA_TARGET to 0 disables ASMM.

Dynamic Sampling   Dynamic Sampling helps improve server performance by determining if there are (or might be) more accurate estimates for predicate selectivity and statistics for tables and indexes. The statistics for tables and indexes, in this brave new world, now include table block counts, applicable index block counts, table cardinalities, and relevant join column statistics. The CBO (since the RBO has now gone the way of the Atari and the Commodore 64) uses these more accurate estimates to better judge what EXPLAIN PLAN it will use for executing the given SQL.

You can make use of this feature to estimate the selectivity of a given single table where clause when the collected statistics cannot be used, or if they are likely to lead to significant errors in CBO estimation. You can allow it to guesstimate statistics for tables and indexes if there are no statistics available for those structures. And you can allow it to do the same for indexes and tables whose statistics are simply too far out of date for you to be comfortable in trusting.

This feature is controlled by the use of the OPTIMIZER_DYNAMIC_SAMPLING parameter. The default value for the parameter is 2, which is the lowest setting that can be used if you want to turn on dynamic automatic sampling so it can gather the necessary stats. Setting it to level 0 turns off dynamic sampling altogether.

Making It Sing

There are some interesting things that you can do to the structure of your data to trick your database into performing far better than it might otherwise. Setup and maintenance might be something you're less than enthusiastic about, but the benefits may well be worth it in the end.

Materialized Views

Materialized views are schema objects that are typically used for pre-computing complex formulas and storing the results, for summarizing and aggregating data, for replicating data, or for distributing copies of the data to locations other than the primary location in order to allow people to access the data where it's being used. All of these are excellent ways to speed up data access. What's the difference between a "regular" view and a materialized view? Good question. Regular views don't physically hold anything other than the definition of what is being sought. They are a grouping of complex queries into a single representation of what appears to be a table but which in reality contains no data until the view is accessed. Materialized views, on the other hand, are more like indexes. They take up space, physically hold data, and are usually used as a way to speed up queries.

How can materialized views assist you with performance? Using the setting where initialization parameters enable query rewrites, the Cost-Based Optimizer can be told it has the option of using materialized views to cut the cost of queries by redirecting certain queries (or even certain parts of queries) to the materialized view and thus improve query performance. The optimizer transparently rewrites the request (or even a part of the request) to use the materialized view instead of the base tables.

If you find out that one of the worst performing queries that runs frequently has a formula in it, you can materialize that query and allow the formula to run once, causing the query to run far faster every time it's run. For example, every month accounting runs the same query, with the only difference being the date they run the query for. And they don't just run it once; half a dozen people run it over and over during the first week of the month. Therefore, you could find the query, determine how best to run it for a given date range (month –1 would give you last month's data and you could even compute the previous quarter based on what your company's quarters are), create a materialized view on that query, and schedule the materialized view to refresh on demand, or as scheduled at 5 a.m. on the first day of the month.

Do you have users who only access a given subset of data and have to pull that subset across a dialup line to a laptop while they're on the road at a client site? Let's say your business distributes packaged foods to convenience stores. Larry, your candy salesman, is responsible for convenience stores in a tri-county area. He needs to be able to determine what is in stock, and figure the lead time on the candy that's in greatest demand for his area that isn't in stock currently. Why have his queries from his laptop or his mobile device search the entire database for that kind of information? If you know you have parts of your business that can be compartmentalized, why not take advantage of this information? Thus, you should create materialized views that are customized to each smaller line of business so that queries can run as rapidly as possible.

One of the most interesting uses of materialized views is their ability to pre-compute joins. Do you have a set of tables that are joined together all the time and always joined on the same columns? Are some of the queries that run with these joins resource hogs? Do users frequently complain about the query times associated with these table joins? Materialized views are great ways to free up resources and make users happy. Find tables that are joined frequently and then pre-compute the joins and store the results in a materialized view. They are optimal in data warehouses or in reporting systems. They have the potential to slow down a transactional system, particularly if you were to build them as "on commit refresh".

Oh sure, it's the best thing since sliced bread, but nothing is all good, right? There has to be something extra you have to do to the database to make it recognize these things and to know to use them. Well, of course there is. Oracle is a smart database, but you have to give it a clue that you want it to use some of its bells and whistles sometimes.

QUERY_REWRITE_ENABLED must be true. You can set this in the initialization file. This tells Oracle that it is allowed to let the CBO know about the materialized views and use them to answer queries. In Oracle 10*g*, the default is true.

QUERY_REWRITE_INTEGRITY is another initialization parameter that's used to determine how and when Oracle rewrites the query. You can control how fresh or stale the data in the materialized view can be in order for it to be a candidate for query rewrite.

The different kinds of materialized view integrity that you can set for your query rewrite are as follows:

- Enforced (this is the default) query rewrite will only be done if the view contains fresh data.

- Trusted query rewrite will be done if the view contains current and correct data.

■ STALE_TOLERATED tells the CBO that it should trust that the materialized view is correct even if it isn't current. Thus, the query is rewritten.

Then you have to deal with the users (this is one of those times when, if you have a bunch of users, you might see the benefit of using roles so you can control groups of users). Grant QUERY_REWRITE to users who will be permitted to have their queries rewritten by the CBO. Or if you want everyone to be able to use this feature, grant it to public.

Let's work with the quintessential Scott/Tiger schema since it's something most DBAs are at least partly familiar with. Let's assume we're trying to compile a listing every month of the department name, the jobs in that department, and the sum of its salaries so you can track where money is going over time.

To accomplish this, you would ordinarily query the table every month using the following:

```
SELECT dname, job, sum(sal)
FROM emp e, dept d
WHERE e.deptno = d.deptno
GROUP BY dname, job
```

Now, with the Scott/Tiger schema, this query won't really be a big deal since it runs in seconds at worst. But what if there were more than two tables, and what if the tables were million- or multimillion row tables?

```
CREATE MATERIALIZED VIEW emp_dept_sum_mv
TABLESPACE MVTS
ENABLE QUERY REWRITE
 AS SELECT dname,job,SUM(sal)
     FROM emp e, dept d
    WHERE e.deptno = d.deptno
GROUP BY dname,job;
```

You would need to be granted CREATE MATERIALIZED VIEW to run the preceding statement successfully. Now that you've created it, gather statistics and refresh the view using the following:

```
execute dbms_utility.analyze_schema('SCOTT','COMPUTE');
execute dbms_mview.refresh('emp_dept_sum_mv');
```

Now test it and see what happens when the original query is run.

```
set autotrace on explain
SELECT dname,job,SUM(sal)
  FROM emp e, dept d
WHERE e.deptno = d.deptno
GROUP BY dname,job;
Execution Pla
----------------------------------------
0 SELECT STATEMENT Optimizer=CHOOSE
1 0 TABLE ACCESS (FULL) OF 'EMP_DEPT_SUM_MV'
```

There are always trade-offs, just as with anything you use to speed up performance. Just like ice cream and chocolate really all do have calories and those are the trade-offs that you have to deal with if you want to enjoy them, and materialized views are no different. Granted, there are not calories in materialized views, but they consume space and you do have to make sure they're refreshed whenever you want to use them to rewrite queries and get the most current data.

Clusters

No, not like in Real Application Clusters (RACs) and not like a computer cluster, but more like the dictionary.com definition (http://dictionary.reference.com/search?q=cluster): *A group of the same or similar elements gathered or occurring closely together; a bunch.*

In Oracle, a cluster is a storage construct that provides you with an alternative method of storing each block of data in such a way that it can make some queries run much faster. It's made up of a group of tables that are typically queried together and have their data stored in shared data blocks. The candidate tables are grouped together because they share common columns on which joins are typically made, and where tables are most often queried together.

Given earlier releases of Oracle, there's also the concept of hash clusters, which allow the database to optimize data retrieval. Hash clusters provide an alternative to the traditional storage of tables and indexes, and can also be used when clustering tables together isn't an option. In a typical single table storage with an index, Oracle stores rows of data in the table according to key values contained in a separate index. To retrieve the data, Oracle has to access the index, determine the location of the data, and then load it. In a hash table, you define the hash cluster and then load your tables into it. As you load the data, resulting hash values correspond to values determined by the hash function. Oracle uses its own hash function to generate a distribution of numeric values (hash values) based on the cluster key (which can be a single column or multiple columns in the hashed table). This can be faster for retrieval because an index-based retrieval takes at least two I/O operations (one for the index, one for the data) while a hash table retrieval takes one I/O operation to retrieve the data and none at all to determine where that row is located.

Because the data from the included tables are stored in the same data blocks, disk I/O may be significantly reduced when the clustered tables are joined in queries. If you know that you have tables that are nearly always queried together, you can define the cluster key column or group of columns that the cluster tables have in common. In an insurance company, this might be a claim number column in the claim table, invoice table, and payment table. By specifying the cluster key (and adding the tables to the cluster), the cluster key value is stored once rather than once for each table no matter how many rows in each table are associated with the cluster key. This means that not only are the queries quickened, you could also significantly reduce the storage necessary for related table and index values.

Again, there are trade-offs in clusters just like in ice cream, chocolate, and materialized views. Tables that are frequently queried independently of each other may not be as good a candidate for clustering. Also, because the rows are stored in the same data block, the tables involved in the cluster may not be good candidates if there are significant amounts of inserts, updates, and deletes occurring on the individual tables of the cluster.

NOTE
While retrieval is quicker with clusters, inserts and updates are somewhat more expensive timewise.

Looking at an insurance company example, it's important to note that, unless the claim number is stored in the individual rows in the invoice line item table—storing line_item with claim—invoice and payment won't make sense just because line_item and invoice are queried together most frequently. Therefore, you need to sit down and consider carefully the table decisions you should make concerning clusters when you decide to go this route. It may be more advantageous in this case to create two clusters, one for claim and payment and one for invoice and line_item, and then take the I/O hit during those times when you query both invoice and payment in some combination. Good design concepts should always be considered when looking at any of these constructs. The biggest impact will always happen when good design meshes with cool new features.

Summary

Tuning can become an obsession, so it's a good idea to have a general goal in mind when starting out. Without a goal, how will you know when enough is enough?

There will always be more tuning that can be done; bottlenecks move, and when you have cleared one, another will raise its ugly head. It is like the circle of life, always turning, always moving from one place to the next. You could find yourself enjoying the adventure of tuning, or you could decide that you're a victim of obsessive tuning disorder. So buyer beware.

CHAPTER
5

Database Down!
Bring It Back Alive!

 henever I hear "database down" I think of the 1978 movie *Gray Lady Down* where the nuclear submarine Neptune sinks after hitting a freighter and the folks up top have 48 hours to rescue the crew. It's at those times that I can hear the sound effects associated with submarines in my head, as well as the background music, and a sense of fear grips my heart. Okay, so I should get a life, not just rent one from Blockbuster. But the analogy is still close.

You rarely have the luxury of 48 hours when it comes to rescuing your database, however. What usually happens is you have a dozen or so managers in suits standing in your cube doorway at six in the morning wondering how long it will be before the database is back up and running. Rather nerve-wracking. So in this chapter, we'll look at some of the best ways to get those pesky managers out of your cube as gently and quickly as possible.

Database Down

While it really doesn't happen often, there are times when your database does crash and burn and you find yourself looking at a SQL prompt that says a shared memory realm doesn't exist or that Oracle is unavailable. Of course, this is when you're lucky enough to find out that the database is down before your users do. When they find out first, you find yourself scrambling to answer questions while furiously typing and misspelling words that you know you know how to spell (like sqlplus, or sysdba). I'm a pro at consistently misspelling "select" any time I find myself under pressure, either from me trying to get things back under control as quickly as possible or due to those dozen pairs of manager eyes boring into the back of my head.

The most important thing when confronted with a down database is to get it back up and running. Then afterward, you need to figure out how, if possible, to keep it from happening again.

Restarting

The first thing to do is check the alert logs. See if anything jumps out at you as a reason for the database being down. For example, did one of the DBAs in your shop do maintenance last night and forget to bring the database back up? Not that this would ever happen, but just for grins check and see if the end of the alert logs might show this is the case. Of course, if someone with just the wrong access decided to go out and kill a bunch of background processes, maybe because they seemed to be taking a lot of the resources on the box, and it was too late at night to bother the DBA with stuff like that, there won't be anything in the alert log or, at best, not much of one.

If there's nothing glaring in the alert log that tells you something horrible happened (like someone deleted a bunch of data files or maybe all of the control files are gone) simply try restarting the database. You might be surprised. Whatever caused the database to crash might turn out to be a simple and transient thing, and your database will be revived simply by using the startup command.

The most important thing to users and to management is getting the database restarted. However, sometimes a restart will wipe out important information, including evidence of what happened, and you won't be able to find out what happened. Try to at least dump out the contents (if possible) of some of the v$ views to help in your analysis before restarting. Once the database is accessible, you can worry about getting to the root of the problem (sometimes referred to by cranky upper management as Root Cause Analysis, or RCA).

If It Doesn't Start

Okay, you've tried the simplest and most straightforward solution—simply restarting the database—but it didn't start. Now what?

Well, you start what could arguably be seen as the fun part of being a DBA (if you're a truly warped individual, which I am, and if you enjoy a real challenge). You have to try to figure out why it isn't starting (hopefully as quickly as possible) and get it back up and running.

If It Doesn't Stop

Yeah, sometimes the database gets stuck … up. Not only stuck in the up position, but since "stuck up" implies that you were trying to shut down the database, no one can now connect to it because a database shutdown is in process.

It's normal for shutdown to sometimes gets stuck, that's a given. Since "normal" implies you're willing to wait for all connections to disconnect, there have to be connections out there waiting for someone to do something. The solution? Kill off all sessions connected to shutdown immediate or (gulp) do a shutdown abort.

Okay, so that's no big deal, right? Sure, but what happens when shutdown immediate gets stuck? The emn0 background process sometimes forgets it's running, goes to sleep, and just won't wake up. Sometimes Oracle weirds out and refuses to be cooperative for some other reason.

If shutdown immediate gets stuck, there are only two ways to bring down the database. One is to kill –9 on Unix, or kill Task Manager in Windows. This is usually used only as a last resort, or by overly anxious operators with just a little too much knowledge. The other is shutdown abort. Yes, this is a valid way of shutting down the database. Of course, so is pulling the power plug or pressing the reset button, but Oracle will assure you that it's a valid shutdown method. It still makes my stomach knot, but I've actually done it. Of course, I start up as soon as the database is down and then perform shutdown immediate again so the shutdown is in as stable a state as possible.

Finding Out Why

Okay, so we haven't gotten it started, and we need to find out not only why it won't start, but what brought it down to begin with. Chances are that, when you tried to bring up the database, if there was an issue that caused it to not come up, it was either sent to the screen or the alert logs and you have some idea of what didn't work and maybe what the error was that meant it didn't work. This is an excellent place to start. You can look in the manuals to find out what the error means, or you can make use of some of Oracle's valuable resources to help you figure out what happened and where to go from here.

The oerr Utility

The Oracle Error (oerr) utility is provided to you, free of charge on Unix and Linux, as a way to help you quickly find information about the errors you're seeing in your database without having to resort to searching with your favorite search engine or running to the manuals to find out what exactly an error message means. By using the following command at the operating system prompt, you can quickly see what Oracle is trying to tell you.

```
oerr <prefix> <number>
```

The prefix is usually the three characters preceding the hyphen in the error that's displayed (perhaps ORA, MSG, PLS, or something else) while the number part of the command is the number to the right of the hyphen. For example, did the dreaded ORA-00600 appear in your alert log? If so, you might be able to get more information by running the following command:

```
oerr ORA 00600
```

In this case, as you can see next, the information you get back will probably be less than useful, as ORA-00600 can cover many different kinds of errors, but you can still get some idea of how the command works and the format of the output, although to allow it to fit within the confines of the book, I had to take liberties with a couple of the line breaks.

```
$ oerr ora 00600
00600, 00000, "internal error code, arguments:
[%s], [%s], [%s], [%s], [%s], [%s], [%s], [%s]"
// *Cause: This is the generic internal error number for
// Oracle program
// exceptions.  This indicates that a process has encountered an
// exceptional condition.
// *Action: Report as a bug - the first argument is
// the internal error number
```

While the original Oracle-provided version of this utility runs on Unix but not Windows (because it makes use of the AWK command, and not every Oracle installation assumes you've installed MKS Toolkit or CYGWIN to emulate Unix on Windows), there are ways to make a similar utility run in a Windows environment. This will make you very happy if you happen to be one of those who have Windows environments without access to a Unix alternative on which to run the command.

I like to tell SAs who want to debug errors how to use oerr. They can then look up errors themselves, which is a big help if they can field even a few user problems.

One notable utility that ports the functionality of oerr to Windows was written by Yong Huang, and uses Perl as the vehicle that allows the script to work. This script is well commented and is freeware. Don't feel like typing all that much? You can get the script from Yong's web site (http://rootshell.be/~yong321/freeware/Windowsoerr.html). Yong maintains an interesting site with a lot of useful information on Oracle as well as on Windows, and offers a truly geeky program that allows you to use a mouse in DOS that was written in assembler (this may not be as useful as it once was, but it's fascinating

from the perspective of someone who really doesn't have much of a life—
not that I find reading code to be a fun pastime, you understand).

```perl
#!perl -w
#Perl script in Windows simulating the Oracle oerr utility in Unix
#I assume you installed Perl for Windows on
#the same machine you installed
#Oracle Documentation. This script should be run by oerr.bat.
#See the following URL.
#This script is published as freeware at
#http://rootshell.be/~yong321/freeware/Windowsoerr.html
#(C) Copyright 2000,2004 Yong Huang (yong321@yahoo.com)
#Please modify $dir, $colon and select $fsp, and $lsp.
#On your computer, open the Oracle Documentation homepage with
#a Web browser
#and find the error message page. E.g. for Version 8.1, it may be
#Oracle8i Server -> Oracle8i Error Messages (in section References).
#Find the URL for the message page
#(if it's in an HTML frame, View Frame Info
#in Netscape, Properties in IE). Take the string before
# "\TOC.HTM". Follow my
#format below. E.g., on my machine, the URL for error message
#Table of Contents
#page is
#    for 9.2 Enterprise Ed
#       file:///C:/ora9idoc/server.920/a96525/toc.htm
#       C:\ora9idoc\server.920\a96525\toc.htm in IE
#$dir shown next should use "/" not "\", no "/" at the end
#(Additional work is needed if you use 8.1.5 documentation)
#$dir="C:/ora8idoc/server.817/a76999";
$dir="C:/ora9idoc/server.920/a96525";
#$dir="C:/ora10gdoc/server.101/b10744";
#For Oracle8i only. Ignore this paragraph if your doc is > 8i.
#$colon=":";
#Let's say you look up ORA-00600. Click it. If you see
#      ORA-00600 internal error code...
#please leave the above line commented out
#so $colon will not be set.
#For very old versions, you may see
#      ORA-00600: internal error code...
#then uncomment $colon=":".
#Error message toc.htm page searches individual error message files.
#We need to
#collect all those file names. $fsp is the file search pattern.
#If Oracle8i (except 8.1.5), use this
#$fsp='CLASS="TitleTOC"><FONT FACE="Arial, Helvetica, sans-serif"><A
```

```
HREF="([^\.]+\.htm)';
#If Oracle 9i, use this
$fsp='class="TitleTOC"><a href="([^.]+\.htm)';
#If Oracle 10g, use this
#$fsp='<h2><a href="([^.]+\.htm)';
#In each error message file, we identify the line that has
#$code you intend to
#search for e.g. ORA-01555. Different versions have different
#HTML markup. Pick
#a line search pattern below for your version.
#$lsp="<STRONG>"; #if Oracle 8i (except 8.1.5)
$lsp="<strong>"; #if Oracle 9i
#$lsp="^<dt>.*?"; #if Oracle 10g
##### No need to modify beyond this line. #####
##### But hacking is welcome. #####
if ($#ARGV!=1)
 { print "Usage: oerr facility errornumber
 where facility is case-insensitive and not limited to ORA
 Please open oerr.pl with a text editor and modify
#\$dir if you haven't done so
 Example: oerr ora 18\n";
   exit 1;
 }
open TOC, "$dir/toc.htm" or die "Can't open toc.htm: $!";
while (<TOC>)
 { if (/$fsp/)
 { $allfile{$1}=1 if defined $1;
#use hash to ensure uniqueness
#Last version uses array which contains some
#   filenames more than once
#That's very bad when running against Ver. 7.3.4 Documentation
#push @allfile,$1 if defined $1;
 }
}
close TOC;
$facility=uc $ARGV[0];
$code=$facility."-".(sprintf "%05d",$ARGV[1]);
#e.g. ORA-00600, IMP-000001
#05/21/00 note: Found another inconsistency in Oracle doc:
#Image Data Cartridge
#Error Messages use "," instead of ":" after facility-errorno,
#e.g. "IMG-00001,"
#This is the only one I find that uses anything other than ":".
#If you need
#"oerr img [errono]", better comment out the line
# $colon=":" which may
```

```perl
#introduce the problem described in last paragraph.
#Inconsistent documentation
#style always causes trouble.
$code .= $colon if defined $colon;
$flag=0;
#print join("\t", sort keys %allfile), "\n"; #for debug
foreach $file (keys %allfile)
 { open INP, "$dir/$file" or warn "Error opening $file: $!";
   while (<INP>)
    { exit 0 if ($flag==1 and /$facility-/);
       #if (/<strong>$code/i) #Actually 9i uses <strong>, 8i <STRONG>.
if (/${lsp}$code/)
       { &rawprint;
         $flag=1;
       #print "This is in file ".$file.".\n"; #for debug
       }
       elsif ($flag==1)
       { &rawprint;
       }
    }
   close INP;
 }
sub rawprint
 { s/<.*?>//g; #de-HTMLize
   print unless /^$/;
 }
```

There are, of course, other versions of this kind of utility, but I really like the way this one was written and the perspective Yong takes regarding his code.

The oerr won't actually tell you what caused the error in most cases and won't likely provide you with information on how to fix the problem, but at 3 A.M. when you're freezing in the server room trying to get out to OTN (http://otn.oracle.com) or Tahiti (http://tahiti.oracle.com) and can't, it's a handy little tool to have. I don't know about you, but for the life of me I can't remember the difference between an ORA-12345 and an ORA-01234 without a little help. For what it's worth, oerr says ORA-12345 indicates a lack of CREATE SESSION privileges, while ORA-01234 indicates someone is trying to end the online backup of a file that is busy.

ITar

ITar is a word that can strike fear into the heart of the most fearless DBA. An ITar is the Internet trouble action request, your personal help line to someone in Oracle Support. But there are times when Metalink can be your best friend. What, you may ask, is Metalink? Metalink is the online support venue for Oracle licenced users. You access it at http://metalink.oracle.com and you need to have a valid CSI number (your service number) in order to aquire an account. Believe it or not, there are people who have to support Oracle databases without the luxury of having their own CSI number and therefore without access to Metalink.

These can seem like a lot of trouble, but they can be worth their weight in gold if just one of your issues gets resolved in a reasonable amount of time (as compared with your struggling to figure out something on your own). The analysts who get assigned to your ITars have an internal knowledge base at their fingertips from which they can draw nuggets of wisdom that would often take you an eternity to stumble upon yourself in your troubleshooting.

Metalink really is a very good resource for troubleshooting your database issues. They have a search facility that provides you with answers or ways to think through issues. Forums are also available where you can post questions and issues, and talk with others who've experienced similar problems. Often Oracle employees monitor these forums and answer questions if they don't believe that support's intervention is warranted. Of course, if you have truly unique situations and you're posting questions that are so complex and unusual that no one else could possibly have the same issue, the question is usually met with dead silence or the suggestion that you log an ITar.

Note 166650.1 from Metalink offers valuable information on how best to work with Oracle support. I highly recommend that while trying to resolve an issue yourself, you should log an ITar. This way not only will you have someone helping you defuse the situation, but you'll be able to maintain a running dialog of what you've tried and what Oracle suggested so that the next time you find yourself in a similar situation, you'll have a starting point to fall back on.

It's important to note that Metalink is a wonderful tool, but it's a little quirky. Putting too many phrases into the search criteria will cause you to not get back any hits, even though the general search is for any of the words. Also, when you're creating an ITar, it's important that you know exactly where your cursor is if you're considering using the backspace key on your keyboard. If your cursor is in the wrong place and you backspace, you've just lost all your hard work and will have to enter information into the form again from scratch. I hate typing, and more than anything I hate having to retype something I already typed in.

Something else to remember: include as much information in your ITar as you can. This will provide the analyst with the background she needs to start working on your problem. Don't think something is relevant? Don't be too sure.

Remember, you've been the one pulling your hair out; your support analyst has no way of knowing what you know. He or she hasn't been the one staring at your screen for hours, poring over log and trace files, trying and failing at every turn. Explain the problem the way you might to your mother or the way you might explain *exactly* what you want your child to do—again, include lots of details, in writing, so both of you know what you're talking about. If you have doubts about whether or not you've given enough detail, have your favorite trusted developer or systems analyst look at your explanation of the situation and see if they can make heads or tails of it from your description. The analyst who gets assigned your issue isn't familiar with everything you've tried or with the details of your systems; give all the details you can.

Your analyst can weed out the information he doesn't need as you go, and it's less frustrating for you if you put it in to begin with than to have to update a severity-one ITar with requested information when your database is still not functional. And don't be afraid to make your ITar a severity one if you have a down database that's impacting your business adversely. Support frowns on too many severity-one ITars for test or development databases, but if it is impacting your ability to move up code to production that's needed for your business, or it's keeping you from fixing a production database so it doesn't crash, they're usually very understanding.

There are two other notes relevant to ITar creation that are very handy to have as reference material. Note 280603.1 tells you how to close an ITar (or service request). Yes, always close a service request. If you don't, it will remain in your analyst's queue until she gets frustrated and soft closes it for you for lack of attention. If you know what fixed the issue, put the resolution in the verbiage of why you closed it. This will help the analyst help the next guy who has a similar problem, and it will also be in the ITar so you can retrieve the information later if you find yourself looking at the same issue again. Note 235444.1 provides you with much needed information on how to prepare information and systems for a test case with Oracle support.

Sometimes when Oracle support people can't reproduce a similar situation in the lab, they need your help to contrive a situation where your issue occurs. When trying to help your analyst reproduce your situation in her lab, it's important you provide her with step-by-step information. While you probably aren't thinking in these terms when you're "in the moment" so to speak, it's important to remember that your analyst doesn't have your background information in this situation and will be happy to have all the help you can give her. This note walks you through all the steps needed to help Oracle help you.

It's important to remember that, as with any support or help desk functionality, it's all potluck when it comes to the analyst you're assigned and their ability. Your analyst may be great with some issues, but not yours. So try your best to work within the system and deal with the analyst you're assigned, but if they start reading you the documentation, run screaming to their manager and request an analyst who can help you. Don't expect your analyst to be a magician or a mind reader. They each have their own strengths and weaknesses. Though they're likely to have more resources than you, they don't know everything and they certainly don't know all of the things that you have already tried unless you tell them. Not only that, but they're not just working on your issue; they're probably working on a dozen ITars simultaneously, and keeping all the details straight can be a true juggling act. They're human just like you. Bear with them. Regardless, the help system often works, and if nothing else, it gives you a second set of eyes that might see what you're missing.

Oh, and don't be afraid to escalate your ITar if you aren't getting anywhere with the analyst to whom it's been assigned, and you've honestly tried to work things out. Sometimes an analyst is too busy to spend the time that your management thinks needs to be spent on an issue, or he simply doesn't have the relevant experience to provide you with the information necessary. If you've been updating your ITar and answering analyst questions to the best of your ability yet are still getting nowhere, don't be afraid to escalate the ITar, and the issue, to a higher-level analyst. You will quickly lose credibility, and get a reputation with support as a reactionary whiner if you try to escalate issues that you haven't been working actively, or that simply don't justify continuous support (like requesting installation media or information gathering), but if you're confident you're justified in escalating an issue, do so. Escalation is often looked on as a doctor's second opinion or a mechanic's assurance that the problem with your car really is the water pump and not just a lack of antifreeze. While Note 120817.1 isn't necessarily designed with the average DBA in mind (it is, after all, entitled "Oracle Applications Welcome Basket"), it has very relevant information in it that you can use—most particularly in this case: how and when to escalate an issue.

As an aside, ITars are no longer just a way of having troubles taken care of or having questions answered. They're now the mode of choice to request from Oracle, whether concerning an enhancement of the database or one of the products and applications surrounding it. While it seems like it's taking human-to-human communication a step further out of the Oracle Support equation, it does allow you to be very specific and have a written record you can use to determine what your enhancement request is doing.

Tools

So what tools are available to you to help determine what's causing all your heartache? What can you use to tell you why your bright shiny database went belly up? This section will give you some places to look, as well as some places you might not have thought about.

Alert Log Monitors

One of the most obvious places to look for problems is in the alert logs. Remember back a couple of chapters when we were looking at making the alert logs into external tables so SQL could be used to scavenge information from them? Well, that isn't really practical if your database is down, so you're going to have to search through them manually. If you want to be the eternal optimist and consider your downed database as lucky, you're fortunate, thanks to the alert log's linear nature. Whatever caused the problem with your database, if it's anywhere in the logs, is likely to be found near the very bottom of the file. So running "tail" on the file for the last couple dozen lines might give you a clue to the problem (if you're running on Unix or Linux), or simply scrolling to the bottom on Windows may do the same.

If you have CRON or AT working on your system, you can set up scripts to run under these utilities as alert log monitors so the system will alert you when errors start showing up in the alert logs. One thing that's nice to have is a little script that checks the alert logs for ORA errors, e-mails you (or your cell phone or text pager) when an error occurs, and then renames the alert log to something like alert<sid>.date so you can easily find, near the bottom of the file, the error condition when you go looking for it. In this way, you not only keep your alert logs at a reasonable size, you have easy access to the error condition. Running this little script every minute or every ten minutes or every hour will allow you to catch many error conditions either before they crash your database or very near the time of the crash. They don't require that the database be up and functional at the time.

Oracle Enterprise Manager (OEM), which has gotten more and more useful over the past few releases and is now more of a tool than just a pointy clicky way to do your job, can also be set up to alert you whenever there are error conditions occurring in your database, or whenever your database is down. Sometimes these features are short circuited by the fact that the database has indeed crashed, but at least they can be set up to monitor crashes and you will (lucky dog that you are) be the first to know that your database is down.

Database Monitoring

OEM is also a useful tool for just monitoring the database. You can set it up to alert you when your data files are getting low and when you're in danger of your application crashing because either it can't get to the database or the database won't let it process information. While many of these issues aren't exactly database down, they can appear to be to your user community.

You may be able to see that the database is, indeed, up, but your users might be reporting that they cannot access the database. This means that the database is down as far as they're concerned. If the database isn't responding to requests, if the listener just isn't listening, and web listeners are not listening or Oracle Names or LDAP servers are not responding the way they should, then in effect the database is down.

Whatever you use to monitor, it needs to be able to determine if the archive log destination directory is filling up. It should be able to determine if objects are getting close to their maximum number of extents or to their maximum available size on disk. Has the maximum number of user connections been reached? While with the use of locally managed tablespaces this should never be an issue, there are still organizations running with dictionary-managed tablespaces because someone somewhere heard about a case where locally managed tablespaces performed worse than dictionary managed.

If you want to see if your issues are connected to free space in the tablespaces of your database, you can set up this script to run automatically (or on command) to check space issues.

```
select tbs.tablespace_name,
tot.bytes/1024 total_bytes,
tot.bytes/1024-sum(nvl(fre.bytes,0))/1024 bytes_used,
sum(nvl(fre.bytes,0))/1024 free_space,
(1-sum(nvl(fre.bytes,0))/tot.bytes)*100 pct,
decode(
greatest((1-sum(nvl(fre.bytes,0))/tot.bytes)*100, 90),
90, '', '*') pct_warn
from dba_free_space fre,
(select tablespace_name, sum(bytes) bytes
from dba_data_files
group by tablespace_name) tot,
dba_tablespaces tbs
where tot.tablespace_name = tbs.tablespace_name
and fre.tablespace_name(+) = tbs.tablespace_name
group by tbs.tablespace_name, tot.bytes/1024, tot.bytes
order by 5, 1  ;
```

This script will show you all tablespaces, their free space, used space, and available space, flagging those tablespaces that have less than 90 percent free space with an asterisk in the last column. While this doesn't bring anything back, it can help you keep the database from going down to begin with.

But tablespaces don't just run out of free space. Sometimes there's sufficient free space in the tablespace, but you could be nearing the maximum usable number of extents available to the object if you're using dictionary-managed tablespaces. You'll want to watch numbers as they decrease in this case because once the available number of extents reaches 0, you'll begin to get errors in your application, and users will notice and start complaining.

```
col name noprint new_value dbname
col value noprint new_value block_size
set verify off
SELECT db.name, value
FROM v$database db, v$parameter pr
WHERE pr.name = 'db_block_size' ;
SELECT
```

```
fre.tablespace_name,
SUM(fre.bytes/1024) free_space,
COUNT(*) num_free,
MAX(fre.bytes/1024) largest,
/*AVG(fre.bytes/1024) avg_size,*/
GREATEST(NVL(mnt.max_next_extent,&block_size),
NVL(mni.max_next_extent,&block_size))/1024 grt_extent,
SUM(DECODE(GREATEST
GREATEST(NVL(mnt.max_next_extent,&block_size),
NVL(mni.max_next_extent,&block_size)),
fre.bytes), fre.bytes,
TRUNC(fre.bytes/greatest(NVL(mnt.max_next_extent,&block_size),
NVL(mni.max_next_extent,&block_size))),0)) min_usable
FROM
dba_free_space fre,
(SELECT tab.tablespace_name,
MAX(tab.next_extent) max_next_extent
FROM dba_tables tab
GROUP BY tab.tablespace_name) mnt,
(SELECT idx.tablespace_name,
MAX(idx.next_extent) max_next_extent
FROM dba_indexes idx
GROUP BY idx.tablespace_name) mni
WHERE
fre.tablespace_name = mnt.tablespace_name(+) and
fre.tablespace_name = mni.tablespace_name(+)
GROUP BY
fre.tablespace_name,
GREATEST(NVL(mnt.max_next_extent,&block_size),
NVL(mni.max_next_extent,&block_size))
ORDER BY 6 desc,1  ;
```

The output from either of these scripts can easily be parsed using a shell script, or Perl, and scheduled using cron. If you don't rely on Oracle Enterprise Manager to automate the monitoring of your database, and you're running on a UNIX operating system, cron is a good way to automate monitoring.

Another critical part of monitoring is at the file system level. One of the most important file systems to monitor is the archive log destination. Another, depending on how diligent you are with cleanup, is the directory into which the logs are written. The following is a simple script you can use to monitor a file system (in this case called /archives) that sends you an e-mail whenever the file system reaches 90 percent full:

```
USED=`df -Pk /archives
          | tail -1 | awk '{print $5}' | cut -d % -f 1`
if [ $USED -ge 90 ]
then
echo Filesystem /archives is at $USED percent | mail
you@your.co.com
fi
```

Another simple script to run, this one to make sure your database is up and running, employs the time-honored tradition of using GREP to see if background processes are running.

```
running =`ps -ef |grep smon |grep <SID>`
if [ $running != <SID> ]
then
echo DATABASE DOWN |mail you@your.co.com
fi
```

History

Okay, now, consider that you're going to start receiving information on crashes, space, and other monitoring information. What will you do with it? You can just react to the information when it comes, and then go on with your day-to-day activity, or you could start to compile this information, along with the steps you took to alleviate the condition. You can build yourself a maintenance schema for each instance, or create a central instance and into that repository store all of the situation that you come up against and what you did to rectify the situation. In this way, you can have a running history of not only what's happened in the database, but an affidavit that shows users and clients that you're both proactive as well as reactive, and that you do have a clue what's been going on in your database.

Panic Mode

Panic mode is not a place where you want to be. Let's say you've tried to restart the database and found you can't simply start it with the startup.

Now what? What if someone dropped a data file or a whole tablespace without your knowing it? What happens if your users have production passwords and have managed to drop an interface table to Oracle E-Business Suite and they can't process payments for certain kinds of vendors? What if the sky is falling and Henny Penny and Foxy Loxy have, in their panic to clean up the server, dropped active database files but didn't tell you for fear of upsetting you, the database god or goddess? Relax. Take a deep breath and get a cup of coffee or tea and settle in for the adventure.

Panic isn't going to accomplish anything and it may well get you into more trouble than taking the extra time to approach the issue with a calm open mind. You are in control and you can do this.

If nothing else, there are people out there who can, and will, help you. http://www.freelists.org/webpage/oracle-l is the URL for a very useful and helpful listserv, the Oracle-L list. There are very knowledgeable DBAs on that list who are more than willing to help with problems and issues. I'm not sure about all of them, but many look on helping as a way to learn something new, or to help someone else not make the same mistakes they have. There's expertise on this list on everything from Perl with Oracle, to RAC, to tuning, to how to get the right results from the most horrendous query imaginable. These resources are available to you even when you aren't having database issues and just want to discuss differences in doing things, but when you're looking at a database full of helpless data and have no way to get to it, they can be a far more invaluable resource.

Hot Standby Database

So, management wants to make sure that, if the database does go down, you have a backup database to use, a database that you can quickly bring back to life to return the organization to its previous condition. More detailed information on Data Guard and physical and logical standby databases can be found in Chapter 6. Suffice it to say that you can make use of Data Guard technology to make sure you have an available and viable database for your users.

Problem Resolution

Okay, so you have a problem. Since you're the DBA, they'll at some point expect you to resolve it—which means someone is going to know you exist.

Keep in mind though, the faster the resolution, the less people who'll ever know there was a problem.

No Oracle Connectivity

Okay, so you can connect from the server prompt on the database server, but the users can't seem to connect. Perform some obvious steps first. Check the log files for your connectivity (Net8, SQL Net, *name du jour*). Ensure your environmental variables are set and inherited by the connection running the listener. These kinds of errors are almost always caused by a misconfiguration in the user's environment.

Use Sql*Plus both from your client computer and at the server level to connect to the database with a valid user ID and password as well as the service name. Make sure no one has suddenly decided they needed to update their own version of the client software. Sometimes installing a new version, regardless of reason or version, can cause brand-new issues. Sometimes the issue concerns an incompatibility between two versions of the client software installed on the same computer, while sometimes versions of tnsnames.ora and other configuration files have gotten overlaid by the software. Either way, it's always because the installation of the software has messed something up and the user is often very reticent to fess up to having changed anything. Have them check their PATH variables as well. Sometimes something has gotten updated, changed, or deleted that used to be in the PATH when the user was last able to connect.

Tnsping <sid> from the database server, and then do it again from a client machine. Ping the database server from a client machine. Telnet from the client machine to the database server. Even if you can't log in, as long as there are no errors returned from the telnet attempt, there's little chance there aren't any network connectivity issues from where you are to the server. Now have the users who are raising issues do the same thing.

Start the listener. At worst, you'll find that the listener is already running. At best, you'll discover the listener is down and that restarting it will fix the problem.

Database Links

One of the most aggravating issues that DBAs work with are database links that just don't seem to work. Sometimes they're user-defined database links that used to work but that now have all of a sudden stopped, or they are database links that users are trying to define that simply won't work as they should. One common problem with database errors is when you think you should be connecting just fine, but you start getting ORA-12154. Often, this is caused by the user misunderstanding which configuration files are being used and assuming that the local version of the file is what's currently employed. When a client issues a database link connection command, the address is not resolved on the client; it's resolved on the server that the connected user's session is connected to.

For example, let's assume that the client has the following in their tnsnames.ora file:

```
DEVDB = (DESCRIPTION=
(ADDRESS=(PROTOCOL=tcp)(HOST=myhost1)(PORT=11234))
 (CONNECT_DATA=(SID=DEVSID))
)
```

And the server has the following:

```
DEVLDB = (DESCRIPTION=
(ADDRESS=(PROTOCOL=tcp)(HOST=myhost1)(PORT=11234))
(CONNECT_DATA=(SID=DEVSID))
)
```

If the user creates the following database link:

```
SQL> CREATE DATABASE LINK MYDBLINK
CONNECT TO scott IDENTIFIED BY tiger USING 'DEVDB';
```

the link is likely to fail and will need to have its definition changed to USING DEVLDB. If there is a tnsnames.ora file on the server, it should either be in the %ORACLE_HOME%\network\admin directory, or a symbolic link to the file should be located there. If one doesn't exist there, copy one to the directory and modify it so it contains the appropriate entries.

Verify the information on the link from the DBA views.

```
SELECT DB_LINK, HOST FROM DBA_DB_LINKS;
```

If all else fails, rename the sqlnet.ora file on the client. If that doesn't work, try renaming the one on the server. Double-check the entries in the tnsnames.ora file. If you're still getting nowhere, and the database link still fails, try pretending that the tnsnames file doesn't exist anywhere and build the tnsnames entry into the database link itself.

```
CREATE DATABASE LINK MYDBLINK
CONNECT TO scott IDENTIFIED BY tiger
USING '(DESCRIPTION= ADDRESS=(PROTOCOL=tcp)(HOST=myhost1)(PORT=11234))
(CONNECT_DATA=(SID=DEVSID))';
```

By defining the database link in this manner, you'll not only be sure about what user ID and password the link will connect as, but you can be certain about what server definition will be used for the connection and what entries are on any given tier (since the person defining the link likely won't be the only one using it) and that the link will function.

RDA

Oracle Remote Diagnostic Agent (RDA) is a set of scripts, customized to each platform, that are designed to provide information on the overall Oracle environment and assist Oracle Support with problem diagnosis.

While Oracle Support encourages the use of RDA as a means of gathering information so they can debug issues, it can help you in the same regard. Use of this tool greatly reduces ITar resolution time by minimizing the number of requests from Oracle Support Services for more information. If for no other reason, it's a beneficial tool that should be used whenever possible prior to opening an ITar, and as a way of debugging an issue yourself.

For a list of all available RDA versions and platforms, please see Note 175853.1 on Metalink. Currently, it's supported on VMS, Windows, Solaris, HP-UX, Tru64, AIX, SuSE, and Red Hat Linux. Naturally, it can be adapted to other platforms with only a little tinkering. Errors will indicate utilities that aren't supported on different platforms.

RDA collects useful information for overall system configuration as well as data that's useful for corrective issues related to the following products:

- Oracle RDBMS Server

- Oracle RAC Cluster

- Oracle Application Server (*i*AS 1.0.2.*x*, 9*i*AS 9.0.2.*x*/9.0.3.*x*/10.1.2, HTTP Server)

- Oracle Management Server and Intelligent Agent (Grid Server, Agent Server, DB Control)

- OLAP products (Express Server, Financial Analyzer, and Demand Planning Server)

- Oracle forms and reports

- Oracle networking products

Test Cases

Okay, so maybe you need to provide Oracle with a test case or maybe you just want to have a place where you can re-create the database so you can figure out why things broke.

Cloning is a good way to not only provide test cases on cleansed data but also to help you fix the problems in a production-like test bed.

Copy the code tree for the database binaries along with the data files and all data associated with the database to a different location or a different server. Own them as another user so you can be sure you don't have any way to mess up your other databases. Change the values in $ORACLE_HOME/rdbms/lib/config.c to reflect the new owner of the binaries and relink the Oracle binaries to work in the new location.

```
cd $ORACLE_HOME/bin
relink all
```

If you're on the same server, you'll need to rename the database. If you're on a different server, you could start monkeying around, but feel free to leave the database name the same. I, personally, am never that confident and always change the name to something outlandish so that I know beyond a shadow of a doubt where I am at the time.

Summary

Recovering from disasters isn't much different than recovering from any backup. Practice when it comes to the art of recovery is important. Clone your production database to a backup location and use it as a practice arena so you can practice fixing things as they break. Having your own private playground is often one of the best tools a DBA has. If you can break a database in every way imaginable (or better yet, have someone else think up ways to break it), and then recover or restart or do whatever is called for in the given situation, you'll better know what to look for the next time your database goes down.

CHAPTER
6

High Availability

igh availability is a warm and fuzzy term that's frequently bandied about in meetings and which is often set as a goal for many systems. However, it's frequently like an organization's mission statement, ill-defined and less than concrete, and is something that's used to make other people think that what's actually happening in an organization is more than what's *really* happening. Just how high *is* high? And to *whom* is it available? But all rhetoric aside, what are they talking about (the powers-that-be in any organization) when they speak of high availability? Do they know realistically what they want?

High Availability

There are a lot of things you can do to assure high availability to your users. These different opportunities can be brought into play under different circumstances. High availability (HA) means different things to different people at different times. Sometimes, HA concerns performing simple maintenance in such a way that you don't have to deny access to the database as often. Whenever faced with minimal maintenance tasks, tasks that don't mean having to restart the database, and you choose to perform these maintenance tasks online with users accessing (or potentially accessing) the database, that's a form of high availability.

Simple High Availability

There are simple things you can do to provide high availability to your end users. They aren't always things a DBA thinks about as high availability, but in actuality it is. It may sound simplistic, but it's a professional touch your end users will appreciate.

Online Reorganization

Historically, the bane of many users' and DBAs' existence was having to take down the database for reorgs. It could mean extended downtime, depending on when and for what reason the reorganizing was occurring, and it usually meant extended planning, preparation, and meetings. Oracle can't do anything to eliminate the planning and preparation, but because you won't need to keep your users out of the database for extended periods of time, you can eliminate many of the meetings (I don't know about you, but even one less meeting makes for a much happier me).

In large, very active databases (those where reorganizations are often necessary and there isn't much downtime available) online table redefinition is one of the ways you can make use of Oracle's newer features to give users access to the database while doing your maintenance. When a table is redefined at any level online, it's accessible. Online table redefinition allows administrators to modify the physical attributes or storage parameters associated with a table, move tables to different tablespaces, add, drop, or alter partitioning, or even change between index-organized tables and ordinary heap tables, all online. Even more important, you can often convert from LONGs to LOBs online, convert from unique indexes to primary keys, or rebuild indexes online. Something that's also important to remember is that it's often possible to change the definition of a table without invalidating the packages or procedures dependent on the redefined tables. While nothing will help if you change the columns involved in the stored program units drastically (for instance, changing a column from VARCHAR2 to number), many stored procedures are dependent on the signature of the table rather than its definition.

Flashback

Everyone makes mistakes. Most of us have had those "oh, no" moments where we realize we've just done something totally wrong and we desperately try to figure out how to undo it. There's a cartoon my kids watch where the main character has an "undo" watch that allows him to go back in time, knowing what he knows now, and undo (or sometimes make worse) what he did the first time.

Flashback Query is Oracle's version of an "undo" watch. It allows you to go back in time and selectively undo something done in the recent past or do a bulk undo of something that might have been done and committed already. So the next time someone comes to you and tells you they just deleted 32,852 rows from a production table and have already shut SQL*Plus (implicit commit), and now are asking desperately if there's any way to get the data back, you can say "Yes." Flashback provides a SQL interface through which you can analyze an error made in the recent past and undo it.

With Flashback, you can recover at the row level, the transaction level, the table or tablespace level, and even at the database level.

Introduced in Oracle 9*i*, Flashback Query lets you reconstruct data that may have been deleted or altered and offers a mechanism that allows developers to provide self-service interfaces that permit end users to correct their own errors without having to run to the DBA all the time (of course, this means you have to loosen the reins and allow someone else to exercise some control over the database).

Oracle started out with Flashback Query. They have expanded their Flashback offerings since then and now it includes some vastly different offerings, all of which will likely come in handy in your DBA adventure.

Flashback Version Query, on the other hand, provides you with the ability to look at changes at the row level over time. Using this ability, the DBA can easily trace changes back through time to a given user, application, or transaction. This can help you track down logical corruption of the data and correct it. It can also be used to allow developers to see what their code is really doing (the next best thing to Expediter for nonmainframe platforms) and correct the errors in the code before they go live.

Flashback Transaction Query gives you the ability to see all the changes associated with a given transaction. Given this information, compensating SQL statements can be created to undo all changes to all rows associated with that transaction. Again, this lets you and your developers analyze and detect errors in the programmatic logic, or in the database logic in the database.

Flashback Database, meanwhile, allows you to see the state of the database at a given point in time. The logical alternative to this would be to recover the database to a certain point in time, but this can take hours (on a good day) or days (depending on the issues that end up being involved). With Flashback Database, you can rewind all the changes to the entire database (provided you have sufficient undo data available) to the point in time where the corruption occurred. This is a means by which you can recover the database to a point just prior to the corruption (logical corruption or user error). This is often the only way to unwind some errors connected to an Oracle 11*i* instance's back-end database because of the interconnected schemas/tables/tablespaces.

Flashback Table takes the undo ability to the table level and allows you to unwind the changes to a given table back to a given point in time.

Flashback Drop lets you undrop database objects. New in Oracle 10*g*, Flashback Drop provides a safety net to catch objects that somehow magically drop themselves. Whenever a user (any user) drops a table, Oracle puts that table into a recycle bin where it will remain either until the user decides to deliberately remove it from the recycle bin or until space constraints cause Oracle to remove the table by overwriting the space where it's stored.

Hardware Failure and High Availability

A great deal of the high availability that goes with eliminating or limiting the impact of hardware failure is where Oracle's Real Application Clusters plays a big part. Oracle's Real Application Clusters (RAC) is a product that, due to its seeming complexity, can strike fear into the most intrepid heart.

It often seems like RAC is more trouble than it's worth, given it can also become expensive and has (under its various names over the years) proven difficult to configure. But more and more organizations will find themselves able to meet a client's needs for high availability thanks to RAC. It's also becoming more stable and easier to configure and maintain. While none of this really means anything if you don't have a use for it, it can mean all the difference in the world if you do. To that end, let's look at how you can learn more about RAC and maybe get some real work experience under your belt.

Oracle Parallel Server (OPS) had been around for years. While you may not realize it, the first bug was filed against Oracle Parallel Server in version 5. So you see, the concept has been around for many years. In the beginning, OPS allowed multiple instances to share the contents of their buffered storage while accessing a single Oracle database. This meant there were multiple memory locations (multiple SGAs, if you will, and multiple redo log threads), but only one set of data files and control files. There was one drawback to the OPS architecture, however. OPS required that all data blocks be available to all instances at all times. In OPS, these blocks were shared via disk (rather than the cache fusion interconnect, the way they are now).

This required a rather difficult process—the integrated distributed lock manager or IDLM—be running in the background. This process was responsible for making sure data blocks were constantly sent back and forth between the instances.

The redesign of the OPS product, which grew into Real Application Clusters (RAC), meant the introduction of Cache Fusion, allowing all the data block buffers of all the running instances within the configuration to be resident within a special area of shared RAM memory that could be accessed by all instances simultaneously. In Oracle 9*i*, there was no longer any need to point back to the disk as a means to share the blocks. They were shared simply over the interconnect. This change in how the different instances shared information from their memory regions meant the elimination of much of the inefficiency that went along with the use of disks to share the blocks. The ability to make use of the high-speed interconnect meant that RAC became more viable to even more organizations as a solution to their high-availability needs.

This means that not only are the inefficiencies overcome, but also the resulting system is faster and more reliable than could have been achieved with just the OPS architecture. One thing that might be of interest when you're looking to possibly implement an RAC environment is that, while it's designed to protect against catastrophic instance failure, it can also allow for highly distributed load balancing to make the best use of your computer hardware.

This means that, should any one instance fail, or should any hardware associated with any given instance fail, Oracle's Transparent Application Failover (TAF) will capture any currently running transactions and redirect them to one of the nodes not affected by the failure. This is similar to the way you'd redirect transactions to a replicated database in a replicated environment, but is handled automatically, with no intervention, and with no need for you to code anything.

Sounds great, right? And it is, but there are some downsides. TAF can fairly elegantly restart SELECT statements, but it doesn't support the restarting of INSERT, UPDATE, or DELETE statements that were in process in the lost instance. PL/SQL package states are lost with the loss of the instance, also, which means that all stored procedures need to be restarted. TAF doesn't support the carryover of anything that was altered with an ALTER SESSION statement unless it was written to the SPFILE, and global temporary table failover also isn't carried over to the surviving instances.

Remember, however, that RAC is all about keeping the database up and running, and keeps at least one instance into the database functioning to allow applications and users to connect and reconnect if the connection is lost. It does this without having to rely on replication and without having to go through an immense amount of work to get the users either connected or reconnected.

One final disadvantage with RAC is that there is, as yet, no reliable rolling update capabilities, so when you need to update the Oracle software, you have to shut down all the instances and the database to do it. While this doesn't occur all that often, it's important to remember, because RAC is touted as *the* high-availability solution and implies no downtime (claims that can seem misleading if you don't understand what's going to happen). Indeed, organizations often read entirely too much into what RAC can do and are disappointed to learn that their expectations can't be met. While RAC is much better than anything to which it can be compared, sometimes managing expectations can be much harder than managing databases, not just with RAC, but with anything that any hardware, software, or database solution can accomplish.

While RAC has begun gaining a greater following and more people are choosing to migrate their applications to an RAC environment, it isn't necessarily the high-availability solution of choice for everyone. Many are implementing their own versions of database replication rather than relying on technology that they don't necessarily trust. This is unfortunate because RAC has become a much more stable product and many huge organizations have chosen it as their failover solution. Fear shouldn't influence your decision about whether or not to implement RAC. The choice should be made based on information and testing if possible. Therefore, that's what we'll cover in the remainder of this chapter: information on RAC, information on where it is or isn't applicable, and help in understanding just what this animal is.

What It Isn't

There's a lot of misunderstanding today about what exactly RAC is. But being the contrary type, I decided to start with what it isn't. This way we can clear up some misunderstandings and create a foundation on which to build our RAC.

Grid

A great deal of confusion surrounds the fact that the "g" in Oracle 10*g* stands for Grid and that one of the central pillars of Oracle's Grid is RAC. In fact, you can't have one without the other. This is a big misunderstanding. Not only can you have Grid without RAC, you can have Grid without any database. Many organizations have done just that for quite a while now. In fact, the introduction of databases into a traditional Grid environment can add complexity and difficulties that many people using Grid would prefer to do without. Making databases more Grid friendly is partly what Oracle is doing with Oracle 10*g*.

Grid is the underlying conceptual architecture that allows computers to be tied together (often commodity servers) in such a way that they can donate their processing power to a pool and the brokers of the Grid. The pool of resources can then divvy up the resources to the jobs that are requesting them. In this way, many smaller, more inexpensive computers can be harnessed together to do jobs that would take the power of a Cray to accomplish under other circumstances.

RAC isn't the Oracle Grid solution, per se, but many pieces (including OEM) are part of the Oracle offering that make it a Grid-like product. OEM now can monitor and control more of the processes at the operating-system level, and this is one of the key components of Grid. OEM, in fact, can control so many aspects of the system, and so many aspects of a Grid system, that it is called 10*g* Grid Control, which fortunately moves people away from thinking of early versions of OEM as tools simply for junior DBAs who were learning the ropes. The part that databases play in all of this is evolving, but the capability to gather data from several different (federated) databases will likely be a necessity, because in reality most organizations have a mixture of databases in which their data resides, and they'll want to analyze all of that data, not just some of it.

The Only Answer

While 42 may be the answer to the meaning of life, the universe, and everything (according to *The Hitchhiker's Guide to the Galaxy*), RAC is not the answer to every problem or every situation. RAC does not deal with the failure of disk devices where database files are located. Remember, RAC is one database with multiple instances—if you lose a datafile, you have still lost a datafile. RAC also does not deal with connectivity to a lost site (as in the case of potential disaster recovery) if all servers on which the instances are running are co-located at the same site or facility. If you lose connectivity to the buildings or you lose the buildings entirely, you still won't be able to make use of RAC's ability to connect to the databases. This is true even if only connectivity into and out of the network is affected. Internal clients (those to whom connectivity is still established) will be able to remain connected, but anyone trying to connect from the outside will be unable to do so. Don't let upper management who've read something somewhere about RAC being better than sliced bread tell you that you have to use RAC because your application has to be available 24/7. While RAC can help assure high availability, it is not necessarily the only solution, and may not be the solution to your situation. You can instead utilize Data Guard to run a secondary logical or physical database to which you could fail over within minutes if necessary. Highly redundant hardware can allow you to maintain high availability if necessary.

But is extreme high availability really necessary, or just something management decided should be important because it makes for a good PR line?

If you don't have SLAs (service level agreements, or agreements with end users or clients that dictate when your systems have to be available and the financial ramifications of not meeting those deadlines) that say you have to have your data available with virtually no downtime, then you may not need Data Guard or RAC. A cost benefit analysis should be done on some level to decide if the cost (in hardware, networking, training, and licensing fees) will make it worthwhile to implement RAC at an enterprise level. Just because you can, doesn't necessarily imply you should, or even that you would in any way be better off with it.

That said, the fact that you can play with it for little money makes it a toy that you're not only likely to play with just because you can, but once you learn the ins and outs of the product, you may be more likely to find areas in your life where you can apply the technology appropriately. And who knows, it might prove to be a handy little ability later.

For Everyone

Just as RAC isn't the answer to every problem or every situation, it also isn't for everyone. There are places and times when implementing an RAC will make life more elegant for the organization and it makes sense over time. But if you're a smaller organization and you have limited data needs, don't buy into the theory that bigger is always better and that you have to have an RAC just to keep up with the Joneses. It won't fly. That's not the reason for any organization to buy into technology that doesn't fit their needs. Look first at the situation. Then realize that RAC comes free of charge with even Oracle 10*g* Standard Edition and that a simple two-node cluster can be very inexpensive to set up and run. The decision, however, should be based on your situation, not on the technology's coolness factor.

What It Is

Okay, so now we know most of what it isn't, but what then *is* RAC?

RAC is an architecture that allows multiple instances (the memory segments, the System Global Area or SGA, and all processes that allow the end user to make use of the database) that write to a single database (the datafiles, control files, undo and redo structures, temporary tablespaces, and the like) to share their information over a high-speed interconnect. This interconnect allows you to more rapidly process queries and access data (more quickly than is possible with disk-based transfers, but slower than what you can expect from just memory) from any node of the system without having the memory structures necessarily be a bottleneck. The high-speed interconnect allows the different nodes, and therefore the different instances, to talk together without having to worry too much about finding one's self in a situation where there's an update anomaly. An update anomaly exists when not all rows (or tuples) are updated and you have incorrect information in the database, sometimes due to design flaws in the constraints, and sometimes due to failures that occur during processing of the update statement. RAC will never be the solution to truly bad design situations, but it can help with some failures in processing.

Want to Try It Out?

Want to try it out before you buy? Don't want to invest in the hardware, the OS, and all the necessary associated software and licenses only to find out that, after all the time and money spent, it isn't for you after all? Feel like learning on your own, but not investing several thousand dollars, minimally, to do it? Why not build yourself a single-node RAC on a PC running Linux as a way to try before you buy? If you want to test without the heavy investment, you can opt for RAC on a single node, RAC on a single VMware node, RAC on multiple VMware nodes, or even RAC and Network Block Device. You can realize the following benefits with one of these configurations, but it's important to remember that none of these is supported as a production environment. They are meant only as a way to learn the technology and test it to see if RAC is the solution for you.

Remember, OTN is your friend, so go out and register for an OTN account (http://otn.oracle.com). It's free to register and there are vast amounts of information, manuals, articles, and downloads available for you to get started with just about any Oracle product still supported. All of these products, all of the pieces of the RAC puzzle that aren't hardware, are readily downloaded. You may just find that they, even the non-Oracle ones, are really great tools that you can add to your toolbelt and pull out later when you least expect it. It's been said that, when all you have is a hammer, everything looks like a nail. Sometimes it's good to have a 5/16" Allen wrench in your pocket so you can make better use of your skills and talent. What are some of the benefits of trying RAC out this way over even a limited full-scale implementation?

No Need for Fencing

While it may be true that fences make good neighbors, in the case of an RAC, fencing makes for more difficulty and less simplicity. Fencing? Is that the kind with wires and posts or the kind with foils and masks? Well, neither.

Fencing, or I/O fencing in this case, is the mechanism used to keep nodes of a cluster (nodes that are having problems for one reason or another) from accessing one or more file systems as a means to protect those file systems from being corrupted. Cluster management software monitors the health and connectivity of all of the nodes in the cluster as a means of determining which nodes are performing correctly. If a node fails for any reason, the cluster manager fences that node off from the rest of the cluster. It does this because, if a node fails or loses contact with the rest of the cluster, the locks it holds will become unavailable to other nodes in the cluster. Such a condition can eventually bring down the entire cluster.

The failed node cannot be permitted to rejoin the cluster while locks it's holding still exist. If the node attempts to write to locks it thinks it's holding from before it failed, it can end up writing to locations that are being written to by other nodes in the cluster and cause a serious corruption of data. Fencing prevents the node from rejoining the cluster by disabling the path between the node and the file system (the database, in this case).

So setting up the facility to manage the nodes in a cluster requires additional expertise (usually at the operating-system level) and knowledge of the different methods of fencing (each of which has its own advantages and disadvantages). Single-node RACs don't run into this issue, because if the node fails, everything fails; thus, there's no concern about held locks that can't be accessed. This can allow you to more easily learn RAC without having to learn everything associated with it. Learning one thing at a time can make life so much easier. Once you master those things that a single-node RAC can provide you with, you can expand your horizons and learn more if you wish.

No Need for Oracle Cluster File System or Raw Devices

Oracle Cluster File System (OCFS) is a GPL (general public license) product that presents a consistent file system image across all of the servers in an RAC cluster. The OCFS product allows administrators to take advantage of a single unified view of the file system that's made available for the Oracle database files (datafiles, control files, and archive logs) and configuration files (SPFILE), easing the overall administration of a production RAC implementation. OCFS was designed to overcome the 255 raw device limit on Linux distributions, but it also brings with it the ability to use standard OS tools for backups.

While the tool is a very worthwhile addition to a DBA or Sysadmin toolbelt, it isn't necessary to install it simply to support your trial implementation.

Raw devices are typically difficult to manage; even more so when you're simply trying to test out or learn the technology. A raw device, also known as a raw partition, is a disk partition that's neither mounted nor written to via the file system, but is accessed directly using a special device driver. It's left to the application to determine how the data is written and accessed from the disk. Significant performance benefits can be realized from using raw devices, but performance isn't necessarily what you're looking for when implementing a simple single-node RAC.

No Need for Multiple Oracle Homes

While in a typical RAC implementation you need to install the Oracle RDBMS binaries on every node that will have its own instance, because you're installing on a single node, you simply install one set of binaries in one home and have one Oracle user that owns that set of binaries. In order to have more than one instance, allow that user to have multiple profiles, and use one profile to be sourced for each instance.

```
su - oracle
. rac1
```

```
echo $ORACLE_SID
test1
echo $ORACLE_HOME
/oracle/product/10g
su - oracle
. rac2
echo $ORACLE_SID
test2
echo $ORACLE_HOME
/oracle/product/10g
```

To mimic the balancing of client-side load, use Listener for each instance in the RAC. To mimic the server-side load balancing, each Listener listens to each instance. This means that information for each instance needs to reside in each listener.ora and tnsnames.ora file and that you have one of these files available for each instance.

Oracle Installer needs to find the Clusterware software in order to install the binaries. This means you must have the Clusterware software installed and running before you attempt the binaries.

Clusterware contains the operating-system dependent components of the implementation that control the way the operating system reacts in the RAC environment and the way that Clusterware controls the RAC. The two primary pieces of the Clusterware software are Cluster Manager (CM) and Interprocess Communication (IPC).

Init File

One of the biggest, most obvious things you'll notice when dealing with RAC are the initialization files. While the files init<SID>#.ora will be located in each $ORACLE_HOME/dbs directory, the naming convention of these files is somewhat different than they would be in a non-RAC environment.

The first thing that may strike you is that there's a number following what you know as the SID for your database. You may also note that, contrary to what Oracle suggests, it does not appear that there is, indeed, an SPFILE anywhere to be seen to govern the RAC. The SPFILE is stored, often in the datafile directories, in a location where all instances can find it (which the init file points to) and uses the SPFILE as a means of getting to the parameters. An interesting configuration would be to place your single SPFILE in a location where all the instances can find it (for example, the directory structure where your datafiles are located). Then, point each init<SID>#.ora file at that SPFILE so the instances can source the file when they start. In that way, all changes made with the ALTER SYSTEM command that would ordinarily get written to the SPFILE get written to one central file and you don't have to concern yourself with all of your instances having the same values—they have to by default. Oracle suggests in its documentation that you back up the server parameter file using the tried-and-true command:

```
CREATE PFILE FROM SPFILE;
```

This is an excellent suggestion for everyone, not just those dealing with an RAC environment. It captures any changes that have been made to the system using ALTER SYSTEM commands so that those changes can be easily recaptured if you lose your SPFILE or it becomes corrupt or someone makes a bonehead change that makes it impossible for you to start the database using the SPFILE or, worse, edits the file with a text editor having forgotten you can't edit the SPFILE. Thus, there are many reasons you might want to back up the SPFILE regularly on any system. It's just good maintenance practice. What they don't necessarily say, however, is that in the case of an RAC, if you're using an SPFILE and you use the command the way it's cited, you may end up causing yourself plenty of headaches. When you use the CREATE PFILE FROM SPFILE command, it will do exactly what you suggest. And if you're using standard naming, it will overwrite the PFILE that contains the reference to the SPFILE with the contents of the SPFILE. Not necessarily a bad thing all in all, but you may end up with instances out of sync with each other because someone made this mistake on any given instance, and overwrote some of the INIT files with the SPFILE contents, and some still have their PFILES calling the regular SPFILE. Suddenly, it's a maintenance situation. But wait! What if you know all this and you're trying to protect yourself by creating a PFILE under another name so you can make some changes and then propagate those changes (for example, changing where the UTL_FILE directory points to) to the database without destroying the integrity of the SPFILE and PFILE setup that you have in place? You could just create the PFILE under another name and make your changes, start the database, and instance with the new PFILE by doing the following:

```
STARTUP PFILE=initMYPFILE.ora
```

Then, you'll want to make those changes available system-wide, so you need to re-create the SPFILE by doing the following:

```
CREATE SPFILE FROM PFILE
File created
```

Cool beans. Now I'm good to go, right? Not so fast, speedy. Think about what you just did. Or better yet, try to start up one of your other instances with just the STARTUP command and you'll quickly figure out what you did. You can't start the other instances because your SPFILE now only has the entry in it to point to the SPFILE itself.

A better solution all the way around would be to always parameterize the CREATE PFILE and CREATE SPFILE commands regardless of your naming standards and your database and instance situation. This way, you can look at what you're really doing and think through what those changes will mean. Then afterwards you can intelligently decide if they're really the ones you want to make.

```
CREATE SPFILE='/path/to/my/spfileSID.ora'
from PFILE='/path/to/my/initSID.ora';
```

Recall, of course, that the ALTER SYSTEM UNSET command can undo many changes created by the ALTER SYSTEM SET command, but remember, too, that you actually have to get the instance and database to a point where you can effectively issue that command and have it take effect.

Parameters

The parameters in the initialization file are applicable to all instances associated with the RAC. That's not exactly what you're after? Want to have greater control over the way each instance acts? Want to fine-tune each instance individually? That's easy: you can ALTER SYSTEM from each instance and the parameter file will hold not only the base settings, but also the individualized settings for each instance.

```
*.OPEN_CURSORS=500
mysid1.OPEN_CURSORS=1000
mysid2.OPEN_CURSORS=750
```

Single-Node RAC on Linux

Metalink Note 241114.1 tells you step by step how to go about implementing a single-node RAC. While they point out very plainly that it isn't a supported configuration in a production environment, there are people who've configured some of their test systems in this manner so they can ape a real RAC configuration without having to invest in a lot of extraneous hardware. In this way, you can test programming changes that you want to move up to a production RAC environment, and see how RAC will behave under different circumstances,

While in a single-node configuration, you don't really have to set up your environment with I/O fencing (this is the magic model that tells the database one of the nodes has died or stopped responding, which is very useful for preventing data corruption in a multinode RAC because you really don't want a node in an unstable state writing to the shared disks on your database). Instead, you can mimic a multinode environment by setting up fencing in the *mode du jour*. This not only gives you the ability to model your environment as if it were a multinode RAC, but will give you the experience of actually setting up I/O fencing on a Linux machine. Looks very good on a resume (wink wink).

RAC on a Single VMware Node

Want to try a different configuration? Why not try RAC on a single VMware node? It is, if that's possible, even easier than it is on a Linux installation. VMware is software that provides you with the ability to have a virtual infrastructure. The virtual machine is scalable and can run Windows, Linux, and NetWare operating systems while accessing the host machine's resources, such as CPU, memory, disk, networking, and peripherals.

It doesn't have to be expensive to try out this type of configuration, either. You just have to do the following:

1. Install VMware (5.0 or 4.5.2), which is available for a 90-day free trial if you register.

2. Install RHEL (Red Hat Enterprise Linux) 3 U2 (not free unless you already have access to a machine that has this loaded and ready) and the RHEL3 VMware skeleton.
   Or:
   Install (SuSE Linux Enterprise server) SLES8 sp3 (not free, again, unless you have access to an existing installation to play with) and the SLES8 sp3 VMware skeleton.

3. Install the Oracle Cluster File System (OCFS) v1, which is free and open source.

4. Install Oracle RDBMS with Oracle RAC 10*g* Enterprise Edition (requires download and CD Burn).

5. Create a sample database using DBCA from the Oracle 10*g* companion CD (requires download and CD Burn).

6. Optionally load OrderEntry Swingbench (the download is free, and it can be used to stress test the database).

7. Add ASM to the existing database using ASMLib Drivers.

Full instructions can be found at the Oracle-on-Linux VMware Cookbook http://www.oracle.com/technology/tech/linux/vmware/cookbook/index.html.
Want to see the data center edition? It's available for download at http://www.oracle.com/technology/tech/linux/vmware/index.html. All of this is pre-installed and ready for you, so what are you waiting for?

RAC on Multiple VMware Nodes

The VMware GSX/ESX server permits you to allow sharing of plain disks with multiple virtual machines that are running on the same host, provided that the disks in question are SCSI disks. While this approach is very powerful and more closely apes a true RAC type environment, it allows you to try your hand at very complex environments including multiple NICs, switches, and disks. It also means that your learning curve is a little steeper and that the setup to get you up and running is a little more complex.

RAC with Network Block Devices

Need to implement an RAC environment using PC technology? By using Network Block Devices, you can allow standard shared disk subsystems to be replaced by a native Linux technology called Network Block Device (NBD). NBD maps remote files to a local block device (for example, /dev/nb0) via the TCP/IP network. In this way, an existing computer (not even necessarily a Linux machine) serves as the data storage device for all of the clustered nodes (Linux PCs) instead of having to invest in expensive disk arrays.

Once you have NBD compiled into the Linux kernel, you can use the remote file server as one of its own block devices and TCP/IP will handle the routing of requests to the remote file system, which will then reply with the requested data. What's more, this remote resource doesn't need to be an entire disk, or even an entire partition of a disk. It can be a directory or a single file.

For best results, both your client and server machines could be running RHEL, the most recent release supported. From Sourceforge, you can download the NBD source (nbd.sourceforge.net/) and as root do the following:

```
bunzip2 nbd-2.7.3.tar.bz2
tar -xvf nbd-2.7.3.tar
cd nbd-2.7.3.
./config

make
make install
```

This creates the new empty files at the NBD server.

As root, use the following:

```
dd if=/dev/zero of=/u01/oradata/rac/system.01 count=300 bs=100
```

Then, run the NDB server as shown next:

```
nbd-server <your port> <Your filename>
nbd-server 4999 /u01/oradata/rac/system.01
```

This installation means that NBD client must be run as root, because of the kernel aspects of NBD, which you have to install before you can actually run it.

```
rpm -Uvh kernel-unsupported -2.4.21-4.EL.i686.rpm
```

Please note one last time that this stuff is all for testing and trial only. It isn't supported by Oracle for anything in any way other than learning RAC and trying it out on a limited scale.

Before loading the NBD module, first see if it's already running.

```
lsmod |grep nbd
modprobe nbd
lsmod |grep nbd
```

Now, run the NBD client.

```
nbd-client <data server> <port> /dev/nb#
nbd-client test2 4999 /dev/nb0
```

Now that you have your block devices configured, it's possible to access your remote data.

Remember, for Oracle RAC to access the shared disk, they have to be raw file systems.

```
raw /dev/raw/raw# /dev/nb#
raw /dev/raw/raw1 /dev/nb0
```

Like to play pretend? Well, next, you may be able to play "let's pretend to be using RAW without actually having to carve up the disks."

What, There's More?

Want to get even more creative, but do it on the cheap? Why not create your own RAC cluster at home? There is a fascinating article configuring a true two-node RAC for under $2000 utilizing Linux, a couple of middle-of-the-road PCs with low-end hard drives (40GB), and Ethernet and FireWire cards. Jeffrey Hunter's article "Build Your Own Oracle RAC 10*g* Cluster on Linux and FireWire" can be found at http://www.oracle.com/technology/pub/articles/hunter_rac10g.html. While it is also not a supported configuration by Oracle, Hunter, or anyone else, the article is a step-by-step guide to how one man implemented his own RAC configuration. It allows you to learn on your own and discover where you can improve your knowledge in the process.

But what about something that isn't RAC but that might meet more of your needs? RAC is one of today's favorite buzzwords (or is it buzz acronyms), but there are other high-availability solutions you could implement. I'll discuss those next.

Data Guard

Data Guard is Oracle's standby database management, monitoring, and automation infrastructure that allows you to create, maintain, and monitor one (or more than one if management is really enthused) standby database. These standby databases are a way of protecting your data from any failures, whether catastrophic in nature, like a hurricane or tornado, or hardware related. Again, nothing is going to provide you with that magic, elusive, silver bullet, but then, you aren't likely to have to protect yourselves or your database from werewolves, either. And if you need to, none of these database-related solutions is likely to help a whole lot.

With Data Guard, your primary database runs as it normally does. Productivity goes on, users are all happy, and things are running smoothly. As mentioned earlier, you can then have one (or more than one) secondary site, which can have a logical standby database or physical standby database. The difference? Well, Figure 6-1 shows you graphically the overall architectural aspects of Data Guard.

Physical standby databases are an identical copy of the primary database, block by block, with data type, schema, index, structure, and all. The synchronization of this database is accomplished by recovering the redo logs received from the primary database to the standby. The underlying functionality that Oracle uses in applying the redo logs to a physical standby database is redo apply technology. Oracle also uses standard recovery techniques to drive the log application on the standby database.

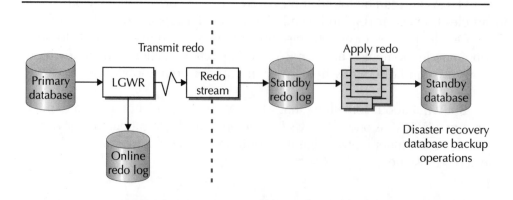

FIGURE 6-1. *Data Guard architecture*

A logical standby database contains the same logical information as the primary database, but the physical organization of the information can potentially be different. The logical standby can be opened for read and write, and thus could double as a reporting database if you so chose and are so licensed. They are nearly fully functional databases, except for the minor inconvenience that not all data types are fully supported in a logical standby. To keep the database in sync (and that really is the point, isn't it?) with a standby database, Oracle's Log Apply Services applies the primary database's redo logs to the logical standby database by using the SQL Apply technology. To do this, they automatically turn the redo log entries back into SQL statements, and allow them to be re-run on the logical standby. Not ready to rely on all this yet? LogMiner can be used to do the same thing, turning redo logs back into SQL statements. Logical databases are often more attractive to upper management because it doesn't appear that they're as big a waste of valuable database dollars since they're not just sitting around waiting to be used. Instead, they can be called into use by providing an alternative location against which reports can be run, thus freeing the primary database from the often immense overhead that this can cause and allowing it to run more efficiently as a transactional database. Logical standbys can sometimes be problematic, particularly if you're dealing with transactions that include nonsupported data types. In Oracle 9*i*, the list of nonsupported types was fairly extensive and included some that precluded the use of many implementations. Oracle 10*g* brought with it a support for more data types, including LONG, LONGRAW, NCLOB, BINARY_FLOAT, BINARY_DOUBLE, and IOTs, as long as the IOTs don't have overflows or LOB columns.

These standby databases can be located in the same facility as the primary database (though for disaster recovery purposes, this isn't a practical solution) or at a remote site hundreds or thousands of miles away.

If for any reason the production database becomes unavailable, Data Guard can switch to one of the standby databases and allow that database to take over the production role. This lets you fail over in case of an emergency, or plan outages for maintenance purposes that will minimize the end user's downtime (either real or perceived) and prevent any possible data loss.

What's really neat about standby databases, if you don't take into account the fact that you're using more disk space and you probably have increased licensing costs, is that you can change the role that any given database plays in the system, changing a primary into a standby, and a standby into a primary, without having to worry about data loss. You can either switch over to an alternative role, or fail over to it.

Switching over reverses the roles that the databases play. The primary becomes a standby and the standby a primary. This is usually the option taken when scheduled maintenance needs to be done to the primary system. It is elegant in its design, and means that neither database needs to be re-created at any point in the transition. Plus, switching back over to the original roles is just as simple and painless as the original switch.

Failing over, on the other hand, is an irreversible step. This is typically done in the event of a catastrophic database loss. Data Guard forces the transition of the standby to the role of primary and assumes that the old primary is a total loss and will never be used again. In order for the database that is failed over from to be used again in the Data Guard configuration, it must be reinstantiated from the new primary database, and then becomes the standby for the new primary. Sound like a good bit of work and a significant amount of hassle? That's why failover is only done in the case of catastrophic loss.

Protection Modes

Okay, so what's the trade-off? This just sounds too good to be true. There has to be some downside, some decisions that have to be made somewhere along the way as to what an organization can (or must) do without so they can make use of this. Well, of course there are. Don't be silly.

Because there is extra overhead associated with the use of this feature (the logs don't magically get transferred or applied), there will be some impact on the primary database and on the server as a whole. Decisions have to be made concerning what applications and associated databases *have* to provide maximum database performance and can tolerate minor data loss, and what applications must be assured no data loss at nearly any cost (including the cost of some performance degredation).

Maximum Protection

Maximum Protection mode offers you the highest level of data protection. Data is synchronously transmitted from the primary database to the standby database as transactions occur. No transaction can be committed on the primary database unless that redo data has been made completely available to at least one of the standby databases that is configured in this mode. If for some reason a standby becomes unavailable, processing stops on both the primary and the standbys. It's guaranteed there will be no data loss on the system. This also means, however, that transaction for transaction, the information is transmitted to both the primary and at least one standby (overhead) and the transmittal has to be acknowledged by the standby and written to the standby redo log file. While it might wait a considerable time to be actually applied to the standby, having it acknowledged and available is critical. This is one way to alert you that there's an issue with the standby databases. It may not be the most desired method, but it is effective.

Maximum Availability

Maximum Availability mode is very similar to Maximum Protection mode, in that it strives to assure zero data loss. One drawback is that while it strives to assure zero data loss it doesn't always achieve it. The trade-off is that the performance is often slower than what users might be used to.

If for some reason the standby database becomes unavailable, processing can still continue on the primary database. Whenever the condition causing the inaccessibility is cleared, resynchronization of the standby database with the primary database occurs. While there is still overhead associated with the process, at least processing on the primary database will not stop because of a transient communication issue between the databases. If for any reason the standby can't be reached, the protection mode is temporarily dropped to Maximum Performance until the resynchronization is complete.

Maximum Performance

While Maximum Performance mode provides no guarantee that there will never be any data loss, it does offer better performance than the Maximum Availability and Maximum Protection modes. In Maximum Performance mode, data is transferred asynchronously rather than synchronously to the standby database. Commits on the primary database do not have to wait for the standby to acknowledge the receipt of the transaction. If the standby suddenly becomes unavailable, processing continues with little or no noticeable effect on the primary database.

Oracle 10*g*

Oracle 10*g* Release 2 has brought to the table many enhancements to Data Guard as well. Now you can set your system up so that Data Guard will automatically fail over to a predetermined synchronized database in the event that the primary database is lost, with no manual failover invocation necessary. Following this failover, you can allow Data Guard to automatically reinstantiate the old primary to be a new standby database, again with little to no direct intervention from you. Interestingly, Oracle 10*g* also enhanced Oracle 9*i*'s ability to combine RAC technology with Data Guard, thereby allowing you to create RAC primary databases and RAC standby databases much more elegantly than was possible before. That's not to say it couldn't be done before, but the manual intervention that was necessary before is now handled almost entirely through the Data Guard Broker interface with the Oracle Clusterware software. This allows Clusterware to exert control over the timing of critical operations during state transitions (switchover and failover), protection mode changes (should you choose to make any), and state changes when necessary.

This combination is referred to as Maximum Availability Architecture.

Maximum Availability Architecture

Maximum Availability Architecture (MAA) is Oracle's more elegant solution to providing the ultimate in availability to organizations. It combines a primary database that is RAC-configured with a set of RAC-configured standby databases that can be either logical standby or physical standby.

But wait, that's not all. Lucky users will also realize that their applications probably are no longer all built on the client server model. More and more applications are built on the application middle-tier model. Neither RAC nor Data Guard addresses this issue at all. And let's face it, many applications operate using Oracle's application layer. So just how do you get from the users to the middle tier of the database? When users can't get to their data, they really couldn't care less how the database is running. That's why MAA also provides for the best practices of other components in the system.

Application servers (or middle tiers) provide access to application services from user machines (whatever those devices might be). Redundant application servers or middle tiers improve the overall functionality of the application because transactions can be distributed across multiple host machines. Yes, this redundancy comes at a cost, in hardware and software, and puts extra pressure on DBAs to not only perform the added tasks, but to understand the new features and idiosyncracies of the application server. Often, middle-tier high availability is accomplished by having clusters of server farms with identical middle-tier hosts in all cases providing the same functionality.

Infrastructure, infrastructure, infrastructure. A high-availability network includes redundant devices (there's no single point of failure in this configuration), which can mean redundant DNS servers to route traffic between primary sites and secondary (or tertiary) sites, load-balancing routers to route traffic to any available database node or application tier in the cluster with fewer physical switches in the whole process. But infrastructure isn't just about networking. Redundancy can be carried down to any and all hardware components in the system, with storage arrays that are fully redundant (not only when it comes to physical disks, but also controllers, power supplies, and connectivity to the array itself).

But let's face it, no man is an island and no technology exists (or exists for long) without sound operational practices to back it up. Any system that consists only of the hardware and not the ultimate software (human software) components will eventually fail. The human factor in the design of these systems, and the ongoing human aspect in their monitoring and maintenance, is critical to the detection of potential problems and recovery from any unforeseen outages that do occur, and the ongoing planning for future growth and upkeep will always be critical. This means not only keeping everyone who is relevant in the loop for anything associated with the system, but also having redundancy in people as well as hardware. While I'm all for self-preservation and job security, I also know that I'll never be allowed to fully grow beyond where I am today if there's no one else in the pipeline who can step up to the task at hand and provide the support I'm providing now. This is true of any position in an organization—although the higher you go, the less cross training there seems to be.

So what's next?

Grid

I guess Grid would have to be the ultimate in high availability. If you have a nearly unlimited amount of computing resources (storage, CPU, redundant networking) all based on commodity components, and you build your databases and applications in such a way as to leverage the ability of any one component to fail over from one place to another, be it hardware or database or software or connectivity, you can see where utility computing and computing on demand might be the ultimate extension of high availability, not to mention productivity and performance.

Grid is a shift in the concept of computing that provides for the use of commodity-level resources that can be easily snapped into and out of the network, as well as the redistribution of resources across all the hardware available, for the purpose of both high availability and leveraging efficiencies that may not exist when servers sit idle 50 percent or more of the time. While Grid is touted for its increased efficiencies and its ability to make better use of existing organizational structures, there's no reason to believe that the trend will simply stop at making efficient use of existing resources for existing demand. By extending the abilities that we already have (RAC, Data Guard, and Grid Brokers that allow use to redirect the flow of information and processing based on load and demand), it isn't that big a leap to allow Grid to become an even bigger piece in the maximum-availability puzzle.

Summary

Okay, so you won't use this information to become an RAC expert, or a Data Guard expert, or by any means a high-availability expert, but at least now you have a leg up on learning, which may give you the ability to look an interviewer in the face and say, No, I've never used RAC in a production environment, but I've implemented it on a limited scale and can both set it up and configure it, being confident in operating it on this level.

What's more, and hopefully what's more important, is that you now have one more thing to contemplate during that thirty-seven seconds of free time in your day while the coffee's brewing or while you're sitting at a red light.

I know we're "given" this technology with a certain set of suggested guidelines, but what's to stop us from being just a little more creative and extending those guidelines to include novel new supported (or at least supportable) ways of using the technology.

CHAPTER
7

Other Stuff

his chapter is a montage of things that really don't fit anywhere else, but that are important enough to spend time looking at. Some are GUI tools that help you do your job. Whether or not you really like or want to use GUI tools, Oracle provides them so at least you don't have to reinvent the wheel while doing your job.

OEM

Oracle Enterprise Manager (now Enterprise Manager in Oracle 10g) is a set of GUI tools built to help the DBA administer the database and much of the operating system in Oracle 10g. There are tools to help you to monitor the environment and to automate tasks, to alert you to situations that require your attention, or to take action in day-to-day situations so you (the DBA) can handle other things. These can be one-time or repetitive tasks that can be scripted and put into place to be run from a central location either on demand (by command or in the event a certain situation occurs on the database) or on a set schedule.

Management Server   Management Server (OMS) is the part of the middle tier that handles communication with the intelligent agents, and provides management and monitoring tools to help you maintain your Oracle database. You can set up and configure the OMS and associated repository database (where the data for historic tracking goes) using the Oracle Enterprise Manager Configuration Assistant. (Don't forget to add the repository database to your backup schedule so you can recover it if there are any issues.) The management server uses the GLOBAL_DBNAME parameter in the listener.ora file as the source for discovering the databases on your server(s), so it's important that every database you want to have monitored be available to OEM and OMS in the listener file. Don't forget... the values assigned to the parameters are, as always, case-sensitive.

```
(SID_DESC=
    (GLOBAL_DBNAME = Database_Name)
    (SID_NAME = mysid)......
```

The Console   The console is a GUI through which you can schedule jobs and events. It monitors the database, several server processes, and even many of the application processes.

Intelligent Agents   Intelligent Agents (OIAs) are autonomous daemons that have to run on the target database and that are responsible for taking care of running the jobs and events scheduled through the console. These processes are responsible for discovering targets you can manage through the OMS (database servers, web servers, listeners, and such), for events you've registered to have monitored in Enterprise Manager, and for executing tasks that are associated with the jobs that you submit to be run.

I've never been big on the use of GUI tools to do my job, but realistically I know that today more than ever it's necessary to make use of the tools available. When DBAs are being asked to do more with less and less in the way of resources, any tools you can find to help are a blessing.

Standalone Use

You can, if you choose, run OEM in standalone mode. While many of the most useful features of OEM are available without the associated background processes, there are objects that can't be fully managed in this mode. In Oracle 10g EM, this is no longer true. Even in standalone mode, you can start and stop the databases, start and stop the application servers, and monitor much of the system without the rest of the infrastructure running.

You cannot start and stop the database or web server or application server, nor can you share administrative data among multiple administrators in Oracle 9i. Nor are there any proactive notifications available for impending situations. This is no longer true with Oracle 10g Enterprise Manager. Automation of most common administrative tasks in the new version is contained in the dbconsole. There's no automation of common administrative tasks. Backup tools are unavailable. Data management tools are unavailable. You aren't allowed to customize, schedule, or publish reports.

Perhaps one of the most interesting tools that's unavailable in standalone mode is being able to run OEM from within a web browser. It's a Java-based application when not used through a browser, and can be a resource hog if you let it. Once upon a time, not too long ago, I had a dedicated PC on my desk that did nothing but run the OEM console because it used enough resources that my main PC would have been limited to a few applications at any one time (even Outlook didn't like it very much when it had to run with OEM console). You can, however, create database objects, and compile program units to run EXPLAIN PLANs and maintain the database structures. You can monitor the health of the database, view initialization parameters, and even alter some of them.

When using standalone mode, your database options are limited to those databases that are found in the local tnsnames.ora file since the dynamic discovery of new nodes is limited to use of the intelligent agents. If you know the full qualification of the database, you can manually fill in the values for Sid, the host name, port numbers, and the net server name to allow OEM to bypass the tnsnames.ora file and connect directly.

After you've connected in standalone mode, you can connect to the management server (provided that one is available) and work that way by shutting down and restarting the OEM interface.

It's often advantageous to work in standalone mode when you're concerned with someone changing parameters in the database without intending to, or without you knowing it, or when you're in a location where web access isn't available

One of the biggest reasons to use OEM in this way is to simplify the job of database administration and to allow junior DBAs a quicker way to start learning the ins and outs of database administration and thus more quickly become a productive member of the database administration team. This can help *you* by allowing them to take on more responsibility sooner, and help *them* by giving them an extra boost of confidence. Think about it. It's one way to mentor those who'll likely be taking our places in the coming years and allowing them to gain a feeling of independence sooner.

Many of these people don't have a deep enough understanding of the underlying ramifications of their actions and would never dream of admitting to having done something so completely moronic as to simply run an update on the initialization parameters on every database in the system without regard to what those changes might do. Or they might decide that instead of checking all of the databases every morning to make sure there are no issues in the alert logs, they'll just schedule a job that will e-mail them if any such issues arise. Then they put in the e-mail address of the LAN rather than just themselves. While it still won't tie their hands enough to keep them from dropping every tablespace or table or package in the database, standalone mode in Oracle 9*i* can help to limit the damage they can do at any given time. It won't eliminate the risk completely (even this sense of security is gone in Oracle 10*g*), but it can help to keep some things from happening. Let's face it, the fewer variables you have to consider when determining what went wrong (even if what went wrong can be attributed to the DBA) means fewer blind alleys you have to go down.

Intelligent Agents

Okay, so anyone who's ever had to deal with these quirky little beasts knows that names can be deceiving. While I can picture these little daemons running around in trench coats and souped-up sports cars, figuring out what is going on in your server, I also know that they can be the most cantankerous and stubborn little buggers to get running correctly.

What do they do? They're responsible for talking to both the operating system and the OEM management server or console (although they don't require either of these pieces to allow them to be functional). They check for events that might be occurring and present the results of the event tests to the management server for reporting later, they run the jobs you define one at a time or on a schedule, and they collect the output of these jobs so you can view the pretty output later and figure out whether or not the job did what you thought it ought to be doing. They also handle requests to send SNMP traps for events (provided that the operating system they're running around in supports SNMP). So, I guess in a lot of ways, they really are kind of like spies, or special agents for the government.

These independent little guys don't even require that a database be available to support their running. This means that they can report back to you that your databases have crashed or that your web servers have crashed, or even that your databases are back up. This is very handy for remote administration, because they can simply page you when your database has gone down or is acting weird.

Intelligent agents are installed using the universal installer and can be installed as part of a larger installation of Oracle. Or they can be installed independently of any other Oracle software on a system. This means you can gather information about middle tiers of your application—for example, servers where *i*AS or Oracle 11*i* is running—without having to install the database, and they can be installed after other systems are already operational.

If you have more than one version of Oracle Intelligent Agent installed on a server, you will want to disable the older versions (they've gotten progressively less quirky as time has passed, so you're better off running the newer ones) by renaming the DBSNMP executable for the older versions. While this will only prevent someone from accidentally starting the service, it will at least prevent the accidental foot shooting. Nothing will stop someone who's determined to damage your database or application like that, other than taking away his or her server access.

Blackouts

Many people who use OEM even with the assistance of the Intelligent Agents don't realize that they have the ability to set blackouts on their servers. Whenever they need to do anything at the server or Oracle level, they simply shut down the Intelligent Agents, perform the maintenance and then restart the agents. This much intervention isn't necessary. You can set transient windows of time when the agents ignore certain events on the system.

Blackouts allow you to perform maintenance without the agents telling you every minute (or every five minutes) that something unusual is going on in the system. By setting blackouts, you can allow the agents to run and gather information about things on the system not related to what you're maintaining, while still allowing you to work. You can black out jobs, events, data collection, or entire servers for differing periods of time.

Ironically, you are likely using a GUI interface to view the information gathered by the agents, but in order to set the blackouts for the agents, you have to use command-line commands to do it. Be careful, though, when setting blackouts. Communication is critical. Blackouts are not modifiable once they are set (they have to be cancelled and re-created) and they can only be cancelled by the user who created them (so if your fellow DBA sets one himself, and then goes out of town on a three-week vacation, you're stuck with the blackout for three weeks, even if the job is done).

Table 7-1 provides you with a list of the commands and what they do with respect to setting agent blackouts

Blacking out servers or other targets is a handy thing to keep in your DBA toolbelt. Many organizations have set themselves up so that OEM is monitoring their systems and so that pages are sent to pagers or cell phones whenever there are issues with any target they're monitoring. Setting blackouts for targets that either you know are having issues you're working on, or targets that you have down for maintenance for the duration of the maintenance, can save you (or those you work with or report to) a lot of aggravation

Command	Result
agentctl start blackout [-d [DD] HH:MM] [<*target*>] (-d option is used to specify the duration of the blackout in the format of DD HH:MM where: DD indicates number of days HH indicates number of hours MM indicates number of minutes)	Defines a blackout for an entire target server
agentctl stop blackout [<*target name*>]	Removes a blackout
agentctl status blackout	Displays the status of a blackout
agentctl start blackout <*target*> -d <*duration*> -s <*subsystem/s*> By default, all jobs, events, and data collections will be blacked out	Blacks out specific subsystems (jobs, events, historical collections)

TABLE 7-1. *Commands That Set Agent Blackouts*

associated with the pages. With Oracle 10*g*, what you can monitor is extended across the organization.

Using Jobs

Jobs, in connection with Oracle Enterprise Manager and Intelligent Agents, are implemented as TCL (Tool Command Language) scripts with Oracle extensions (OraTcl). You can use and customize some of the canned jobs that come with OEM, or you can create your own jobs and submit them with the Run TCL job task associated with the Intelligent Agent.

Jobs are anything that you have historically scripted and can be run against the database, the node on which the database or the Intelligent Agent is running, the Listener, or the web server. These jobs can run SQL statements, perform DBA tasks such as starting up and shutting down the database, or starting up and shutting down the web server or Listeners. If you can script it, you can call the script from a job and therefore run it as a job. You can see historic information on jobs that have been run by selecting the History tab of the OEM Console, or you can see information on currently running jobs by selecting the Active tab.

You can view the active job's name and target (if the show target check box is selected), the target type (listener, node, web server or database or other managed targets), the owner of the job (administrator submitting the job), and the status of the job at hand (submitted, scheduled, started, pending deletion, "fixit"—if the fixit job has been submitted, or "fixing" if the fixit job is already executing). You can see the date and time when the job was scheduled by the Intelligent Agent. Right-clicking a job in the Active tab allows you to view published reports associated with the job, view or edit the properties of the given job, create another job just like this one, copy this job to the library, or remove the job entirely.

In my past life, we set up jobs that ran SQL scripts to alert us when tablespaces were running out of space and which would extend the file if there were room on the file systems to do so. We scheduled jobs that would copy the archive logs off to tape and then move the archive logs to a backup location whenever the primary location was starting to hit a size threshold. We even scheduled a job that shut down all of the databases every Saturday night so the operators wouldn't have to do that and be faced with making the decision of having to "kill –9" jobs that they didn't know what to do with, like smon or pmon or arc.

The history page is where the job goes when it is no longer active. You can add the status of completed, failed, or deleted to the preceding list of statuses available on the History tab. A finish time is also available so you can see what day and time the job finished on the given target.

From the Job menu on the menu bar, you can create or duplicate existing jobs, edit an existing job's parameters or schedule, and copy a given job to the library so that other administrators don't have to run around re-inventing the wheel. You can view a job or remove a job, clear the history, or refresh the history page.

The job library is a handy tool. It is very similar to a regular library of scripts and utilities that you might have squirreled away somewhere that you use regularly and that you have had with you for years. In the case of these libraries, however, they're stored centrally and accessed by multiple administrators.

Setting Events

The event system in OEM is a tool that allows you to centrally monitor and manage the data associated with enterprises from one or two small databases to multipetabyte databases across a number of servers on a multitude of operating systems or hardware platforms.

When setting up a job, you need to determine what targets you want to have monitored for the event and select the tests you want to run. Many events are predetermined in the event library of OEM. You can thus determine the threshold values you want associated with a given event (do you want the tablespaces to get 90 percent full before you're alerted, or 95 percent full?), and how often you want those values checked (every minute, every hour, at 6 a.m. every Tuesday). You can even set up a fixit job that will run and fix the issue at hand if you believe the event is fixable through an automated process.

For example, every five minutes I want to check if all my databases are up and available. If they are, the event system can go back to sleep. If they aren't, it should e-mail me and let me decide what to do about it.

Be creative when considering what to do with jobs and events. It's a great feature that you can have them alert you or your cell phone or pager whenever there's an issue with the database, but what about keeping track of what you've been doing, which tablespaces are really the hot ones (the ones you're always getting asked to add more space to), and what time of day you're seeing those pesky ora-<*insert number*> errors. Why not set the "to do" list up to include inserting as much information as possible about the event or job (the duration, what it was for, whatever) into a table which you can then query to see what's really going on in your system?

Oracle intends for Enterprise Manager to be used to maintain the database (with Oracle 10g you're going to find your hands tied to a great extent anyway, because a lot of its maintenance has to be done via the GUI interface), so why not use it for something that will make your job easier each day? You could use this information for your own trending, determine what will need to be set up to perform differently, or when you'll need to add space to a file system or tablespace. You decide on the information you want to track for each event and each job, and create your own set of tables that will let you be as productive as you want to be.

OAM

Where Oracle Enterprise Manager is the utility of choice for administering the database, Oracle Application Manager (OAM) is the web-based utility for the administration of the Oracle 11*i* E-Business Suite. In earlier releases of Oracle 11*i*, you had to log in to the server or interface to determine what services were running and the health of those services. If you're connected to the network or have broadband connectivity this isn't a big problem. However, if you have to dial in with an analog modem, the downloading of jinitiator can be a major roadblock to remote administration. Because of the OAM web-based interface, however, this is no longer an issue. With web access and knowledge of the passwords, you can maintain concurrent managers, submit and monitor jobs, and maintain workflow and all background processes.

Configuration Information

OAM provides not only administrators but also users and other support people access to current configuration information relevant for all tiers of an Oracle 11*i* Applications system. This can help with debugging issues and in determining where there are problems with the system and where such issues are not necessarily system-wide issues. OAM provides you with tools designed to help you to detect potential configuration problems and mitigate damages done before the issues get too widespread. This can mean that an inadvertently altered site-level profile option setting or database initialization parameter (sometimes SPFILEs can be less than optimal) that does not meet the requirements of the given system or the recommendations of Oracle can be caught early, before too many users are impacted or too much damage has been done. This information can also be used as a one-stop shopping interface for answers to questions asked by analysts when different people open an iTar. Developers who are having issues can go here rather than directly to the tables or to you for help.

Oracle Workflow Mailer Management

The Oracle Workflow Mailer, the centralized way that Oracle E-Business Suite has to route information on jobs that are ready for the next action in line without manual intervention, is notorious for being difficult to manage and acting very flaky. OAM's interface has been much improved from the perspective of reliability and usability. You can now use the OAM interface to monitor and change the status, settings, and throughput of the mailer and its different components. It still requires setup on the server in order for Workflow and its mailer to work correctly, but maintenance tasks can now be accomplished much more easily. You can quickly and easily configure and validate the settings, test the mailer and its components, and reset statuses for temporary outages.

System Alerts

System alerts are handy little constructs that allow the thousands of E-Business Suite system components to report potential problems directly to OAM. Used in conjunction with Workflow, users (you as system administrator or the head of one of the other departments) can receive relevant notifications of system alerts as they're posted by the different applications or components. Once the issue is dealt with, users can classify the alerts as open or closed, and they can attach notes to each alert concerning steps that were taken in resolving the underlying issue and what needs to be done in order to fix it next time or to avoid it completely. The next time that the alert is posted, context information is collected along with associated logs and diagnostic messages to assist the user in resolving issues and preventing recurrences.

Diagnostic Log Viewer

Have you ever been at home (for those of you who don't actually live at your desk) and gotten a call about something that isn't acting quite right? Or you've gotten paged at the airport or other inconvenient place where you may or may not be able to be sure of a secure connection to your servers about something that is a little odd. OAM now provides you with a web-based interface that can provide users with the ability to search the central diagnostic log repository already built into the E-Business Suite to see if they can come up with their own answers, or it provides you with the ability to log in through a browser and see if you can come up with answers for them (not that they don't want to find them themselves, but you are just so much better at this than they are). You can search for messages based on date, the application involved, the component that is giving you problems, and log level.

Patch Advisor

The Patch Advisor can recommend patches specifically targeted to your system. The Advisor is customizable to your preferences and system, and takes E-Business Suite patch data that it has downloaded and then analyzes that data against your system and your preferences. It then recommends patches based on your criteria. In a lot of the same ways that Microsoft's automatic updates make me uneasy, the Advisor part of OEM makes me uneasy as well. However, the Advisor simply advises you on the patches you might want to install. It can then analyze each individual patch, identifying all of the prerequisites necessary for the patch and what's required for your system to accept it. It can also help analyze the impact the patches might have on your system in terms of affected applications (licensed, shared, or in some cases customized) and provides you with a list of affected files (this can be a big help if you've customized—counter to Oracle's supported method of customization—one or more of the core files).

Even more important, OAM provides you with a web-based interface that allows you to see what patches you've applied in any given environment. This feature has more than paid for itself (okay, so it doesn't cost anything extra… you get the idea) in the time it's saved me running queries for developers asking, "Have we applied patch *<insert patch number>*?" Now you can go to OAM, pull back the patches, and sort them by name. Easy as click, click, click, they can answer their own question, often faster than they can get an e-mail back from me, particularly if I'm in meetings or busy with one of the other systems.

License Manager

While it doesn't take away the necessity of running ADSPLICE (the tool through which you can license different Oracle 11*i* elements one piece at a time), OAM does provide an interface through which we can not only enable the license of E-Business Suite products but also country-specific functionalities and languages. In connection with this, OAM also provides access to several useful reports that can tell you what you're licensed for, what's installed as a shared product, what the base character set for the application is, and any licensed country-specific functionalities, languages, and territories. Again, this can save a lot of time and aggravation for you and for those people opening the iTar who are hoping for a speedy answer to their e-mail about whether or not your organization is licensed for projects, or just AP, AR, and

GL. These reports can also help you when you're analyzing whether or not to apply a patch for HR even though you don't have HR licensed or configured. However, because HR is so tied to everything it must be considered anyway.

Init.ora Parameters

OAM will also show you the values that have been set or implied by your settings in the Init(SID).ora file. Oracle 11*i* is a very intelligent animal, and knows minimally what settings will make it most happy. It checks the settings that exist for the current file, and provides you with suggestions for changing the values to make it most content. The listing that OAM provides gives you the parameter name, the current value, the suggested value, and whether or not the changes that it "suggests" are mandatory or not. For example, parameters like _complex_view_merging = TRUE are suggested (as mandatory) to be removed. Other values, like db_block_buffers, if set to 10,000, are suggested to be changed to 20,000. Depending on whether or not you've started your instance with PFILE or SPFILE, you can, through the interface, alter the values of these parameters. Further, if you know the parameter that you (or one of your developers) are looking for the value of, you can use the search facility built into the interface to search for the values associated with that parameter, or look for a wildcard list of parameters associated with some string (like arc for all archiving parameters).

Monitoring and Analysis

One of the demands of many developers and users in Oracle E-Business Suite is the monitoring of performance and other information. While much of this monitoring can be done with scripts by the DBA, it is good to be able to offload some of this responsibility to the users or developers themselves, which OAM allows you to do.

Applications Usage Reports

Applications Usage Reports gives you a quick interface into what applications inside of E-Business Suite users are using, and to what *extent* they're using them. While this might not necessarily be important to you, it can give you quick access to information should you face a SarbOx audit (Sarbanes Oxley) or a SAS-70 audit (Statement on Auditing Standards... SAS-70 is the standard assigned to service organizations, like many IT organizations).

Want to see who has been granted access to what applications? Want to see if they're really using the applications they've been granted? This information can be used to create finer-grained security so you can disable accounts for people who have left the organization or with whom you're no longer doing business, so that there are fewer avenues through which people can gain access to the data in your application. Looking at this page, this set of information can be an eye-opening experience if your security measures have gotten lax over time.

You can even use some of the canned reports to see how many expense reports have been run through your application (if you're using Internet Expense), or how many Invoice Line Items your Accounts Receivables people have processed in a given time period. With this information, you can start to see trends in your business areas—for instance, if you're processing more lines this year than you did during the same period last year, or if you're buying more this quarter than in the previous one. Upper management eats this information up, and with over 10,000 tables to consider having to look at and determine where to get the information, you could find yourself being able to provide requested information in minutes rather than hours or days. A word to the wise ... make friends with some of these reports, know where they are and how to quickly get to them so you have them when you need them. It may even justify your job to be able to tell them, Hey look, not only have you had uninterrupted downtime, but you've processed 21311 invoice lines this quarter because of the interface you have.

Okay, so it's a stretch. But it *could* happen.

Concurrent Manager Processing

Concurrent manager processing is interesting just from a curiosity standpoint. You can see who has been running different concurrent requests (jobs submitted through the Oracle 11*i* E-Business interface), who runs the most requests, which programs run most often, and view concurrent program statistics by name. But that isn't all the information available to you here. You can view all of the requests submitted in the last hour, all those that have errored out in the last 24 hours, and those that completed in the last 24 hours but that took longer than 60 minutes to run (a handy performance tuning tool, and a handy little tool to help your users schedule long-running resource-intensive processes at times other than 9 in the morning). You can even see details on wait times for the different requests, and what processes have been scheduled to run that aren't relevant to your implementation (like the synchronization of workflow tables for an organization not utilizing workflow). This allows you to cancel processes that might be running and accomplishing nothing, thus keeping the load on the CPU and the database to a minimum.

Given enough information from the user community, you can even find what program prints all the invoices printed on the second day of every month so users can cancel that request.

Database Status

The Database Status option allows you to see most of the details of your database from the same central location as the application information. Tablespace status, the name, size, number of extents, wraps, high-water mark, the status of rollback segments and extents, system statistics (including table scans broken out into cache partitions and rowid ranges, user commits, and physical reads and writes), wait events associated with your apps database along with the number of times waited for each, and memory statistics are just some of the interesting things you can look at (if not edit) through OAM. This means that, if you're an Apps DBA, you have a one-stop interface, available through any graphical browser, to view your database statistics without having to go from interface to interface, or even visit the command prompt. What's more, some of your users, depending on their level of authority in the application, can see the same information and leverage it to help debug issues or create elegant customized applications.

Forms Runtime Processes and Forms Sessions

Want to know how your forms runtime engine and forms design are performing? There is even an option in OAM that allows you to see the memory usage, the CPU usage and duration of the run, the PGA used, the UGA used, and the physical and logical reads associated with a forms session and with the forms processes. I think Oracle understands that there may be some tuning associated with the inner workings of the Oracle 11*i* engine and that there will definitely be some tuning that needs to be done with custom forms built as ancillary interfaces to the application. This quick little interface allows you to see what is performing badly and what resources are being hit the hardest.

You can use it as a means to prove that testing may not have been done adequately with an application or use it as an interface through which you can gather data for trending.

Invalid Objects

While I have been told that there are always invalid objects in the database, and that you can simply search for these invalid objects by name, owner, or type by running a SELECT statement against all_objects or dba_objects, this isn't always the most practical solution, particularly if you're in a location where you have limited access to the server or to SQL Plus. Oracle Application Manager provides you with an even more robust thin web interface that allows you to search for invalid objects by name, owner, and type, as well as search only for those that have gone invalid in the last hour or two hours or those invalid objects that have been updated within a given date range. While it's true that there will likely be a number of invalid objects in any database, and that the simple presence of invalid objects indicates only that you have a database that's running (invalids will often be recompiled whenever they are called), having readily identified invalid objects can give you an idea of whether someone has been changing things in your database, or if something has been run that shouldn't have been, or answer a question from an iTar analyst quickly. One of the questions that is on every single solitary Oracle 11*i* iTar is, Do you have invalid objects, how many, who owns them (they are primarily interested in the ones owned by Apps or Applsys usually), and what are they? Having them presented to you in this location, without having to run to the ALL_OBJECTS table and then joining that to however many other tables you end up needing, can take longer to write the query than to go to the interface. While you can't run utlrp.sql (recall, the package that recompiles all invalid objects) or compile the objects directly through the interface, it will let you see what is invalid and, in certain cases, allow you to go back to your developers and tell them that this or that custom program had errors that needed to be addressed because of the installation of this patch or another.

Jserv Environment

Virtually any parameter you want to see the value for that's associated with the inner workings of the Jserv (the Java Servlet engine that runs many of the internals of Oracle E-Business Suite) environment can be viewed through this interface. You can see the memory usage for the Java Virtual Machine (JVM) (or one of the JVMs if you're running multiple Jserv environments) for the system, and view those settings with and without garbage collection set to on.

Site Level Profile Option Settings

Anyone who's ever cloned an Oracle 11*i* instance knows that profile options can be problematic at best. Even if everything runs perfectly (and it has gotten far better over recent versions), there are almost always values in the APPS.FND_PROFILE_OPTION_VALUES table that get stuck and don't get changed. Some of these values end up simply being misleading for the end users (not necessarily a good thing itself depending on what you're doing), making them think they might be in an environment other than where they are, while others are more dangerous. By pointing to a different environment, they can either prompt the misdirection of functions to another environment or cause some functionality to not work properly. While it is the case that there are Metalink documents that tell you that changing the values within this table manually is not recommended or supported, it has been recognized by everyone (including Oracle Support) that changing the values in the PROFILE_OPTION_VALUE column will not leave you any worse off than you already were.

Knowing which ones to change, or which ones have been changed, or which ones have been changed incorrectly, can be interesting at best. At worst, they can be downright ugly. OAM provides you with a view into the FND_ PROFILE_OPTION_VALUES table and shows you all of the thousands of profile options and values assigned to each value. While it does not provide you with a venue to change the values (you still need to change these values through the Oracle 11*i* interface or by following the unsupported but oft-used method of altering the values in the FND_PROFILE_OPTION_VALUES table directly), it does provide you with a look at what the values are, and what profile options they're associated with. Not that any of us have actually updated the PROFILE_OPTION_VALUE column of this table, but it is helpful to have a way to view what those values are, or rather (often) what they should be in another instance in order to help us make informed determinations.

Other Oracle Systems

Think Oracle is "just" a relational database product? Oh sure, they have *i*AS (or AS Oracle 10*g*) and E-Business Suite, but these are really just databases too, right? Well, yeah, but there are a lot of components that people don't use because they either don't know that they exist, or because they are afraid of "new" (read newfangled) technologies, or because they don't see the technology as being worth the effort. But really, a lot of Oracle's extras (many of which are already included in what you've paid good money for) are pretty neat and can be used for many things Oracle may not have anticipated.

Express

Oracle Express? Is that a new train? A new delivery service? Nope. Oracle Express is a multidimensional database and application environment that's been built to assist in building OLAP applications. The components of Express (or the OLAP option) are dimensions (part of the multidimensional portion) and variables. Dimensions are those logical units into which the Express database is broken down. Much like the dimension tables of a data warehouse, they're typically the keys of the database, or the "where" clause limiters of a logical expression. Where product = Teva Sandals, where gender = male, or where date_of_birth is between 01-JAN-1946 and 31-DEC-1950 are examples of such where clauses. In these cases, product, gender, and date_of_birth are the dimensions.

Variables are the objects that hold the data in an Express database. These variables are nothing more than arrays of values (again, like a data warehouse the values are typically numeric) that are described by the dimensions. Extend the idea of an array a little further to think of it as like a table. The Sales variable may have as its dimensions Product, Sales_District, and Sales_dt_time. Three "dimensioned" variables are often referred to as data cubes.

It's not uncommon for an Express database to have multiple variables, each with multiple dimensions (some dimensions, like time, are common to multiple variables, while some are unique to a variable).

The data in an Express database is stored in such a way as to make it much faster for users to process the information to answer their business questions multidimensionally rather than in a typical database structure, even an object-relational structure. This is why it is an OLAP database, because the business often requires slicing and dicing data in ways that are different than those supported in a "normal database" (and for what it's worth, there's absolutely nothing normal about the structure of the Express database other than the fact that it has the Oracle name attached to it).

Express comes in two basic flavors designed to support the customer, regardless of size. Express Server is designed for larger applications and is a multidimensional data store. It can be used in conjunction with an existing data warehouse or as a precursor to a fully functional data warehouse. Depending on need, it can even be built to take the place of a data warehouse. Personal Express is a single-user Express Server and can be utilized by individual people in an organization who desire the ability to do OLAP analysis on data without having to go to the cost and time to implement a fully functional organizational data-mart.

But wait, there's more! There are even tools that go along with the Express Server database product. Express Analyzer is a tool for reporting and analysis against an Express database. Express Objects is an OO tool that allows you to develop applications against an Express database. You can use Express Web Publisher to publish your content to the Web (intranet or Internet) for others to peruse, while Express Spreadsheet is an add-in (something like ADI for applications) that allows you to interface between Microsoft Excel and your Express Server database.

Apache
A lot like *i*AS and E-Business Suite, Express has at its heart the Apache Web Server. It works much the same in Express as it does in any of the other programs.

Connecting
You guessed it—you can't use SQL*Plus to connect to an Express database any more than you can use any of the other utilities you're familiar with to maintain the database or the data within. In fact, in Express, there isn't a typical standard user interface in the way we think about using SQL* Plus to connect. Users have to connect through either a web browser or one of the Windows client applications. The data is accessed via one of Oracle's OLAP client applications, a custom-built application, Personal Express 5 or 6, or through another instance of Express 6.

Oracle Express Client Application	Description
Oracle Express Administrator	Used to create and configure Express databases
Oracle Express Analyzer	Used to create simple applications (called briefings)
Oracle Express Objects	Used to create more complex OLAP applications and briefings
Oracle Express Relational Access Administrator	Used to create and manage OLAP applications that access data stored in a relational database (RDBMS)
Oracle Express Spreadsheet Add-In	Used to access Express data from Microsoft Excel
Oracle Express Web Publisher	Used to make briefings available for use on the Web
Oracle Financial Analyzer	Used for reporting, analyzing, and modeling financial data
Oracle Sales Analyzer	Used for reporting, analyzing, and modeling sales and marketing data

TABLE 7-2. *Client Applications for Use in Connections*

In order to connect to Express, the Express Connection Editor has to be used to create the connection files (nope, not tnsnames, these are .xcf files). Once you use the Connection Editor, you can test the connection through the Express Connection Utility (ECU).

You can connect using any of the client applications in Table 7-2, depending on what it is you want to do and who the user is.

Querying

So, if you can't use SQL*Plus, how can you query the database? You can allow developers to use Express Analyzer to create a briefing through which the queries are run. Further, you could use Express Web Publisher to publish a created briefing or to create a new WebBriefing. Express Objects can be used as a way to develop a functional and efficient front-end to the data, or you can use SPL to write scripts directly in order to send queries to the database. Oracle Express queries are written in what is called Oracle Express Stored Procedure Language (SPL), which is executed using the command-line interpreter

You see, Express isn't a simple product to use, but it is a functional product that is built for a job and does that job well. It's true that it could be more elegant for users to create their own queries, but it's also true that, if you're doing in-depth analytical processing, end users may not be able to efficiently construct the query necessary to return the accurate results.

Backup and Recovery

Because Express is its own kind of animal, it doesn't play well with Oracle's backup and recovery utilities. In fact, because of the kind of database it is, you can't even log in to SQL*Plus and start up the database, let alone recover or restore it. You have to back up an Express database at the file system or mount point level and then back up all of the pieces of the database together since there's catalog information associated with user information, and getting the two out of sync can lead to significant difficulties.

The system database is usually located under the $OLAP_HOME/oes630 directory and is typically very small (unlike the system tablespace in a "typical" database, which can get very large).

This does mean, however, that point-in-time recovery is not an option. You recover to your last backup, period. But, because it is an Online Analytical Processing database, and because this implies that the data really doesn't change a whole lot once it's in the database, and there isn't much loading action going on, that really shouldn't be an issue and thus file system level backups should be sufficient.

Also, because Express isn't really much like any other relational database, you don't have to worry about getting a read-consistent picture of the data. If you're using the personal edition, you have control over when and how data is loaded into the database. Also, whenever a user logs into Express she gets her own dedicated workspace, complete with preserved data as it was at the point in time they attached to the database. This not only assures read-consistent views of the data, but for the duration of the user's session, all of their analysis will be performed on exactly the same picture of the data, regardless of how long the analysis takes or how many different times they run a process.

Hold on to your seats, but there are yet more differences between Express and Oracle's RDBMS. Just when you thought you knew PL/SQL sufficiently well to write fairly efficient code, Express uses something called Oracle Express Stored Procedure Language (SPL) which is written and executed using the command-line interpreter (oescmd).

The following is a Unix scripting example:

```
. $ORACLE_HOME/olap/express.prm     # Set the environment
. $ORACLE_HOME/olap/bin/oescmd      # Start command interpreter
    -> database attach express    " Attach a database
    -> database list
    -> database detach express
    -> outfile 'db_structure.lst'  " Describe database structure
    -> listnames
    -> dbdescribe
    -> outfile eof
    -> database create myexp.db attach      " Create a new database
    -> database password manager
    -> DEFINE HELLO PROGRAM     " Write a program
       PROGRAM
          show 'Hello, lookout world, I can program express'
       END
    -> DESCRIBE HELLO
    -> CALL HELLO          " Execute program
```

Don't like using the command line? Sigh. Yeah, there is, of course, an easy-to-use GUI that allows you to do pretty much the same thing. This product is, after all, designed specifically so that much of the "programming" can be done by the end user or with the end user's direct help, so why not create a GUI to help with the process?

Not cryptic enough for you yet? Not yet suffering from information overload? Just you wait. You can abbreviate the commands used to access and manipulate the Express data (not, however, any of the Express program names). You simply use the first letter (regardless of what that letter is) and the next two consonants for the commands. You can also abbreviate things like width (W) and decimal (D) so that you can get programs that are nearly (okay, not quite, but almost) as cryptic looking as C. Now take a look at the earlier example again.

```
. $ORACLE_HOME/olap/express.prm # Set the environment
. $ORACLE_HOME/olap/bin/oescmd   # Start command interpreter
    -> dtb att express  " Attach a database
```

```
-> dtb lst
-> dtb dtc express
-> outfile 'db_structure.lst' " Describe database structure
-> listnames
-> dbdescribe
-> outfile eof
-> dtb crt myexp.db att " Create a new database
-> dtb pss mng
-> DFN HELLO PRG    " Write the program
     PRG
          show 'Hello, lookout world, I can program express'
     END
-> DSC HELLO
-> CALL HELLO    " Execute program
```

Need to get your ho-hum relational data into an express database? It can be imported into an Express database from the Express Administrator or via a handy-dandy SPL script that can be re-used. Using Express Administrator, it's as simple as choosing File:Import from the menu, but you can't simply call that a real process in the way Oracle refers to processes. It is like other kinds of stored procedures: let the database do whatever it can for you.

The Express Relational Access Manager (RAM) is used to access Oracle RDBMSs and other ODBC connectable data sources directly. This means your OLAP database (Express Server) can now be used for ROLAP analysis (relational OLAP). A little bit of configuration is needed to use the Relational Access Administrator (RAA), a GUI utility that was built for just such a purpose, but it can be done without jumping through too many hoops or reinventing any new wheels. This is the tactic used by many organizations to perform analysis on their financial data already stored in an E-Business Suite Oracle 11*i* database. The data is already there, so you don't have to store it twice, and you can combine it with data that you already have in Express (time dimensions, sales office location information, and so on) to perform very powerful analyses. Accountant types eat this kind of thing up.

Oracle 9i *Lite*

In recent releases of the Oracle software suite, I think starting with Oracle 8*i*, Oracle began acknowledging the fact that more and more business types were requiring access to corporate data from locations other than their desks. In case you haven't noticed, wireless connections for users on the move are becoming more of a product in demand. Persistent wireless connections, however, aren't always practical or even possible. Heck, I can't maintain a consistent connection on my cell phone from where I work to where I live, and that's in a metropolitan area over a scant 18 miles. From a security standpoint, having a persistent wireless connection may compromise the integrity of the data or its sensitive nature, leaving the organization open to litigation or hacking. But the need is there for these remote users to access data.

Enter Oracle Lite Database.

Lite Database

Not to be confused with lite beer or lite salad dressing, where the "lite" refers to something less than the original in some way, Oracle's Lite Database was designed from the get-go to be used in connection with mobile applications in small mobile devices.

Oracle Lite Database is a Java-enabled, secure relational database management system with a small footprint designed to operate on laptops, handhelds, PDAs, and other information appliances. It runs on all versions of Windows from 98 to XP and from NT to 2000 as well as Windows CE/Pocket PC, the Palm OS, and Embedded Linux. I can run it on my Axim, my Vaio, and my Zarus... from the geek perspective alone, this is pretty cool.

Oracle provides myriad interface acronyms (the APIs) through which you can access the database. ODBC, JDBC, ADO, .NET, and SODA are all available to the developer as a means to access the database, which gets installed along with all associated utilities when you install the Mobile Development Kit (MDK). The database is not only SQL 92 and ACID (Atomicity, Consistency, Isolation, Durability—the basic properties of a relational database transaction) compliant, but fully supports Java-stored procedures, 32 simultaneous connections, change capture, and is supposed to come with zero administration, but then they've been claiming they'll have DBA-less databases for years now, and somehow we just keep getting busier and busier. The database is supposed to be small, but small is kind of a relative term. The database is supported up to 4 gigabytes. While it's true that, in a time when petabyte and terabyte databases are becoming almost commonplace, 4 gigabytes isn't anything to really be impressed with, it still isn't what can be thought of as really small. And when you realize that this database is what's running on the mobile device, the fact that we even anticipate the need for 4 gigabytes of storage is kind of impressive.

This database gets synced with the primary database by means of invoking the mobile sync client, and so the update occurs in both directions through what's called a publish/subscribe model.

Mobile Server for Data Synchronization

The Lite Database contains a relevant subset of data found in the primary Oracle database. This subset is stored in snapshots on the mobile device, and the changes to the data, the relevant data on the primary database, as well as on the mobile device, are stored in logs so that only the changes need to be applied in either/both directions when synchronization occurs. Now see, you knew there was something for which those handy-dandy materialized views were good for other than data warehousing and speeding up join queries.

Materialized views are similar to regular views but the data is stored again on disk. They are often used in data warehouses for summarizing and aggregating data to support queries. A materialized view has to be deliberately (either manually or automatically) refreshed when the underlying table's data changes.

Advanced Replication is the technique by which the database, either in part or in whole, is replicated to one or more alternate sites. Advanced replication is usually implemented through updatable materialized views.

Life-Cycle Management

Okay, just the phrase "life-cycle management" brings back bad memories from software design class in college. In this case, however, life-cycle management is Oracle's catchphrase for its application built for the distribution, installation, and management of software, data, and other files on the mobile remote devices that support Oracle 9i/10g Lite. Life-cycle management allows for the management of this distribution to an entire workforce from a central location. Oh, and guess what? Its administration is accomplished through a web-based interface. Yep, more pointy clicky. Somehow, because of staring down the path of least resistance at the world of GUI interfaces as the primary way to do my job, I'm starting to feel again the way I felt when I told people (has it only been ten years) that I was an IMS Cobol programmer. Am I from the Jurassic or Cretaceous period?

Rapid Application Development

Rapid Application Development, or RAD (hey, an acronym I actually recognize), is a programming environment that allows programmers to quickly build working applications without having to reinvent the wheel (or the button in the case of programming) every time they program an application. Basically, it's a set of canned objects that typically have the same features regardless of where they're built, and which you can use over and over again: Visual Basic and Oracle Forms.

In the case of Oracle 9*i*/10*g* Lite, the RAD environment offers developers and programmers multiple platforms in which to develop a set of tools, APIs, and code samples to help them to mold applications surrounding the mobile environment more quickly. Once built, these applications can be bundled up together using the Packaging Wizard (boy, could I use one of those at holiday time) into a single unique file that can then be deployed to the target mobile environments.

Several industry-standard supported development tools also exist that programmers can use to develop these applications, such as C++, Jdeveloper, .NET, PowerBuilder, and anything else that makes ODBC or JDBC calls.

Warehouse Builder

Okay, so I could give you a huge spiel on the wonders of Warehouse Builder. I took the class in Chicago that Oracle put on a few years ago; Warehouse Builder is a great product. It does what it's good at, keeps metadata, and provides you with an intuitive interface through which to build the structures for a data warehouse.

If the only thing you used it for was to manage your enterprise metadata, it would probably be worth the price. Far too many organizations don't have any idea what some of the data elements are for in their systems, and even more have multiple meanings for a single data element depending on the context in which it is found. While we know that this is less than optimal from a design perspective, we can also probably agree that it, as well as other "stuff," happens. We have what we have and in many cases we have to live with it. Having a central repository of information on what data elements are, what they mean, and where they are used, while a tremendous undertaking, is useful for many organizations.

It installs nicely into an existing schema in the database, but put it in its own schema. If you ever have to uninstall it, you'll thank me later. In times past when you uninstalled it (at least with earlier releases of the product), it didn't keep track of what objects belonged to, and which objects belonged to something else, thus truncating the schema. I personally lost several months' worth of coding on a perfectly good customized general ledger system, thus teaching me the necessity of a good backup. Better safe than sorry.

Discoverer

Discoverer is just one more in Oracle's set of business analysis tools, the same way that Oracle Reports and Oracle Express are part of Oracle's offered business intelligence tool set. Discoverer's intended use is to provide end users with an analysis tool that allows them to write ad hoc queries or run predefined queries that have been created to be shared among users. It is easier to "program" Discoverer reports than it is to create similar ones in Oracle Reports. In fact, the reports generated in Discoverer are usually user-written and require little or no programmer intervention.

Discoverer Viewer

One of the tools that's part of the Discoverer tool set is the Discoverer viewer. The viewer is meant to give users the ability to run predefined reports via a web-only interface. While this interface limits the ability of a user to pick and choose what he wants to see, it does help to keep the user from being able to determine what she wants to see and report on. From a security access standpoint, this is a good thing.

User Edition

End users use the Discoverer User Edition as a way to create ad hoc queries and reports. Through this interface, users can create reports, perform data analysis, and publish result sets to the Web.

Administrator Edition

The Administrator Edition is used to create and maintain the End User Layer (EUL). No, you do not have to have access to the APPS password to be able to run reports, create reports, or administer the EUL, so don't let them (whoever "them" is) tell you that they do. The APPS password is like SYS and SYSTEM—only those who really, really, really need to know it should have access to it, and they probably already do.

End User Layer

The End User Layer is a database schema that houses the metadata, the data used to help hide the complexity of the database from the user.

Oracle Discoverer, naturally, can connect natively to any Oracle database and is often used against an Oracle 11*i* database as a way to report on the information it contains, and do so in a specifically designed manner without having to resort to customizing Oracle E-Business Suite (which can be a complex and occasionally painful experience, particularly if you don't customize in the supported manner).

The End User Layer is the location where workbooks are stored when users or administrators create them and from where these workbooks can be shared.

It is not necessary to provide the APPS password to anyone simply for the purpose of creating and sharing workbooks. The functionality exists to allow anyone to create their own and, if given the proper authority, share those workbooks with others.

Oracle Text

Have you ever wanted to be able to find every recipe in your collection that's made using applesauce but not eggs or oil? Or have you ever needed the name of a song that has a car in the lyrics but not a girl, or maybe a movie that has a character named Frank but not Frankenstein? You know that you have all of this information in your database. It was a good idea at the time, and inputting it was easy enough, but retrieving it in any manner close to effective seems next to impossible. Or maybe you have all of the e-mails from your e-mail server stored in an Oracle database so you have a simple way of searching for people who might be sending e-mails containing corporate secrets. Enter Oracle Text.

Oracle Text is an interesting contraption that indexes every (or very nearly every) word in a file or column (blob, clob, VARCHAR, or bfile), and stores the information about that word and all words in the general vicinity of that word (within 100 words is currently the limit) so that you can determine later what you want to search for and what criteria you want to use. There are over 150 different document types that Oracle Text can search through and index.

Not sure what the exact word is you're looking for? Think it might be apple, but it could be applesauce, McIntosh, yellow delicious, granny smith,

MAC, or IPOD? You can use fuzzy searches, wildcards, or stemming ("mouse" would be a hit for "mice" and vice versa) or you can make your own thesaurus so you can define your own relationships between kinds of words as they relate to your particular situation. You can even limit or expand the number of words that you allow to be indexed by changing what the lexer includes.

The lexer? That's the utility whose function it is to separate the document or sections of the document into words or tokens. Punctuation is typically stripped out, and the resulting strings of alphanumeric characters are then parsed for "stop words" (those words that you have either allowed Oracle to decide you don't want to have indexed because of the sheer volume of irrelevant words that would be texted—added to the list of words stored internally so that Oracle can retrieve them for user queries later—or that you have decided will be irrelevant for the same or similar reasons). It is important, however, to keep in mind that just because a word isn't indexed doesn't mean it's ignored completely. The existence of the word in context will be maintained and counted in exact phrase match searches or in searches where nearness counts (within five words of, for example).

In addition, Oracle Text can be allowed to understand alternative spellings of a word (color and colour, for example), diacritical marks from different languages, compound words, and multibyte languages.

Oddly enough, Oracle Text is included in both the Standard and Enterprise Edition of the database, so whatever you have available, you can use to play with Oracle Text. It's the underlying architecture for IFS, Ultra Search, and XML DB. These will all be discussed in later sections in this chapter.

The data in Oracle Text is stored in what is referred to as a datastore. The data can be stored locally on the server either within a column in the database or on a file system that's accessible by the database, or, because Oracle Text can be stored and accessed via a URL, it can be stored remotely on other servers and accessed via HTML or FTP protocols. This means that, with the proper settings and access, and sufficient space to allow you to index the pages sufficiently, Oracle Text could be the driving engine behind a search engine or web crawler. The datastore can even be the output of a PL/SQL procedure.

Okay, so it's stored in there somehow magically. How do you get it back out effectively and efficiently, and in the manner you choose to have it returned? The real magic is in the indexing. You map the words or tokens *inside* the documents to the documents themselves. Each word found in any document is held in the index along with where in the document it's located, and the location of the document itself. This kind of logic is a bit inside out. Normally, you look through a document for a list of words, while Oracle Text looks through its list of words for documents containing those words.

The indexes in Oracle Text are a wee bit different than the indexes you're used to working with in another way as well. Normal indexes update themselves whenever you add data to the database. Oracle checks where the new or updated values should go and updates all relevant indexes accordingly. Oracle Text doesn't. Once the index is built, it is static, regardless of the documents you add to the datastore. The associated indexes don't get updated until you deliberately synchronize the indexes. This has changed as of Oracle 10g, where you can set the preferences on the indexes so they refresh themselves on commit, on a schedule, or using the Oracle 8i and Oracle 9i manual synchronize method. Because of the nature of the indexes and the volume of data that they have to work against, Oracle 10g also brings with it the capability to build and synchronize indexes in parallel. This can offer you tremendous time savings if you have the CPU power to back it up.

To speed up your search, Oracle 10g also allows you to locally partition Oracle Text indexes, making them more manageable and improving the scalability of the indexes overall.

Never thought that you would ever again use those truth tables you created in Logic class in college? Guess again. Oracle Text searches can get incredibly complex, particularly if there are people like lawyers determining what needs to be searched for and in what context the search needs to be. Getting the syntax of the search right is a matter of understanding exactly what is being asked for and the logic and order of operations for the Oracle Text operators.

The pseudo code logic might be something along the lines of: Give me all documents where cat is within 25 words of dog, but not in the same document with chicken, horse, or hippopotamus, and in the same document where dog is not within five words of food and cat is not within 5 words of food but feed is within 8 words of either dog or cat and not within 8 words of man, woman, men, women, or people. And if a lawyer is involved, they might try catching any mistyped words, so they may throw in a few wildcard words like hors* or hip*. The possibilities are endless.

HTML DB

Oracle's HTML DB is not a database, but rather a Rapid Application Design tool that is used to quickly develop web applications against an Oracle database.

Despite the fact that databases are more prevalent today than ever, many organizations still rely on spreadsheets and small personal or small-group databases to present content to end users. These spreadsheets and databases are either e-mailed between those who need access to the data contained, or they are put on a shared drive where many people can access them (albeit sometimes one person at a time). While those tools are very good at what they're designed for, they do not typically present content well on web sites. This is not a judgment call or meant to in any way slight the tools for what they do. They're simply not designed to fill this role. They are not, however, designed to be used to present information to an ever-expanding audience. What's more, there is usually a lot of room for improvement with this kind of tool with respect to security and content.

By consolidating this data centrally, in a database rather than in a multitude of individual spreadsheets or personal databases, you can assure that there's a single point of update or insertion and that everyone is seeing the updates at the same time, rather than, as often happens, having to update different data based on the timing of different people's e-mail. This allows you to be more assured of the validity of the information at any given time. It can cut down significantly on the resources required to e-mail a set of spreadsheets to everyone concerned and saves time due to network latency or due to people not noticing that their mail contains the revised spreadsheets. This can provide you with the security of knowing who is accessing the information at any given time and the ability to provide assurance to an auditor that access to the given information has only been given to relevant individuals, and not to anyone involved in maintaining the e-mail server or to anyone who has intercepted an e-mail (or had an e-mail misrouted to them).

If you need to securely present this information to an audience in a central location, Oracle's elegant solution is HTML DB.

Workspaces

Workspaces allow one or more developers to create applications against the same database with their own database objects. A single Oracle database can house multiple workspaces and each workspace can access one or more database schemas. This means that multiple development processes can occur simultaneously without one interfering with another. There is a wizard that helps walk you through requesting a workspace, at which time you can determine if you need to access an existing schema or if you need to have a new schema assigned to the workspace as well.

While this isn't really a virtual private database in the security perspective, it is a virtual database in that everyone sees the same picture of the base schema and can name their objects independent of what someone else names her objects, and without having to be concerned with what someone else calls his programs.

Application Builder

The HTML DB Application Builder is an interface optimized for assembling an HTML user interface on top of database objects. It comes complete with wizards that help build both data entry and reporting applications.

SQL Workshop

The SQL Workshop is a simple tool that lets you interact with the database through a web browser in much the same way you do with other GUI utilities. These utilities, such as Toad or even SQL*Plus, are handy for when you don't want to use the command line. Through this tool, SQL Workshop, you can query tables, create and alter tables (or rather, generate the necessary DDL to create tables), run SQL statements, and even find information using Query by Example.

What? Oh, Query by Example?

Query by Example refers to a method of forming database queries in such a way as to let the database program display a blank record with a space for each field. Into this, you can enter the condition for each field that you want to have included in the query.

Query by Example is usually simpler than learning to program a complex SQL statement, particularly for users who normally employ something like Access.

Data Workshop

The data workshop provides an interface to help with the importing and exporting of data into and out of the database table. You can import data from a spreadsheet to database tables. You can even create a table, form, or spreadsheet immediately. Further, you can import from a CVS fib or a fill with tab-separated values. You can even import a file with your choice of separators.

What's more, HTML DB provides you with a canned set of templates for virtually everything that a developer will want to create (reports, pages, labels, regions) that encourage developers to separate the user interface from the application logic, and all of that from the data access. Of course, they are working on the premise of, build it and they will come. Speaking from personal experience, however, they usually demand you use best practices, even though they don't have the time or inclination to do the same. But the more encouragement you can give a developer to build applications the right way, the better chance you have that eventually they will.

HTML DB does use its own methodology to render the pages that are processed for the application. This means that pages will perform similarly within the application (or across applications) regardless of who designed the pages or the queries involved and that the developers don't have to trouble themselves with the application of HTML logic. Okay, for anyone who has used vi or Notepad or any of the myriad HTML programming interfaces, I understand that "programming" HTML is not quite as complicated or complex as programming C or assembler, but there is a certain elegant logic that suggests it might be a good idea to have all your pages rendered similarly. At least one won't be exceptionally faster or perform better or have more accurate data or links than another simply due to the programming involved to render the page.

While it is still possible to mangle the logic involved, or to deliberately load the gun and point it at your own foot, HTML DB makes the tendency to accidentally mess up less likely.

Workspace Administrator

Think no one is using HTML DB? Ask Tom's web site at http://asktom.oracle .com has been built on HTML DB since 2003.

HTML DB is built on the already-proven modplsql construct. Modplsql works by calling a PL/SQL stored procedure (like you couldn't have guessed that from the name, huh?) and retrieving the data buffered by the procedure. This does mean, however, that if you run a very long query, because of the way that modplsql works, the browser will not "see" any data, not even the first line of output, until every line of output has been produced and returned. HTML DB simply generates HTML that is presented to the screen via htp.

Until all of the data is available for the HTML, it can't be completely rendered. For this reason, developers still have to understand the concept of correctly joining their data together as well as the concept of Cartesian products and Garbage In Garbage Out. This is partly the reason that HTML DB is designed to build applications, not ad hoc queries (many users are very good at the logic involved in creating a query, many others are not).

Ultra Search

Okay, so one of the things that I didn't know I was getting myself into when I accepted the calling to be an Apps DBA was all of the new products that I would have to deal with, products that I had no idea how they worked, didn't really care a lot about at the time, and never thought I would have cause to install (and therefore no call to ever upgrade). One of the products that I really never cared enough to learn about was Ultra Search.

Ultra Search provides you with a one-stop shop for searching documents across the organization no matter where that document is (provided it is accessible to the network). It was built using the Oracle Text retrieval engine and provides users with a simple retrieval interface through which to search for relevant data. It is, in effect, a corporate crawler that searches out documents, indexes them, and makes them easier to find through a single integrated interface.

You can perform virtually any kind of search through Ultra Search, and as long as you have access to a given document, and you have set up Ultra Search to access that document, you'll be able to find it later using Oracle's search capabilities.

Many search engines give you the ability to search the documents on your available servers. Google provides you, now, with a search engine that basically text indexes every document on the network to which you have access mapped. Why would anyone use anything else? Google is really pretty efficient at documents, but it doesn't search databases. Ultra Search can integrate and pull together information on not only database information but the file system data as well, and provide you with a central location for all information.

Are there security concerns about someone using Ultra Search to gain access to information that would not ordinarily be available to that user? In Oracle 10g, Ultra Search provides you with the functionality to have searches adhere to the security policies of the underlying data repositories.

The irony comes when you find out that people are still able to access data that they shouldn't ordinarily because the security policy in many cases is simply not to tell anyone where the documents are, which would never stop a decent hacker.

Spatial

Once upon a time, there was a product called Oracle MultiDimension that provided a way to store and retrieve multidimensional data in an Oracle database. As is common with Oracle products, the name evolved with the product. MultiDimension became SDO, which in turn evolved into Oracle Spatial. Spatial's primary use is in connection with Geographical Information Systems and is used as a way to implement Geo-References and to use these references as a way to help provide answers to queries dealing with how something is related to a specific location in space (hence the name Spatial).

Using Oracle Spatial you can represent and store features like points, lines, or polygons in a single field in a table in the database.

Spatial was designed for heavy-duty database applications. Locator (free with both Standard Edition and Enterprise Edition) is designed for lighter-weight, smaller applications or for you to tinker with on your own without having to go to the expense of separately licensing Spatial. It brings with it the same functionality that Spatial has, but without any additional cost. Spatial and Locator, however, may make you think way more about Euclidean geometry than you really care to. Also, the type of data stored by Spatial is limited only to data that's numeric and has a bounded range of values.

While contemplating this part of the chapter, I thought about how Spatial is *really* used compared to how it *could* be used. Geographical information can be elegantly stored in Spatial, which means mapping and navigational information, but what else can it hold?

What doesn't Spatial do? It doesn't come with a mechanism for spatial data collection, a sophisticated analytical and visualization functionality provided by many of the traditional Geographic Information Systems (GIS).

So what does Spatial consist of? A schema (MDSYS, yes it has to be named that) that designates the storage, syntax, and semantics of the Oracle-supported geometric data types is at the core of Oracle Spatial. Also included are indexing mechanisms that provide a set of operators and functions which assist you in performing "area of interest" queries, queries involving spatial joins, and other heavy analysis spatial operations. Further, while not included in every release but either downloadable from OTN or to be included in later releases, are administrative Java class–based utilities you can use for manipulating and storing Spatial-related object types.

Mining

Mining is, to a great extent, geographical in nature anyway. You look for deposits of whatever it is you're mining or extracting (oil, coal, diamonds, iron pyrite) in relationship to other things in the ground, or in relationship to other topographical information in nature. In the case of mining things like taconite, Spatial could be useful in storing and analyzing information about blast locations, the purity of taconite in the area around potential blast sites, and where the next logical location would be to blast in order to attempt to assure at least a given purity of magnetic iron filaments.

Manufacturing

You can extend the idea of geography to include things like automobiles, appliances, houses, wheelchairs, or even swimsuits. There's a certain kind of geography to just about anything, thus you can conceptually extend the idea of Spatial to just about any kind of manufacturing. And, hey, combine the data collected in those medical databases on the size and shape of the current average human body, and we might be able to find ways to make office chairs more comfortable, movie or airplane seats fit the changing shape of the world, and swimsuits that do a better job of covering our changing shapes and looking more like outfits to be seen in instead of like a butterfly bandage trying to hold two sides of a deflating pool toy together.

Amusement Parks

As I sit under a tree at Six Flags Fiesta Texas, thinking about geography, watching people wander past my rock on their way from the entrance to the Road Runner roller coaster, waiting for my kids to wander past in their adventures or my husband to return from his hike to the concession stand that honors the free soda all-day bracelet on a 98-degree Friday afternoon, the idea that there is not only a geography to the location of the park in relationship to cities and highways, and fifty bazillion ways to get from there to here, but the relationship between the actions at the park, the traffic patterns of people in the park, and the placement of vendor stands within the park crosses my incredibly unusual mind. The relative profitability of each stand (concession, gift shop, cart) and their relationship to each other in the park and in relationship to the traffic flow and the rides and attractions in the park are all geographical information that you could store in Spatial and analyze.

Future design decisions could be made based on this information. Stands could be placed in locations where they'll be most visited by patrons. Children's rides wouldn't all necessarily be grouped together. Instead, occasional "kiddie" rides would be scattered throughout the park so families on the march together could allow older kids to visit roller coasters while littler people visited something else of interest to them. Fiesta Texas actually does this very well. Benches, trees, and other architectural structures, meanwhile, could be optimally placed so that traffic throughput would be optimized, providing resting places for tired parents and making the overall amusement park visit good for all patrons and more profitable for all its stockholders and stall owners.

Writing

Okay, so maybe this one is a bit of a stretch for most people, but there is a kind of geography associated with a book. It isn't obvious, and it might not happen in my lifetime, but in any book, there is real estate to be covered. There are points in different parts of the book that can be connected, either through the index or the table of contents, to another point in another part of the book. You navigate from one point to another and find yourself at a destination. In a novel, the plot can travel in such a way that something in chapter 1, paragraph 18 relates directly to something that the protagonist says or does in chapter 23, paragraph 82, line 6. There would be a kind of elegance if this kind of plot information were able to be analyzed for popular novels and a person could look and see the design of the book that they enjoy most and extrapolate to those books that they might be interested in later. *Harry Potter*, for example, holds deep fascination for a number of people in my family. We have determined through trial and error and many frustrated nights that we don't equally enjoy the *Redwall* series (no matter how well written and popular it is), but we do enjoy *Eragon* and the *So You Want to Be a Wizard* series. Again, because of the really unusual way that my mind works, I wonder if there might be a way to determine ahead of time what stories my family might enjoy without having to go to the time, expense, and frustration of trying to enjoy books that just don't meet our tastes. True, this might lend itself more elegantly to e-publishing than to typical paper and print media, but it is an interesting thing to daydream about on a hot sticky afternoon.

How Does It Do That?

How does Spatial work? Oracle Spatial depends on Jserv Java Virtual Machine being installed and running for the instance in question. You also have to have interMedia installed and operational, and have Oracle XML Database functional as well. Spatial is an option you have to license separately. The locator is free.

```
Select comp_id, version, status from dba_registry
Where comp_id in ('JAVAVM','ORDIM','XDB');
```

The user MDSYS owns Spatial, so be sure you either create the user or make certain the existing user has the proper privileges and rights in the database. Make sure the account is locked, too. This latter step is important because if the user is created as a part of the installation and automatic database creation steps, the password will be well known and easily determined. MDSYS has a great deal of authority when it comes to the database and you want to make sure it isn't used to hack into it. Don't worry about not being able to install stuff after you get the schema owner created—MDSYS doesn't have to do with who installs Spatial anyway, SYS does.

XML DB

XML (eXtensible Markup Language) is being used to identify and describe data on the Web today. While HTML is a presentation language, and can be used to present XML documents, XML provides the dynamic flexibility that allows a web page to be presented in exactly the way that each current user of the page desires. It can govern the content that the user sees based on that user's preferences and desires. XML can be effectively translated into HTML by using SXTL or some other transformation, but the dynamic flexibility lies in the XML, not in the end HTML created from it.

Oracle handles XML in the database through two very different constructs, both of which reside in the database. The following paragraphs provide an overview of these constructs.

Storage of XMLType is set up whenever an XML table is created or registered with the XML DB. Whenever the schema is set up to contain XML data, Oracle creates a set of tables and views whose purpose is to hold the XML instance documents. These can be viewed not only from within the XML schema, but from the other construct (the XML DB Repository) as well. XMLType can be stored in tables and columns as character large objects (CLOBS) or as sets of objects (referred to as shredded storage). Just like "regular" data, XML data can be accessed either from the local database, or via database links to a remote database. You can index XMLType data with any of the normal indexing methods, including Oracle Text, or it can be indexed with an XMLIndex. The data can be manipulated through HTTP and HTTPS (naturally), WebDAV, FTP, SQL statements, or through Advanced Queuing, Web Services, or Oracle Streams.

You can use the XMLType type wherever you can use any of Oracle's other provided types (date, VARCHAR2, char). You can define variables in PL/SQL code as XMLType, define columns in tables as XMLType, and because XMLType is an object type, you can create a table as XMLType. If you choose to define a table in this manner, the XMLType table can contain any well-formed XML document. Because you can validate that any document stored in XMLType is a known XML structure, Oracle can make its own determination on the best way to query and update the data. If you were to simply store XML in a CLOB or as a BFILE, Oracle wouldn't have the opportunity to make this determination.

Oracle XML DB Repository is the construct in the database that is optimized for handling XML data. The repository contains resources (folders or files; folders can be either directories or containers) each of which is identified by a path. Every resource also has a unique set of metadata associated with it, which includes items like owner and creation date, as well as user-defined metadata. While this repository is optimized for handling XML data, you aren't limited to storing just XML data within it. You can store any kind of data you want in the repository. To access the data in the repository, use the RESOURCE_VIEW or the PATH_VIEW view, PL/SQL through the DBMS_XDB API, or use Java through the XML DB resource API.

Because XML data is inherently hierarchical in nature, Oracle uses a hierarchical metaphor to manage the XML data. Hierarchical indexes are used to speed up the traversal of folders and paths to a level that's often faster than more traditional file system traversal.

Collaboration Suite

Okay, I've put off the inevitable as long as I could, but now it's time for one of the biggest pieces of the Oracle puzzle: Collaboration Suite. Collaboration Suite is the first Enterprise product that applies relational database technology and additional Oracle database security to business communications. By leveraging relational databases, you can consolidate information and use SQL as a means to retrieve information from the database. You can thereby reduce the need for additional hardware and software, and leverage the fact that Oracle DBAs understand Oracle databases and can therefore shorten the learning curve.

Oracle 10g provides a store for e-mail, voicemail, and fax messages that is reliable and scalable and takes advantage of Oracle's core database technology. What's even more important though is that they provide you with a robust web interface through which to access not only your e-mail but your voicemail and faxes as well.

The web interface is more useful and intuitive than most alternatives. It brings drag and drop, and sort and search to the web interface, something few others do. Even better, there are connectors to Outlook and voicemail, providing wireless access and browser-based clients (both Web and wireless). Even more applications can be mail-enabled by integrating Oracle Email's PL/SQL and Java application programming interfaces (APIs) with other applications (canned as well as home grown).

Oracle Email makes extensive use of Oracle Text as the vehicle through which e-mail searching is accomplished. Not only can you search the text of the messages with Oracle Text queries, you can search the attachments (straight attached as well as those that are zipped before being attached) using Oracle Text.

Integration with calendars, fully searchable files (whether attached directly to the Oracle database as LOBS of one sort or another or simply stored as file system files), extended support for XML, and web conferencing all through one interface allows you a much fuller interface through which to access any communication information.

And, because it is based on XML and Java and other standard technologies, it can be integrated with—ta-da!—Oracle E-Business Suite's interface.

E-Business Suite

Don't let them kid you—if anyone tells you that you're the new Apps DBA but not to worry, it will only take at most 25 percent of your time, you can rest assured it will take at least 75 percent of your time and maybe 125 percent of your time caring and feeding this amazing piece of work. I wouldn't suggest that you run screaming from the room, although in retrospect that's not the worst idea, but I would suggest you very gently assure them that, even if you do the barest minimum work on an Oracle 11*i* system, it will most assuredly take more than 25 percent of your time.

Oracle Financials, Oracle 11*i*, Oracle E-Business Suite… it is known by many names, some depending on when those people talking about it first came to understand what it was (like Oracle Financials). Typically, all of these refer to the suite of products that now make up E-Business Suite.

Yes, the product is massive. Yes, it is as powerful as it is massive. No, I honestly don't think any one person can fully understand what exactly is involved in the complete product suite. The documentation alone fills an entire CD and one upgrade patch can be bigger than many whole programs (2 gigabytes zipped, 8 gigabytes unzipped, and this rests on the fact that you've already installed the base product, which ships on upwards of 16 or more CDs). A few releases ago, over ten thousand tables made up the core product, without any notion of additional auxiliary customized applications hanging off the edge. Tens of thousands of program units, views, and synonyms, as well as a liberal use of queues, Materialized Views and even Index Organized Tables make it one of the most complex pieces of software on the market today.

E-Business Suite brings with it its own language and terminology, but can draw in and integrate portions of most other technologies that have become part of Oracle's offerings. Here we'll just touch a little on what the major players are in the product, and if you want to spend your next ten or so years investigating them, feel free to learn the rest.

This section is by no means an all-inclusive set of every scrap of information you need to know to be an Apps DBA. It will, however, give you a grounding in the vocabulary so you don't get that deer-in-the-headlights look whenever someone starts to talking about Oracle 11*i*.

I never thought that those classes I "had" to take to get through my MBA (finance, accounting, human resources, marketing) would ever amount to anything. I thought I was taking classes just to put in the time to get the degree so I'd have a better understanding of business. NOT! When it came time to talk to the accounting types when I was going through my application implementation, I realized that if I didn't learn anything else in those classes (and let's face it, I'm still clueless when it comes to some of the deeper information from those classes), I at least learned the vocabulary necessary to be able to talk to and understand people with whom I would have to work closely for the next umpteen years. I'm more convinced than ever that business isn't as much about the numbers as it is about having the ability to talk about the numbers in a way that makes you sound like you know what you're talking about.

Oracle i*AS*

At the core of Oracle 11*i* is Oracle's application server. Driven by Apache technology with extra stuff thrown in just to make things more interesting, the application server part of E-Business Suite relies primarily on either a scaled-down version of the Application Server (what Oracle 11*i* has typically shipped with) or on the fuller, more robust Application Server that is the core of *i*AS proper that sells on its own. Oracle *i*AS is typically talked about as if its own suite of products includes Modplsql, Developer, Forms, Reports, Discoverer, Single Sign-On, Oracle Internet Directory, Portal, WebCache, and other middleware tools. Most of these are also a part of the E-Business Suite of products, although they're often versions of a different scale than those in *i*AS proper.

Modplsql is a module for Apache that allows calls to PL/SQL, calls to process simply and easily as Perl modules, and other application code to be called in order to process data. Developer is the rapid development arena that allows programmers to produce applications quickly that permit data input and reporting. Forms and Reports are pieces of the Developer suite of products. Discoverer (previously discussed) is an integral part of the Oracle 11*i* suite of products. In past releases, you would have had to buy, install, and configure Discoverer on its own server or as an additional piece of the server on which Oracle 11*i* is running. Now, it's part of the core application that you can simply license and configure. Single Sign-On allows a user to sign into an application interface once, and regardless of the number of different databases accessed by the different pieces of the application, the user isn't required to sign into any interfaces again, as long as the access point through which the user signs on supports it. This means that if you sign into the application as yourself (lfreeman, for example) from a web interface and that interface is used to navigate to all of the required pieces, then the user's connection will be maintained through the original connection.

Concurrent Managers

Concurrent managers are a complex and intricate part of E-Business Suite. They are customizable job scheduling daemons that can be made responsible for many administrative tasks from within the Oracle 11*i* application. They handle batch processing, report generation, self-maintenance of concurrent job output, and jobs can even be scheduled to gather system statistics for the application tables. There isn't a single concurrent manager that fields requests for the whole application. If there were, that single scheduler would end up being a bottleneck and be a place where the application could frequently come to a screeching halt. Multiple concurrent managers can be defined by administrators of the application as a means to help out the core managers provided by Oracle.

Internal Concurrent Manager

The central master manager (the CEO manager if you will) is known as the Internal Concurrent Manager (ICM). It is Chief Executive Officer because it is responsible for controlling the behavior of the other managers that fall under its control. The ICM is the boss. Whenever "concurrent managers" begin, the ICM is the first manager to be started by the application and it must be running before any other managers can start working. Also, kind of like a CEO, the primary function of the ICM is to provide the impetus for others to start up and shut down. It starts the individual concurrent managers, shuts them down, and resets the other managers if for some reason one of them has a failure.

Standard Manager

If the ICM is the CEO manager, the Standard Manager (SM) is company president. The SM's function is to run any reports or any batch jobs that have not been assigned to a specialized product manager. This is a good reason to assign batch jobs to their own manager, so they can be created, scheduled, and during all of this allow for jobs to be load-balanced within the application. Examples of specialized concurrent managers might include the Inventory Manager, CRP Inquiry Manager, and Receivables Tax Manager.

Conflict Resolution Manager

Conflict? Surely there can't be conflict in scheduling or in allowing one program to run whenever it wants to run (or whenever the user wants it to run) regardless of whether or not the data on which it is supposed to operate is available to it or not. The Conflict Resolution Manager (CRM; see, more acronyms) works to check all concurrent program definitions and attempts to make sure there are no incompatibility issues based on the business rules defined for them when they are created or redefined. While the CRM is a manager that apps users are highly encouraged to use, it is really the "optional" required manager, since the ICM can be allowed to take over its responsibilities and itself resolve concurrent program issues.

CM Issues

Concurrent managers are tied incredibly closely with printers. Why? We live in a paperless society after all, so why is it necessary to tie printing to running batch jobs? Okay, first, our paperless society doesn't really exist. And second, just because. Oracle provides you with a mess of printer drivers and printer definitions you can use. There are never sufficient drivers for your needs, however. Instead, find someone who understands printer language and can help you make sure your printer is doing what you need it to. Don't like the idea of strong-arming a piece of hardware into cooperation? Well, in this case, it may well be necessary. Different printers require different sets of special character commands. Seek professional help.

Oh, and any time you change anything with printers, you have to bounce the concurrent managers. They get all touchy and finicky if you don't.

And if you want to make sure your care and feeding of the concurrent managers is adequate, and that they are behaving well, look in the $FND_TOP/ sql directory for scripts that can help you manage the concurrent managers and check the status of the concurrent managers from the command line, without having to resort to going into the application (whether the application proper or even to OAM). I would much rather be able to log into SQL*Plus, where I'm more comfortable, and run some queries to tell me what the database believes is going on in the database, than to take the chance of messing something up in the application and having a mess of users mad at me.

ADI

Application Desktop Integrator is not a central part of Oracle E-Business Suite, but it is an auxiliary piece that's supported as an add-on and which allows users a different kind of interface into the data of the database. ADI is a means by which users can take data that is in Excel spreadsheets or delimited text documents and upload them into the database.

Users commonly manipulate data in spreadsheet format for things like Journal Vouchers, budgets, and assets of the organization. They then want a simple and elegant way to upload this data into Oracle Financials. ADI is the interface through which they can do this.

The idea that you can take information out of the database, finesse that information in a spreadsheet or in Access, and then take that information and upload it back to the Oracle database makes me shudder, but it is apparently a common enough activity that there has been a product specially designed to allow accountants the ability to do this.

Web ADI is a newer interface that can be configured with more recent releases of Oracle 11*i*. It provides a web interface through which users can perform many of the same processes they perform using the client server ADI. This can mean you no longer have to go to every computer after every upgrade to make sure that nothing has broken—everything is maintained centrally. Yes, of course there are drawbacks. Some of the functionality that's in the client server version is still lacking in the web interface. The one that springs to the minds of most users is the inability to use wizards when you're using the web interface.

Interestingly, you must have previously installed Excel on the computer that you use ADI on.

FSG

FSG, or Oracle Financial Statement Generator, is a piece of the application tied to the General Ledger module that's used to generate financial statements. Balance Sheets, Profit and Loss Statements, Cost Center Statements, and Statements of Cash Flows are examples of the kinds of reports that accounting types tend to like to put together. They can use FSG to help them do this. FSG allows organizations to define their own application reports, schedule these reports to be produced automatically, adopt a consistent style for all customized reports for the organization, and then have them magically published to a secure location for use by managers, all without having to resort to customizing the core functionality or creating add-on modules just to get the reports they need in the format they're used to seeing them in.

Workflow

Oracle Workflow is really pretty slick. It provides a conduit through which work can pass from one user to the next in a logical and structured manner so that the business processes that are already in place in your organization can be modeled in the application and maintained in a fairly efficient manner. Naturally, there is a wizard, or workflow builder, to help you with the modeling. I personally think that modeling clay would be more fun, but getting the information from the model at that point and into the computer would be difficult to say the least.

Workflow routes documents from one user to the next automatically, building in the approval process that you define for your business rules. It's actually more robust than that even. There are things that many businesses do that need to loop through processes more than once. Some business rules suggest that parallel processing needs to happen to a document, and when all pieces of that document have been processed adequately, the parallel paths reconverge at a common spot to continue on through the process.

Workflow can route information to any user or group of users in the organization, whether or not they have to act on the information in order for it to be fully processed. Sometimes the CEO needs to be kept in the loop of information but isn't required to act on every invoice or payment processed by the organization. Workflow can be set up so that she has e-mail notification showing up periodically to let her know what's going on without the necessity of her having to log in to the application and taking active response so that each one can be forwarded on its way.

Customization

Okay, so with 10,000 tables and umpteen-thousand other objects, how can Oracle E-Business Suite not have everything you could ever need or ask for? Believe me, there's a lot of room for customization. Maybe your organization needs to print these really cool things called invoices and would prefer the invoices print on the custom invoice stock they've invested in and which has been a standard in the organization for years. Or maybe the employees would like to get paid, or the people to whom you owe bills would like to get paid (imagine that), and you need to be able to print checks in such a way as to make sure the numbers that get put on the checks line up somewhere near where they're supposed to. Have you ever looked—really looked—at checks? No two are exactly alike and sometimes the spacing from one to another is incredibly different. Or maybe you have an application that needs to make use of information that's the same (or similar) to what's already in Oracle 11*i*, and you want to be able to integrate that application into the framework you've spent so much time and effort implementing.

Oracle lets anyone customize Oracle E-Business Suite, provided that they customize it in a supported manner. Don't change things that Oracle provides to you directly; instead, build your own "stuff" and make each of your customizations an add-on. Anyone who's ever spent hours running patches knows that just when you think you know what a patch is going to do, it will often overlay an object you never anticipated. If you overwrite Customize The Canned Invoice Printing Report program with a custom one, you'll never know when a patch that gets applied (whether it should overlay that report or not) will have the need to change one of the programs called in connection with a report you've chosen to customize. Simply re-overlaying the new report with one you've saved off for such an eventuality will eventually mean you've broken something that was fixed and now have to start over with your customization effort. Why take the chance?

Oracle recommends you use a custom-naming standard when customizing E-Business Suite. Make your custom objects (tables, program units, indexes, whatever) start with four characters, then an underscore, and then the rest of your custom name. Why? Simple. Oracle has reserved the "right" (and let's face it, it IS their software product) to name their core objects with two letters, followed by an underscore or three letters, followed by an underscore. If you follow the direction that Oracle has set out, when they run out of names that they can create using their current standard (xx_ or xxx_) they'll know how best to take the next step and add to their standard, while allowing your custom code to remain safe.

If you do create custom objects (tables, views, forms, reports, program units) you need to register those objects with the application so it can make use of them. Which is why you created them, right, to be used? A user with System Administrator responsibility (and unless I miss my guess, that's probably going to be the DBA) needs to log in to the application and register a new custom application with the Oracle 11*i* application. This application can really be anything you want to name it (provided you protect yourself and follow their laid-out convention). By doing this, you protect your code and objects from future upgrades to the application. Create a custom directory structure under the $APPL_TOP directory into which you can place your new code. Follow the directory structure layout of the existing applications, like AP or GL, so whenever someone has to maintain your code, they have a better chance to find where it is—such as reports in the reports directory, forms under forms, and SQL under sql. This way, your code is centrally located and you can honestly answer yes to your support analyst when they ask you if your customizations follow convention. Now, create another Oracle userid and schema to own the custom database objects. It's not as if there aren't sufficient userids out there (for example, AP, GL, HR, and LMNOP), but by creating your own, you make sure your stuff is protected when you upgrade or patch. Finally, generate synonyms for anything you've created in the database schema so other programs calling yours won't have to necessarily append your custom schema to the beginning of every program that gets called.

Passwords

And now it's time to talk about passwords in Oracle E-Business Suite. Every installation of E-Business Suite comes with standard passwords. Change them. Don't let anyone feed you anything you think sounds odd, such as why they need to have the APPS password in production or why you can't ever change the passwords for any of the application users. Developers should create programs that can be run by anyone with a given responsibility or with a given set of privileges granted to them. APPS is like SYS or SYSTEM: it offers ultimate power in the database and there's no need every developer must have the ability to alter tables in production or attempt to manipulate data at the database level. Oracle was thoughtful enough to provide you with this wonderful interface through which data manipulation can occur, thus everyone who can possibly use it to do his or her job should.

Oh, there will be times when you have to take drastic measures and run something directly in the database as the APPS user. There will be an issue with the data or the structure and Oracle Support will need something to be run in this manner. FNDCPASS (under the $FND_TOP/bin directory) provides you with the means to alter the APPS password, and any other application's user's passwords. No one ever knows who it was that dropped that production table or deleted all of the information that used to be in that set of tables (yep, there is even Referential Integrity in E-Business Suite).

While disasters happen and accidents happen even more frequently, it's important that you don't have to load the proverbial gun for them, hold their hand while they aim it at their toes, and explain to them how to pull the trigger. It is much better to have users who are less than happy with the rules in place than a whole lot more users who can't do their jobs because you have to recover the database. Plus, think about it this way: With the incredible RI included in E-Business Suite and the way every product relies on every other product's data, point-in-time recovery for 10,000 tables suddenly becomes very interesting.

Summary

So you see, Oracle isn't just a relational database anymore. There are dozens of products covered by its umbrella, and there's no way for everyone to know everything (or even most of it) to any great depth. This chapter was designed as a teaser to introduce you to some of the more interesting auxiliary things that reside under the name of Oracle so you can better decide which ones interest you more and on which you might want to do more research. Dig around on OTN or oracle.com and see what kind of interesting things you can learn about these products. Have some fun and realize that, at some point, you'll find yourself hooked on something that intrigues you to enough of a degree that you just have to get out there and start playing with it yourself.

Don't say I didn't warn you.

CHAPTER
8

Will It Work?

oor software quality and database design can be tremendously expensive to an organization. Companies depend on software and databases for development, production, and distribution, not to mention for sales support, accounting, human resources, and payroll. Even if you're buying a database product, or perhaps a middle-tier application that will run on your Oracle back-end, you need to make sure that, in your environment, it runs and that there aren't any defects in its design just sitting there waiting for you to find them. While it's pessimistic to go into testing feeling there are flaws in the design, you need to be aware that chances are good that *something* was overlooked in the process. Even when you prove there are no flaws, certain inefficiencies get introduced and are often uncovered through testing.

Testing is frequently the one procedure not given enough attention during implementation. Management wants to be sure programs work, but they don't want to waste the time or man-hours to make sure that all the likely scenarios are checked out and actually work. All too often even the most minimal of testing takes a backseat to time savings when it comes to the project plan. Ironically, when testing is cut, changes often have to be backed out because they don't work or they have broken something critical, or data gets corrupted due to unanticipated side effects.

Planning and Organization

Planning and organization are as critical to the testing process as they are to the development and programming of the product itself. Planning is crucial to a successful testing effort partly because it plays a significant role in setting the expectations of management, end users, programmers, and testers alike. It takes into account the budget, the available employee hours, the available clock hours, and the available schedule and performance in test plans and assures that the testing takes place in an effective and efficient manner. It also makes certain that tests aren't forgotten or repeated in the process unless necessary for regression testing or to prove that uncovered and undocumented features have been either documented or removed (preferably removed).

Develop a Test Plan

Test plans outline the entire testing process, the individual test cases, and the anticipated outcomes of the test cases. In order to develop a solid test plan, you have to systematically explore the program and ensure thorough coverage to all pieces. The formality in developing a concrete test plan establishes the process and does not depend on random testing or accidental testing for the chance uncovering of inconsistencies. You should also test various "they will never attempt to do this" scenarios as well. Believe me, even if you think no sane person would ever try something, somehow one of your users will.

Testing, like development, can easily become an all-consuming task. This is another reason why application specifications and resulting test plans need to be as concrete as possible and should define the minimum acceptable results necessary to ship the application out to end users. It's important to make sure everything meets the minimum requirements, but not necessarily to assure perfection.

One of two approaches is typically taken when planning the testing portion of application design. One is the waterfall method; the other, the evolutionary method.

Waterfall

The waterfall method of testing is an oft-used and traditional approach. It is defined, and often driven, by the development team where each team member works in phases. These phases vary from requirements analysis to the ultimate testing and release of the application to the user community.

For the testing team, this means there's little opportunity for early intervention or for input into the process, and that the testing team has to wait for the final specs and then follow the predetermined pattern set out by development. Typically, specifications are, shall we say, set in warm oatmeal rather than in stone. This ties the hands of the testers and means that problems are identified late in the process, therefore making them much harder and more expensive to discover and then correct.

While the waterfall approach can be a very robust method, it's usually best suited for smaller projects with limited complexity, or for modular projects where each module can be taken through the process and signed off individually. More complex and robust full applications can suffer significant setbacks when this approach is taken.

Evolutionary

An earlier intervention alternative to the waterfall method is the evolutionary approach to testing where you develop the overall application modularly, test each module, fix the inconsistencies uncovered in the testing, and then retest the results of these alterations until you feel somewhat satisfied with each result. This piece is then left as is and auxiliary pieces are added to the periphery of the already-built modules. Testing then continues, not on each module but on the appended core module after each additional piece is added. The application, and therefore the testing involved, ends up being more complex with each iteration since it must be assured that the functionality of the original remains unchanged by the additional modules. Thus, the added pieces have to be tested to make sure they meet the requirements but don't break the system.

Because testing is introduced early in the process and becomes an integral part of it, there are lower-cost opportunities to reappraise the overall requirements, refine the design based on inefficiencies or inaccuracies uncovered in the process early, and help the application be better understood by the team overall. This can be a side benefit if you also get the documentation team involved in the process at the same time as the testing team because the documentation then becomes a living document rather than a sticking point at the end where everyone has to be called on to remember everything. Going back in to add or remove pieces as they're written is much easier and more elegant than trying to rework an entire document after it's written and pieces of information are forgotten.

Time is saved using this method because you're constantly able to deliver a working useful product to end users, and additional functionality can be added on with each release. While this leaves the door wide open for scope creep and for the requirements to grow, often exponentially, it also means that the user community has more input into the process, which seems to make them very happy and more forgiving of errors. Functionality can be added in either priority order as set out in the original specifications, or it can be added if the user community discovers something critical was left out of the original specifications.

The test plan thus becomes evolutionary at the same time the product becomes evolutionary. Rather than suddenly trying to develop one huge test plan to test the entire application and all functionalities and areas where bugs can enter the equation, you should start your testing efforts small, keeping the initial plans and use cases and then building on them as the application becomes more fleshed out. You add sections to the plan as you add sections to the application, allowing depth and breadth in new areas to be built in as each part is constructed and put to use.

This evolutionary process also allows you to incrementally make changes to the database rather than make alterations in one fell swoop. By making changes in this way, the overall impact of the new application, or the new code, can be spread over an extended period of time, thus minimizing its impact on end users.

Of course, there is a place for everything and everything in its place, and testing is no different. Evolutionary testing is less appropriate for small applications or modifications to existing applications where inaccuracies or inefficiencies, or the need for additional functionalities, is uncovered. In such cases, it makes more sense to use the waterfall method.

Requirements-Based Testing

Regardless of the method you choose to use for testing, it's important that the testing effort be based on requirements, and not just requirements for performance of the application, but requirements for the data in the database and the reaction of the database to the application and its use. It also provides the basis for all testing efforts of the product. Testing identifies the defects that create, cause, or allow behavior that may not be anticipated based on the specifications. This is one of the reasons the testing team should be actively involved in not only the test plans or the testing but also in the specification writing process. All requirements should be written in as unambiguous and concrete a fashion as possible. It is critical that the specifications be written as concretely and with as many measurable deliverables as possible. They must be testable in a way that ensures the program not only functions as programmed but that it complies with all of the specifications as well. Perhaps most importantly, all requirements in the specifications and all tests and test results need to be binding because the end users and the customers demand that they do so. You need to design test cases at the same time that the specifications are being written so you can meet all the requirements. The actual act of developing test cases forces everyone to think more critically about your specifications and programming.

What Testing Is

Testing is finding out what difference the new changes made in the existing system or what functionality performs other than anticipated in a new system. Testing is quality control. It is the steps you take to ensure no new bugs are introduced to a system, that existing bugs are either fed and healthy or eradicated, and it is the means by which you can prove that you have done due diligence in your efforts to create a good software product for your end users. Testing is not just checking to see if all the pieces work as expected, but also checking to see that nothing breaks if used incorrectly. It's not enough to test that every menu option works; you need to test to see what happens if you enter a choice that's not on the menu.

Important

The cost of application downtime can be extensive. Users depend on your database to be available and efficient so they can do their jobs. Lost man-hours are a big cost of downtime. But consider the application. If the application is used by external users as order entry or by internal users to process payments to the company or pay bills owed by the company, there could be substantial dollars involved in every single minute that the application is unavailable for any reason. Poor testing, or worse, no testing, can result in applications that are unavailable or that produce incorrect data.

But the cost of application downtime goes far beyond simply immediate money. It can radically impact customer impression, your market share, and your ability to win in today's highly competitive business environment. Reputation and goodwill are as important in the modern landscape as are cash flow and balance sheets. While it's true that without a profitable business, goodwill means nothing, it's also true that reputation, brand name, and goodwill are critical.

A Tool

Testing is not the magic silver bullet that will make all your database troubles go away. It does not do that for database troubles, or software issues, or performance issues, and it will not make all of your users magically happy on day 1. What it is, however, is a tool. It will give you a guide, a metric, so you have a way to measure how closely you've come to your ideal—how closely you've come to your ideal product, your ideal database design, and your ideal project.

Testing reduces the overall cost of developing the project. While realizing these savings in the early stages of the project development cycle is unrealistic since it often appears to delay both programming and underlying database design efforts, delaying testing efforts until the latter stages of the project will likely greatly increase the amount it will cost and the time it will add to the overall project because design inefficiencies are easier and less expensive to correct if caught early. It's not unrealistic that catching and repairing problems early could save a considerable amount of money and time. If they are not repaired until later, the cost of the repair could nearly double.

The testing process not only ensures that your application behaves exactly the way your user community expects it to (change and unpredictability are two things which users complain loudly about), but it can drastically reduce the overall cost of ownership by providing software and an underlying database design that performs as promised. It's also important to consider the learning curve that often accompanies the implementation of many new projects or software, the temporary loss of productivity, and the human errors associated with the changes.

What Testing Is Not

Testing is not a way to get around poor design. It's not meant to provide information on what the performance of the application should be, but rather to judge whether the performance is adequate to meet projections. It isn't supposed to help you find bugs so you can tell people what not to do, it's there to help you find those bugs so you can fix them.

What Good Testing Does

Testing, or at least *good* testing, uncovers all of the places where data corruption will occur, everywhere that there will be an impact to performance (positive or negative impact), and assures that the specifications have been met (does it do what was expected) without having unanticipated side effects (it doesn't do bad things that it wasn't expected to do).

Functional Testing

Functional testing is usually where companies focus their attention when it comes to testing. Does it do what users asked it to do? Does it meet the written specifications and does it put the right data in the right places in the database? Is it in the right format? Is there any noticeable obvious logical corruption?

While attention is most often directed at this kind of information, it's not sufficient to just do a cursory job of testing. It's important to have a test plan and stick to it, and if you have to retest later, to stick to the EXACT same plan you used before. The same processes and procedures, the same data, and preferably the same people should be involved with each iteration of testing in order to keep your variables constant.

The Proper Environment

It's important that you have a proper testing environment. It needs to mimic what the proposed production environment will look like as much as possible. Having a duplicate set of hardware available for use in the process is optimal. You shouldn't try to perform your testing on the same hardware where you're currently running production systems, even if this is the environment you'll eventually be using for the new system. It isn't worth the risk should your two systems clash severely. Even though it will eventually be the environment where the systems will coexist, the risks of testing in this way are too great.

While the temptation might exist to simply import production statistics into a test environment as a means to fake out the system to make it think it's production-like, it's important to note that, while importing statistics will often make the CBO think it's running against far larger tables, during testing efforts the same will not apply. You need to have at least a similarly configured database (with all the same parameters set in the test as those in your ultimate target environment, or as many of them as possible) with at least production-representative data, if not amplified data, on which to run your tests. It is important to not only test what would happen if the application were currently deployed, but to see what would happen when deployed six months or a year down the road.

It's not possible to infer that if you get X results on a system that has two processors that you'll get a response that's three times better than that if you run the same system on a server with six processors.

Limiting Variables

When testing, you need to limit the dependent variables you end up testing. This is one reason that a duplicate of the production database is critical even if duplicated hardware is not available. You need to make sure you're testing software changes or database changes or whatever changes are involved in the new system and not changes associated with the differences in the database.

This is also why it's critical that each piece be tested independently of every other piece, and independently from any other testing effort that might be going on in the same system. At the very least, separating the data into separate schemas is important so that the impact of the given test is all that's being measured.

Collecting Results

The test plans that define the acceptable results of the tests and the acceptable measurements expected from the tests should be collected centrally and stored in locations accessible by everyone.

Once you've collected the results, what better place to store the test plans and the results than in the database. By storing the results in a database, or by creating a database for the purpose of storing tests, test plans, and results, you can easily provide your users with access to it.

Unit Testing

Once again, it's time for a little more vocabulary.

- **Unit**   A unit is the smallest compilable (or interpretable) component of an application, and is the smallest complete conceptual piece of the database. It's typically the work of one programmer or at most a small team of programmers and does not include any called subcomponents with which it communicates.

- **Unit Testing** In unit testing, only a single component is tested. Any called or calling components are replaced with components that have already been tested or with stubs or simulations. Each unit is tested in isolation and the results of these tests are captured to assure that no individual component is introducing inaccuracies to the application.

It's important to understand that it's not enough just to pay lip service to testing. You can't just write the test cases and scenarios. You have to run them as well. Often, unit testing is done by the programmer or by a member of the testing team in isolation. Before any piece of code can be released to further programming or testing (or even be released back into the application), if the alteration is to the existing code, it has to fully pass all tests that are set out for it. This is one reason why adequate specifications are necessary. More than one DBA has had to face the daunting task of backing out of a change or recovering from the inadvertent alteration of data by code that has not fully passed all tests. The excuse usually runs somewhere along the lines of, I didn't think it was a big enough change to worry about.

The primary goal of unit testing is to take the smallest testable piece and isolate it from any other pieces of code as much as possible. Then you can determine if the piece in isolation performs exactly the way you expect. Each unit is tested separately and all test results are analyzed for conformance to the ideal. Many times, a misplaced semicolon or a badly constructed statement is uncovered in unit testing and the potential results of the implementation of such code is headed off and fixed early on, again, when the cost of discovering them and fixing them is lower and the time needed to fix the errors is less. In this way, the time taken to perform unit testing once again proves invaluable.

It's important for any DBA to remember that not only does data live in the database, but also stored program units, triggers, and other structures, and testing one can minimize the ramifications to the whole.

While some people may consider it a waste of time to develop drivers or stubs that are written to limit testing of the code in question, it is useful to create a library of calling programs and stubs that make use of different numbers and types of parameters as a means of assuring that proper (or maybe improper) data is used so that all aspects of the code can be tested. Proper data will test that the code does what it is supposed to, but improper data can prove that the error checking and error handling also does what it is supposed to do.

It is often proposed that testing be accomplished at a coarser grain than unit testing, that several units be tested together, or that units be grouped together and tested in connection with each other. Management, either management of the project or of the organization, often suggests that the time taken in testing can be aggregated and thus save time overall in the process. But think about it. What if even three units are tested together at the same time, or even in parallel with each other? If an error is detected in the data during the testing efforts, or during the post-testing reporting, to what unit do you attribute the corruption? Is the error connected to unit one, unit two, or unit three? Or is the error connected not to any one of the units individually but only when they're taken as a whole? Side effects are often caused by interconnection interfaces or by a combination of units working at the same time but not individually. Finding the ultimate cause of the error or corruption can be far more difficult, complicated, and time-consuming if the units are not tested individually first.

Once each of the units is tested singly, you can go on to the next step of testing them as a module or application.

Component Testing

You guessed it. Before going any further, more vocabulary is called for.

- **Component**   A component is one or more individual entities that contributes to a whole, a building block. While it's true that a unit is a component, the integration of one or more components together is also considered to be a component. This can potentially be an extension of unit testing if the units, together, make up a single entity themselves. Several pieces of code, taken together, make up an Oracle Form. The Form can itself be considered to be a component if it is a piece of an even larger whole.

- **Component Testing**   Component testing is often the same as unit testing: the same test cases, the same data, the same nearly everything, except that all stubs, drivers, and simulators are replaced with pieces that would be the actual called or calling programs.

Two units or two components are said to become a component when they're integrated, or when they've been compiled and linked together, or when they have successfully passed integration tests that encompass the interface between them.

This means that testing unit one and unit two together with the interface between the units can be considered component testing. By extension, unit one-two and unit three together with the interface interconnecting them can be considered yet another component test.

Integration Testing

Integration testing is the logical next step to unit testing. It combines component testing (two already-tested units together with their interface) as a means to tackle a bigger picture by testing aggregates of multiple units in realistic scenarios. Units are combined into components and further aggregated into larger and larger parts. The overall idea of integration testing is to test all of the combinations and eventually expand the concept of component testing to check the overall product in connection with those that feed it and those to whom it provides input. Each unit is an island and these islands are tested themselves. The island chain is tested as a whole, followed by the country, the continent, and, finally, the world.

Unit testing uncovers those problems that occur because of a single piece of the equation, while integration testing reveals those problems that only occur when the units are combined.

A test plan that requires you to test each individual unit assures the viability of each before combining. The test plan then assures that all components test accurately before moving forward. This makes it easier to quickly address issues as they're uncovered rather than being overwhelmed by a slew of them at the end of the project.

You can accomplish integration testing in one of three ways: top down, bottom up, or the umbrella approach.

The top-down approach requires that you test the highest-level modules to be integrated first. In this way, you allow the highest-level logic and data flow to be tested earlier in the process. This tends to minimize the need for drivers to be developed to feed data into the process; however, as no system exists in a vacuum, it does not completely do away with the need for external data if that's one of the drivers of the application. The need for downstream components, however, sometimes tends to complicate both testing and test management, and it means that lower-level utilities are tested relatively late in the development cycle. Often, these lower-level components are critical from a database perspective and top-down integration testing often sees poor support for the early release of limited functionality.

The bottom-up approach to testing, just like the bottom-up approach to most anything else, requires that you deal with the lowest-level units first. In this case, the lowest levels are tested and therefore integrated first. This means that utility modules are tested early in the programming process and the need for downstream stubs is minimized. There is, naturally, a downside, however. Bottom-up testing requires a more extensive use of upstream drivers that are available to feed the different components of the testing their inputs. And, like the top-down approach, there's at best little support for the early release of a product with limited functionality.

The third method is sometimes referred to as the umbrella approach. The umbrella approach requires testing that proceeds along functional data paths and flow control paths. The inputs for different components are integrated in the bottom-up pattern, and at the same time the outputs for each function of the tested functions are then integrated in the top-down manner of testing. This means you have a testing approach that can provide a degree of support for the early release of narrow or shallow products and of products that have limited functionality. Because you're testing the inputs and outputs to the components, and therefore, by extension, the inputs and outputs of other components, it minimizes the need to rely on that library of input and output stubs and drivers. Its major drawback? It is far less standardized and structured than other approaches. It's also less systematic, thus leading to a greater reliance on regression testing.

An Example and a Counter Example

I guess a good way to explain more fully might be to work through a little example.

Let's say A, B, and C are three separate units. According to the specifications, Unit A feeds data to Unit B. Both Unit A and Unit B can also feed input to Unit C based on business rules and logic. Figure 8-1 shows, graphically, the data flow that can occur in this set of units of the system. Charts are often helpful when preparing the testing plan so you're sure you've covered all processes when creating test scenarios.

Thus, unit test plans for the set would be Test A1, Test B1, and Test C1.

Component tests would test Unit A and Unit B and the interconnect between the two. This would be Test AB1. Unit B and Unit C and their

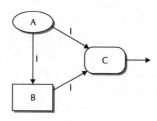

FIGURE 8-1. *Data flow*

interconnect would be Test BC1, while the components Unit A and Unit C and their interconnect would be Test AC1. Units A, B, and C and the interconnect between A and B, as well as that between B and C, would comprise component Test ABC1. Each of these tests needs to occur independent of the others.

Integration testing can then be constructed to test all paths to C as well as all paths that should fail to navigate anywhere.

Concrete measures should be gathered so that all tests and their results can be reported to users or customers and clients. All scenarios, whether possible, impossible, or improbable, should be tested out.

As a counter example, a lesson learned (or a don't-do-that tale) lies in the following little story.

Once upon a Y2K project, there were parallel remediation processes taking place in different departments of a very large organization. Accounts Payable, Accounts Receivable, Purchasing, Sales, Marketing—each department in its turn went through the process of database remediation (in this case, the databases were DB2 and IMS, rarely Oracle, but that doesn't play a big part in our little tale) and program remediation.

Purchasing Systems and Accounts Payable Systems were very closely tied together, sharing databases and programs, and feeding each other with data and information. Accounts Receivable, by contrast, was somewhat of an island unto itself. Both had IMS databases and a number of Cobol programs.

Purchasing Systems and Accounts Payable Systems had thousands of programs, millions of lines of code, and tables that were intricately linked.

With a badly programmed interface, the company would not be able to buy anything, or pay for the things they had already bought.

Accounts Receivable had its own set of IMS databases. Without its programs or databases, they would be unable to process payments to the company.

AP and Purchasing went through their processing, were tested and re-tested, and the data was closely watched to make sure no corruption would be introduced into the system. Sets of programs were tested and the entire system was tested repeatedly using valid dates and invalid dates while the flow and data were watched. The database and flat files against which the programs worked were monitored and studied and reported on to management and were refreshed once at the beginning of testing but weren't refreshed again unless some data corruption was uncovered and as a result fixed. Only after the error was corrected was the database refreshed and the entire process restarted from the beginning. Testing proceeded first in the online system, as if end users were really doing things, and then later in the batch system, as if batch processing was occurring against the systems on which the real pretend people were operating. One program out of the several thousand had one date error on a report page at the end of the remediation effort, but this occurred in the date that the report was supposed to have been run, not in the code that performed the overall processing. The remediation was completely successful and the extensive back-out plan that the group had laid out was completely unnecessary.

Accounts Receivable proceeded a little differently. There were several hundred programs involved in this effort and the strategy of testing the online programs as a set was followed. Afterward, the databases and files were refreshed and the batch processing was run against the new data. Following the batch processing, the databases were refreshed again, and the online processing was once more tested. All of the results were reported to management. Everything appeared on the surface to be as it ought to be, but the batch processing caused unexpected data corruption (not the dates, but the data following the dates in the copybooks) and incorrect data was put into "fields" where it didn't belong. Because the end-to-end scenario wasn't tested, the corruption wasn't uncovered in the testing phase and made it into production. The resulting production data corruption (caused by errant batch processing) meant that the company was unable to process payments to the organization for more than ten days.

The head programmer for both departments got the monthly award of excellence for their hard work. The head purchasing programmer got the award for making sure that all bills got paid and that every buyer in the organization could do their job adequately. The head programmer got the same award the following month for spending long hours working overtime to clean up the corruption and both reprocessing all of the payments and catching up on the intervening payments that didn't get processed while the repair work was under way.

Pay me now (when the project is under way) or pay me later (when the corruption happens or when the project is nearly over) but pay you will, and often the payment later will be a much higher price.

Load Testing

Load testing is the systematic and (often) automated exposure of an application to expected real-world conditions used to predict system behavior and both pinpoint and diagnose any undiscovered errors in an application and its infrastructure before the application is deployed in the environment. Load testing is typically used to analyze the following three aspects of an application's quality of service:

- **Performance**   The actual response times versus the expected or anticipated response times

- **Scalability**   Throughput—Can the application withstand the amount of data being thrown at it during a typical load, and can it withstand the stresses given the amount of data it receives during a peak load period?

- **Reliability**   The availability and functional integrity of the application and the system it's riding on

Of the three, reliability is often the one that gets the short end of the deal. People want faster, bigger, better and frequently aren't as concerned that the new change hasn't introduced undesirable side effects into the equation, such as data corruption, or missing or misstored data.

There are many types of load testing, just as there are many types of loads to be tested in an application. Each type of load testing checks for the performance results of a given function and provides information on a discrete set of tasks or a discrete set of information.

Some load tests check the peak stress levels for an entire application. This is done by simulating something that typically exceeds the maximum expected number of users of the application for a short but realistic period of time. The time period tested, just like the amount of work being done and the number of users being tested, should exceed realistic expectations by some percentage. The results of the excessive load should also be within acceptable parameters so you can assure users that the response expected will be within tolerable limits.

Other load tests might be designed to maintain a given number of users apparently performing processes for days at a stretch. This is done as a way to uncover memory leaks in the application or the underlying database structures.

Still other load tests might be set up as a means to stress a single application component—for example, one of the middleware components such as the iAS Web service, in order to verify its performance singly, before testing the performance of the overall composite application. This can be done outside of testing during an application testing cycle.

Regardless of the specifics, all load tests aim to make an application more reliable by identifying where, when, and under what circumstances the application breaks.

How to Determine Possible Loads

How can you test possible loads before implementing the application and finding out exactly what's happening instead of contemplating what the load might be? This is a tricky proposition at best. You'll need to have an understanding of the number of users who access the application, anticipate how many hours a day the application will be in use, how fast a user can possibly process a transaction, and how many transactions an hour a super-user can possibly process. Always assume the estimates given to you are low or at least inaccurate. Multiply the maximum number of users by 20 percent so you have a buffer zone for the peaks that you don't anticipate. Multiply that by the number of hours a day users will access the application and then multiply that by the maximum number of transactions that super-users could process an hour. Got that number? Now multiply that by a 10-percent fudge factor, which will make sure you have adequate load. The result is the number you should use to be certain your application can handle the maximum load possible.

Regression Testing

How do you insure that your new application software won't negatively affect existing production databases, applications, or processes? One of the best ways to test that the existing overall applications aren't adversely impacted is to check the current applications using the test cases. But how do you do this without actually impacting production data or the system and end users of the current system?

One good way to do this is to create a representative regression-testing database, which can be a clone of your production database.

Clone

Backing up the production database can be done as a full cold backup, or as a hot backup complete with archive logs. Afterward, take this backup, copy it to tape, and then keep the tape safe for the duration of the testing effort. The backup, naturally, needs to include the trace file, which was created by issuing the BACKUP CONTROLFILE TO TRACE command.

Re-create that backup as the database against which the regression tests are run. If you keep this database backup, you can use it as the baseline against which all future tests are run on the units, components, or the system as a whole. While you as the DBA should be the one who re-creates this database as a means of providing testers with an environment for testing, this isn't always the case. It's okay to test on a nearly duplicate environment, but if at all possible, precise duplication of the database should be what you strive for. You, as well as members of the QA team or IT team, need to make sure the data available for testing is representative of the data in both the production database and the new application.

So, how do you re-create the new database? Use a backup that you take of the production database especially for the testing process and rename it using the new database's name. Take a "BACKUP CONTROLFILE TO TRACE" and fix it so you can change the database to a new name. Rename the paths to the datafiles, and the redo logs to the location where you've recovered the backup, and then create your new initialization file. You're now ready for testing.

```
STARTUP NOMOUNT
CREATE CONTROLFILE REUSE
SET DATABASE <new database name> RESETLOGS...
```

Once you've created the database properly and it's running correctly, take a cold backup of the database. It's easier and quicker to recover the database from this cold backup than it would be to re-create it from the original backup.

The selective retesting of the components or systems that have been modified should be done as a way to ensure that bugs have been fixed and that no previously working functions have failed as a result of the repairs done on the software or database.

Regression testing is often referred to as verification testing. It is initiated after the programmers have attempted to fix a found issue or after someone has added source code to a new or existing program that may have inadvertently introduced errors.

It's important that all applications be so tested, whether they're web applications or more traditional applications. In practice, web applications aren't tested as thoroughly as traditional applications—in fact, they're often overlooked entirely. Thus, it's important this practice not continue since web applications aren't always the most efficient or dependable. Such applications are also much more vulnerable to attacks and hacking, which can have potentially devastating results on your systems and databases. Needless to say, testing all components is critical to both your applications and users. Regression testing, meanwhile, needs to be done on all tiers.

Regression testing should be done when you modify or implement a program. Re-run the original tests against the modified code in order to determine whether or not the changes have fixed everything or broken something. This is one of the reasons why it's important to keep track of the tests you've already run and re-run the same tests so you can be sure you're testing in the same way and using the same process you did before. While it is important that you have adequate coverage for the changes, the testing, and verifying the testing of the changes, it's also important that you try to spend as little time as possible to do an adequate job or re-testing. Spend enough time to make sure though that you detect new failures and to verify already tested code, but don't waste time digging for just one more if you can't seem to find any more.

Fix bugs and test those fixes promptly. Make sure that not only were the symptoms fixed, but the underlying causes as well. Watch for new side effects of the fixes to make sure your fixes don't create new bugs. Make certain, too, that you document all of the bugs, what was done to fix them, and the database's behavior after the alterations. If you find that two or more tests are very similar, decide which of the tests is least effective and get rid of it. Identify those tests that all programs pass, and archive them. Don't get rid of them, because you may find it necessary to dig them back up, and it would be a waste of time to reinvent what has already been created. Make sure you measure memory usage that can be attributed directly to the application.

Be certain to focus not only on functional issues but design issues as well, find the places where extreme inefficiencies arise, and make sure they run as efficiently as possible within the constraints of the user requirements.

Check that all data changes, large and small, were anticipated and that no corruption was introduced by the application or appeared as a side effect of the application.

Building a Library

One of the most effective approaches to regression testing is to create a library of a standard battery of test cases that you can attribute to the given application. One of the most difficult and important things to do when setting up the library is to determine what test cases to include. It's best to err on the side of caution when determining what to include in the library. Embrace quality tests rather than simply quantity. Automated tests are always good to include as well. So are test cases involving boundary conditions. Response timing should also belong in a library. It's important that any tests that have uncovered bugs be included, particularly if they have uncovered bugs in more than one instance.

Periodically review the regression test library so you can eliminate outdated, redundant, or unnecessary tests. Add new tests as issues arise and as they're required. Go through the library every three or four testing cycles, too, to make sure you're neither duplicating efforts nor missing chances to catch issues.

A second library may often be handy to keep track of those tests developed when a bug arises or when one test is particularly onerous. Numerous tests may end up written and added to the regression test library, and while these tests are good to keep around, and are useful for fixing the bug for which they were created, keeping duplicate tests, or irrelevant tests that have never uncovered anything, is simply a waste of resources. Select only the best of these tests and remove the rest.

Tools

Tools? What testing tools? I thought testing was a tool. It is, but there are tools that are created that are very effective in the testing effort. There are even modules available for testing Oracle E-Business Suite. It is often more effective to invest in the additional software to assist with the testing effort than it is to create the test cases yourself. This is particularly true when you have to work at testing multiple applications at once or applications that are constantly evolving and that are required to work in diverse environments. Organizations with limited resources, or resources that are increasingly under pressure to deliver more and deliver high-quality products with fewer resources on tighter and tighter schedules, often benefit greatly from the additional help that tools can bring.

Mercury WinRunner

One of the popular testing tools for Oracle programs is Mercury WinRunner, which is excellent for enterprise-wide testing. It's the answer to many organizations' needs for functional and regression testing, providing them with a means to capture, verify, and replay user interaction over and over again (load testing is more easily captured with this kind of interface). It also allows them to identify defects and ensures that business processes work whenever deployed. Thus, they can automate repetitive tasks and optimize testing efforts with a single testing tool.

OUNIT

Want to opt for an open-source (and therefore inexpensive) answer? OUNIT might be the tool for you. A product of the utPLSQL Sourceforge development site, OUNIT is a unit testing framework for programmers. It's created using Oracle's PL/SQL language and allows for the automated testing of packages, functions, and procedures. The documentation is available as a part of the utPLSQL download from https://sourceforge.net/project/showfiles.php?group_id=6633 or is available online at http://utplsql.sourceforge.net/Doc/index.html. A discussion group at utplsql.oracledevleoper.nl can provide you with answers to any issues you have.

Optimization

One tangential topic that is somewhat related to testing, yet nearly touches tuning, is optimization. Optimization, particularly when taken in the context of testing, is the process by which you can identify bottlenecks introduced to the system, or to the overall system, by an additional application. While other testing and optimization testing can become nearly as all-consuming as tuning, particularly if there are fuzzy requirements or an overly demanding user community, it is nonetheless something that needs to be done. Care can be taken to assure that scope creep does not overtake the optimization process.

Collection

You should always collect data on the existing system as a means to determine the baseline performance of the system and then compare that to the new application's performance. You can do a preliminary load test of the existing system so you have a realistic set of measurements to use to compare the incremental changes that are introduced by the new or changed application.

This added impact includes measuring the impact of the system or systems on the server's performance and on the performance of other applications on the server.

Analysis

Look at the baseline data and compare it to the data gathered during your testing efforts. Determine if the change in performance of all of the systems is acceptable.

By analyzing performance data, you can develop optimization theories that identify potential bottlenecks. If you can identify bottlenecks introduced by the application, they can either be removed, moved, or minimized as a result of optimization testing.

Configuration

You should also identify, document, and make adjustments in the configuration of the database or existing code. If you can, attempt to make small changes to the target system once problems have been identified through testing. You can then determine how the changes will affect the production system and thus have a chance to alter the settings in the real environment or back out of the settings if they have a detrimental effect on the overall system.

Testing Again

Test, test, and test again to determine if your theories are true. Make sure that the changes you have made are not introducing anything unintended to the system and that everything on the system still performs as anticipated. Without baseline data, it's impossible to determine if your modifications will help or hinder the application.

Summary

Testing often gets the short end of the stick. It's usually viewed as a necessary evil, but it's just as important to the database design or database application programming effort to the success of the project. While testing is no simpler than any other part of the programming process, and requires at least as much planning as any of its other pieces, it is the most critical step in ensuring a successful project that an organization can undertake.

GLOSSARY

%FOUND   Attribute of a cursor used to determine if the cursor affected any rows. Returns TRUE if an INSERT, UPDATE, or DELETE statement affected one or more rows, or a SELECT INTO statement returned one or more rows. Otherwise, %FOUND yields FALSE or NULL. Returns TRUE after fetches if there has been a row returned; otherwise, returns FALSE.

%ISOPEN   Attribute of a cursor used to determine if the cursor has been open; only applicable to explicit cursors.

%NOTFOUND   Attribute of a cursor used to determine if the cursor affected any rows. Yields FALSE or NULL if an INSERT, UPDATE, or DELETE statement affected one or more rows, or a SELECT INTO statement returned one or more rows. Otherwise, %NOTFOUND yields true. Returns FALSE after fetches if there has been a row returned; otherwise, returns TRUE.

%ROWCOUNT   Attribute of a cursor containing information on how many rows have been fetched for a cursor for a fetch statement. Before the first fetch, %ROWCOUNT returns 0, thereafter it will return the number of rows fetched so far, incremented every time the previous fetch returned a row. %ROWCOUNT can also return NULL.

%ROWTYPE   Attribute of a cursor used to provide a representation of a row; typically derived from the definition of the row in the table. The derived record stores data from an entire row selected from the table or that has been fetched from a cursor. Table columns used to define the row and the corresponding fields in a %ROWTYPE have the same names and datatypes.

ADDM   See *Automatic Database Diagnostic Monitor*.

AFTER trigger   Trigger defined as executing its logic following a successful triggering statement. Can be defined at the statement level or at the row level for a table.

aggregation   The process of rolling data values up into a smaller number of values or a coarser degree of storage. For example, all sales might be stored, then all sales for a day might be aggregated at the end of the day, and then all sales for a week aggregated from the daily sales at the end of the week/month/quarter/year depending on business rules and requirements.

ALLOCATE CHANNEL   Command used to manually allocate a channel between RMAN and the database instance. The command initiates a server session on the target that performs the work of backing up, restoring, or recovering.

ARCHIVELOG mode   The database operational mode where Oracle automatically copies the filled online redo logs off to another location on disk as a more permanent means of storing them. This is advantageous when requirements dictate that you be able to recover the database to a point in time other than the last cold backup. ARCHIVELOG mode is necessary for online backups (or hot backups) of the database. Unless you're willing to lose all data modifications since your last full cold backup, or unless you're able to easily and quickly re-create the data in the database from its ultimate source, then your database has to be in ARCHIVELOG mode. Honestly, it's just a matter of time. If you're not in ARCHIVELOG mode, then someday you will have an event that causes you to lose data. At that point, you'll lose all data modifications. If your database is in read-only mode, then this may not be as big an issue. Nevertheless, you have to make the informed decision not to be running in ARCHIVELOG mode.

ASM   See *Automatic Storage Management.*

ASMM   See *Automatic Shared Memory Management.*

Automatic Database Diagnostic Monitor (ADDM)   A separately licensed monitoring utility that allows your database to diagnose its own performance and attempt to determine how best to resolve problems that it identifies. ADDM runs automatically each time after AWR holds the captured statistics on the current workload, thereby making the performance diagnostic data readily available.

Automatic Shared Memory Management (ASMM)   Oracle 10g functionality that automatically readjusts the sizes of the main pools of memory in the SGA (db_cache_size, shared_pool_size, large_pool_size, and java_pool_size). These areas are resized based on existing workloads. Oracle Automatic

Shared Memory Management requires that the database be running using SPFILE. It must have sga_target set to a nonzero number, statistics_level must be set to TYPICAL or ALL, and shared_pool_size needs to be set to a nonzero number. This functionality is separately licensed.

Automatic Storage Management (ASM)   The manager provided by Oracle (should you choose to implement it) that takes control of I/O tuning and extends the concept of striping and mirroring everything into one centrally integrated utility. Allocation of space to datafiles is handled automatically by this utility.

Automatic Storage Management disk   The unit of storage that's added or removed from ASM managed space.

Automatic Storage Management file   The unit of allocation stored in an ASM managed disk group. These files are not visible at the operating-system level or to OS utilities, but are accessible to all Oracle-supplied tools and utilities.

automatic undo management mode   The mode of operating the database wherein the creation and management of the segments needed to hold the undo is performed by the database itself in a dedicated undo tablespace. The only undo management you must perform is the creation of the undo tablespace.

Automatic Workload Repository (AWR)   A repository in an Oracle Database that houses snapshots of all of that database's vital statistics and workload information.

AWR   See *Automatic Workload Repository.*

background process   An Oracle process, a set of which gets started on every instance, typically at instance startup, with the purpose of consolidating those functions that support user processes but that would otherwise have to be handled by multiple Oracle programs running for each user process. Examples are PMON, SMON, LGWR, and DBWR.

backup   A copy of something (for example, the Oracle Database data) that's made of the entire database, one or more tablespaces, one or more tables, one or more datafiles, the control file, or the archived redo logs. The backup is taken by one of several methods: RMAN, Export, or OS utilities.

backup set   A binary file backup of one or more logically grouped datafiles, control files, or archived logs that's produced by the RMAN BACKUP command and that can only be restored by the RMAN utility.

BEFORE trigger   A trigger that executes before the triggering action takes place, often used to assure referential integrity or other business rules. Can be fired at both the statement level and the row level.

buffer cache   The portion of the SGA that's shared by all user processes currently connected to the instance and whose purpose it is to hold copies of Oracle datablocks.

cache recovery   The roll forward part of instance recovery where Oracle applies all changes in the redo log files, committed and uncommitted, to their affected datablocks.

CHECK constraint   An integrity constraint on one or more columns, setting up a condition that must evaluate to true for every row of a given table. If any DML statement causes the condition to evaluate to false, the statement is rolled back. This assumes that the constraints are nondeferred constraints.

checkpoint   The act of flushing dirty blocks from the cache to the disk.

cluster   Optional structure in Oracle used for storing table data physically in the same blocks for one or more logically related tables. Used for improving disk access times.

column   Construct in a table that's used to represent a particular domain of data. Has a name and data type associated with it (and hopefully a comment) and is the named value in the SELECT statement.

commit   To make changes to data permanent.

connection   Communication pathway between a user and an Oracle instance.

consistent backup   A whole database backup that does not require media recovery to be complete. There is no need to apply redo logs in order for the database to be consistent. This can only be accomplished when you've taken the backup after a clean shutdown of the database and before the database has been reopened. Also known as a cold backup.

control file   A special database file that records information about the physical structure of the database. Contains the database name, the names and locations of associated datafiles and redo log files, the date and time that the database was created, the current log sequence number, and the checkpoint information (SCN). If RMAN is used for backups, the control files will also contain backup information. Should be multiplexed. Read at database startup. When RMAN is used, contains considerable backup-related data.

database   A collection of data stored for easy retrieval of related information, which is treated as a unit.

database buffer   Memory structures that store recently used blocks of data within the System Global Area.

data block   The smallest logical unit of data storage in an Oracle database which corresponds to a specified number of bytes of physical space on the disks.

data dictionary   The central set of views and their underlying tables. Used as read-only reference for information about the database to which it is associated.

datafile   A physical file that can be observed at the operating-system level on disk. The file was created by Oracle, is associated with exactly one tablespace in exactly one database, and contains datablocks that are grouped into extents. Datafiles can be associated, as read-only, with multiple databases.

datafile copy   A copy of a datafile on storage media produced by either the RMAN COPY command or an operating system utility.

data integrity   The reliability of the data and its ability to adhere to the business rules set as a measurement of the standards for acceptable data.

DDL   Data definition language. Defines the storage of the data and the definition of the data itself.

dedicated server   A database server configuration in which a single server process handles requests for a single user process.

disk group   One or more ASM disks that are managed as a logical unit.

dispatcher processes (Dnnn)   Optional background processes that are present on the system if a shared server configuration is used. Responsible for routing requests from a connected user to any available shared server process that's running and for returning the process's responses to the user.

distributed processing   IT architecture that makes use of software resources and multiple computers to divide up processing of a group of jobs. The purpose is to reduce the processing load on a single computer and speed up processing of the jobs involved.

DML   Data manipulation language. Statements that manipulate the data (insert it, update it, delete it, or select it) in a database.

Enterprise Manager (EM)   Also known as Oracle Enterprise Manager (OEM), this is a graphical user interface database management tool that's provided by Oracle as a centralized interface through which you can manage your database environment (and in Oracle 10g, more of your overall environment). Also known as Grid Control in Oracle 10g.

fencing   I/O technology used to keep database corruption from occurring in an RAC environment.

foreign key   Referential integrity constraint set so that each value in a column or set of columns in a given table is required to match a value in a related table (either another table, or to the data within the same table) that is either defined as unique or as a primary key.

import   An Oracle-provided utility that's used to get external data located in an Oracle binary file into a database (either the original or an alternative database on the same or different platforms).

inconsistent backup   Hot backup, or open database backup, in which some of the files in the backup contain changes made after the files were checkpointed. Can only be accomplished if the database is in ARCHIVELOG mode. This type of backup needs recovery before the database can be assumed to be consistent. While inconsistent backups are typically made deliberately while the database is open, they are also the backup definition used when a backup is taken after an instance failure, or after SHUTDOWN ABORT (or after kill –9 on a background process).

index   An optional but highly useful relational database structure that's associated with tables, materialized views, and clusters and is used as a means to (usually) speed up query access to data on that table.

instance   The set of a System Global Area (SGA) and the associated background processes that support access of an Oracle database.

integrity constraint   Definition of a rule for a column or set of columns of a table that's used to enforced business rules that have been defined as applicable to the data in the database. The primary goal is to prevent invalid data from being entered inadvertently into the database.

key   A column (or set of columns) that is included in the definition of certain types of integrity constraints (primary keys, foreign keys, unique keys) and is used to describe the relationship or lack of relationship between data elements in a given table or between data in different tables.

large pool　Optional portion of the System Global Area used to provide large memory allocations. Most often used for Oracle backup and restore operations, but that's also available for session memory for shared server configurations.

LAST_CALL_ET　V$SESSION view column containing the number of seconds since the last call made in a given session and usually used to determine just how idle a given session has been.

logical backups　Backups created using the Export utility and stored in a binary dump file at the operating-system level. This dump file can then be read by (actually it can *only* be read by) the Import utility to import the data back into the database. Database logical objects are exported independently of the files that, in the source database, contain those objects and can be imported into different databases and even databases on different platforms.

manual undo management mode　A mode of database operation where undo blocks are stored in user-managed rollback segments rather than in undo tablespaces.

materialized view　A construct that stores the results of a query physically in a schema object. It's designed to speed up access to information and can be indexed.

mean time to recover (MTTR)　The maximum desired time required for you to perform instance or media recovery on the database. Often used as the basis for Service Level Agreements. Influenced by the speed of detection (and who is doing the detecting), the method used for recovery, and the size of the database.

multiplex　To create multiple copies of control files or redo log files to help prevent a downed database caused by the loss of the primary copy.

NOT NULL　Data integrity constraint that's set so a column of a table can contain no null values.

NULL   Absence of any value in a column of a row in the database; indicates missing, unknown, or inapplicable data, is ALWAYS unique, and should never be used to imply any valid data.

online backup   Hot backup; inconsistent backup. A backup of one or more datafiles that's taken while the database is open and the datafiles are online.

online redo log   A set of two or more circular queue files whose purpose is to record all changes made to Oracle datafiles and control files. Should always be multiplexed.

PGA   See *Program Global Area.*

physical backup   Backup of Oracle database–related files (datafiles, archived redo logs, or control files) that has been copied physically from one place to another; made using RMAN or operating-system commands.

PL/SQL   Oracle's procedural language (the PL part) extension to SQL that enables you to mix standard ANSI SQL with procedural constructs, and is often used to store program units within the database.

primary key   One or more columns that are included in the definition of a table's PRIMARY KEY constraint, ensuring that every value in the column is unique as well as not null.

PRIMARY KEY constraint   Integrity constraint whose purpose is to disallow duplicate values and nulls in a column or set of columns.

Program Global Area (PGA)   A memory region that Oracle maintains, containing data and control information for a single process (server or background). One PGA is allocated for each server process; it's exclusive to that server process and is read and written only by Oracle on behalf of that process. A PGA is allocated by Oracle when a user connects to an Oracle database and a session is created.

Real Application Clusters (RACs)   A high availability, scalability solution for Oracle databases where a single database has multiple instances.

record   Used to group data; tuple.

recovery   Using a database backup to recover from an instance or database crash.

Recovery Manager (RMAN)   A free Oracle utility to simplify, centralize, and maintain Oracle backups and recovery situations.

redo log   A set of circular queue-type files that protect altered database data in memory before it has been written to the datafiles. These files, when copied off to another location, become the archived redo log. See *online redo log*.

redo log buffer   Memory structure in the System Global Area designed to buffer the changes made to the database. The entries are stored in the redo log buffers, are next written to an online redo log file, and then written to the archived redo logs, all of which can be used if database recovery is necessary.

referential integrity   The rules surrounding the definition on a column or set of columns in one table that guarantee that the values in the key match the values in another key in a related table (either the same table or another table) and what manipulation actions are allowable on these values or the referenced values included in the definition.

rolling back   The use of rollback segments as a means to undo uncommitted transactions that were applied to the database during the rolling forward stage of recovery or that have occurred as a normal state of processing in the database.

rolling forward   The application of redo records to their associated datafiles and control files in order to recover changes to those files; precedes rolling back in instance recovery.

row Record, tuple, a set of attributes (values associated with a column) or values pertaining to one entity or record in a table.

ROWID A unique identifier for a row in a table in a database.

server process Process responsible for handling communication requests from connected user processes and for interacting with the database to carry out requests of the associated user process.

session A set of events that begins when a user connects to an Oracle database and ends when the user is disconnected (either deliberately or because of an error condition) from the database.

shared pool Part of the System Global Area that contains shared memory constructs and that processes every unique (down to the whitespace and capitalization) SQL statement submitted to a database.

shared server A database server configuration that minimizes the number of necessary server processes and maximizes the use of all available system resources by allowing multiple user processes to share a smaller number of server processes.

SQL Structured Query Language; often pronounced "sequel." A nonprocedural language to access data. Users describe in SQL what they want done, and the SQL language compiler automatically generates a procedure to navigate the database and perform the task. Oracle SQL includes many extensions to the ANSI/ISO standard SQL language.

SQL*Plus An Oracle-provided and -supported tool (either on the client machine or on the server) through which you can run SQL statements against an Oracle database.

standby database A copy of a production database that you can use for disaster recovery or so maintenance can be performed without any impact to the users. Standby databases are updated with redo logs from the primary database as a means of staying current.

synonym   An alias for any Oracle object, whether Oracle-defined or user-defined, which may include another synonym.

system change number (SCN)   An Oracle-defined and -controlled number that uniquely defines every committed version of a database (the state of the database at the point in time when a transaction is committed) at any given point in time.

System Global Area (SGA)   The group of shared memory structures that make up a single Oracle instance and contain the data and control information of that instance.

table   The basic unit of data storage in an Oracle database. Data is stored in a table in rows and columns, which are conceptually similar to a spreadsheet of a two-dimensional array.

tablespace   A database storage unit used to store objects and usually to group related structures together (tables, indexes, materialized views).

tempfile   A file that belongs to a temporary tablespace.

temporary segment   Segments that are created by Oracle whenever a transaction needs a temporary area to complete its execution. When the statements in question finish, the extents allocated to that temporary segment are made available to the system for reuse.

temporary tablespace   Temporary tablespaces, and by extension tempfiles, can contain no permanent database objects and are typically used for sorting. Information on tempfiles can be found in the V$TEMPFILE view.

transaction   A logical unit of work containing one or more SQL statements. All SQL statements associated with a transaction are committed or rolled back together.

transaction recovery   Recovering all committed transactions and rolling back all uncommitted transactions of a failed instance. If the uncommitted transactions managed to get saved to disk, Oracle uses undo data to reverse any changes that were written to datafiles but not yet committed.

trigger   A stored database procedure that is automatically invoked whenever a table or view is modified in a way that meets the definition of the trigger.

tuple   A set of value attributes in a relational database, record, or row.

UNIQUE KEY constraint   A data integrity constraint that's used to require that every value in a column or set of columns be unique so that no two rows in the table can contain duplicate values in the column or columns. Not analogous to PRIMARY KEY, however, because a UNIQUE KEY allows that every value in the column or columns can be NULL since NULL keys are always unique.

Username   The name by which a user is known to the Oracle database server; analogous to userid and schema name.

user process   Used to execute application code or Oracle tool code on behalf of a user.

view   A customized representation of data contained in one or more tables, often thought of as a stored query. Views are primarily conceptual constructs and contain no data directly, instead deriving their data when called based on data contained in the underlying table at the time they are accessed. Depending on the view definition, they can be queried, updated, inserted into, or deleted from; however, it's important to remember that all operations performed on a view affect not just the view, but its base tables.

whole database backup   A backup of all datafiles, redo log files, archive log files, and the control file belonging to the given database.

Index

%FOUND, 324
%ISOPEN, 324
%NOTFOUND, 324
%ROWCOUNT, 324
%ROWTYPE, 324
10032 trace, 161–162
10033 trace, 162–163
10046 trace, 157–160
10053 trace, 160
10104 trace, 163

A

access control
    Discretionary Access Control, 31–32
    Fine-Grained Access Control, 32–45
ADDM. *See* Automatic Database
    Diagnostic Monitor
AFTER triggers, 324
aggregation, 324–325
alert logs, 13
    monitoring using a shell script, 13–14
    monitoring using an external table,
        14–16
    monitors, 212–213
    renaming and moving, 17
    writing to and backing up, 16–17
ALLOCATE CHANNEL command, 325
amusement parks, 284–285
Apache, 267

application backups, 101–102
Application Desktop Integrator, 293
ARCHIVELOG mode, 103–104, 325
ASM. *See* Automatic Storage
    Management
ASMM. *See* Automatic Shared Memory
    Management
auditing, 68–69
    by access, 70
    database connections, 65–68
    objects, 72
    privilege auditing, 71–72
    by session, 70
    statement auditing, 71
    SYSDBA or SYSOPER, 72–73
    transaction success, 70
    turning auditing off, 73
authentication
    operating system, 56–57
    password file, 57–62
Automatic Database Diagnostic Monitor,
    325
Automatic SGA Memory Management,
    192–193
Automatic Shared Memory Management,
    325–326
Automatic Storage Management, 326
Automatic Storage Management disk, 326
Automatic Storage Management file, 326
automatic undo management mode, 326

Automatic Workload Repository, 326
automating tasks, 17
AUTOTRACE, 150–151
availability. *See* high availability
AWR. *See* Automatic Workload Repository

B

background processes, 49, 326
backup pieces, 130
backup sets, 130, 327
 creating, 135
 restoring and recovering from,
  135–136
backups, 98–100, 101, 327
 application, 101–102
 cold backups, 111–113, 115–116
 consistent, 328
 control files, 141–142
 with exports, 142–143
 inconsistent, 330
 logical, 101, 331
 online, 332
 physical, 101
 real-time, 125–126
 requirements, 108–109
 RMAN-managed, 107–108
 suspended, 126–127
 user-managed, 105–107
 warm, 116–125
 whole database, 336
Beck, Christopher, 37
BEFORE triggers, 327
blackouts, 254–255
block media recovery, 102
buffer cache, 50, 327
BULK COLLECT, 74–75

C

cache recovery, 327
Carmichael, Rachel, 23
catalog
 commands, 133

 connecting, 134
 creating catalogs, 133
 no recovery catalog option, 131–132
 recovery catalog, 132–133
 scripting, 137–139
channels, 129
 allocating, 134–135
CHECK constraints, 327
checking object status, 10–12
checking space, 4–10
checkpoints, 327
clusters, 197–199, 327
Clusterware, 235
cold backups, 111–113
 disadvantages, 115–116
 restoring from, 115
Collaboration Suite, 288
columns, 327
commits, 328
component testing, 309–310
concurrent managers, 291–292
CONNECT command, 62
connections, 48–52, 328
 auditing database connections, 65–68
 connecting as SYSDBA or SYSOPER,
  56–62
 connecting normally as a user, 52–53
 connecting with a script, 63
 connecting without a password, 53–55
 connecting without
  TNSNAMES.ORA, 55
 disconnecting users, 63–64
 limiting user connection time, 73
consistent backups, 328
control files, 328
 backing up, 141–142
control structures, 51
copying files, 114
crash recovery, 102
CREATE USER statement, 28–29
cursors, 83–84
 cursor FOR loops, 86–87
 explicit, 84–85
 implicit, 84

processing, 85–86
SELECT FOR UPDATE statements, 86
sharing, 176–177
Cygwin, 14

D

DAC. *See* Discretionary Access Control
data blocks, 328
Data Definition Language. *See* DDL
data dictionary, 328
Data Guard, 242–246
data integrity, 329
Data Manipulation Language. *See* DML
Data Pump, 181–183
database buffers, 328
Database Creation Assistant, 18
databases, 50, 328
    creating, 18–20
    design, 146–147
    monitoring, 213–216
    shutting down, 20–21
    starting up, 21–23
datafile copies, 329
datafiles, 328–329
DBCA. *See* Database Creation Assistant
DBMS_STATS, 189–190
DDL, 329
declarations, 77
dedicated servers, 329
diagnostic log viewer, 259
dictionary cache, 51
directives, resource group, 24, 25
disaster recovery, 103
disconnecting users, 63–64
    See also connections
Discoverer, 275–276
Discretionary Access Control, 31–32
disk groups, 329
dispatcher processes (Dnnn), 329
distributed processing, 329
DML, 329
    BULK COLLECT, 74–75
    FORALL, 74–75

downtime, cost of, 304
duplicate target, 130–131
Dynamic Sampling, 193

E

E-Business Suite, 289–290
    customization, 294–296
    passwords, 296–297
End to End Application Tracing, 191–192
Enterprise Manager (EM). *See* Oracle
    Enterprise Manager
errors, Fine-Grained Access Control
    (FGAC), 36
events, 257
exception handling, 78
executable statements, 77
EXPLAIN plan, 149, 151–156
explicit cursors, 84–85
export utility, 181–183
exports, backing up with, 142–143
external tables, monitoring alert logs,
    14–16

F

failover, 125–126
failures, 109–110
fencing, 233–234, 330
FGAC. *See* Fine-Grained Access Control
Financial Statement Generator, 293–294
Fine-Grained Access Control, 32–45
Flashback, 225–227
FOR loops
    cursor, 86–87
    numeric, 79–81
FORALL, 74–75
foreign keys, 330
FSG. *See* Financial Statement Generator

G

GATHER_STATS_JOB, 186, 188
Gorman, Tim, 4
Grid, 229–230, 247–248

H

HA. *See* high availability
hardware failure, and high availability, 227–229
high availability, 125, 224
    Flashback, 225–227
    and hardware failure, 227–229
    online reorganization, 224–225
history, 216
HTML DB, 279–282

I

IEEE floating-point types, 75
implicit cursors, 84
import utility, 181–183, 330
inconsistent backups, 330
indexes, 330
init file, 235–237
    init.ora parameters, 261
instance failure, 110
instance recovery, 102–103
instances, 50, 330
integration testing, 310–311
integrity constraints, 330
intelligent agents, 253–254
invalid objects, 264
    checking status of, 10–12
invoker's rights, 76–77
I/O fencing, 233–234
ITar, 209–212

J

jobs, 255–256
Jserv, 264–265

K

keys, 330
Kyte, Tom, 11, 36

L

large pools, 331
LAST_CALL_ET, 331
latches, 148–149
least privilege, 31
lexer, 277
library cache, 51
load testing, 314–315
locks, 148–149
logical backups, 101, 331
loops, 78
    controlling, 82–83
    cursor FOR loops, 86–87
    numeric FOR loops, 79–81
    simple loops, 78–79
    WHILE loops, 81–82

M

MAA. *See* Maximum Availability Architecture
manual undo management mode, 331
manufacturing, 284
materialized views, 194–197, 331
Maximum Availability Architecture, 246–247
mean time to recover, 331
media failure, 110
media management layer, 130
media recovery, 102
Mercury WinRunner, 319
Metalink, 209–212
mining, 284
MKS Toolkit, 14
MTTR. *See* mean time to recover
multiplex, 331

N

NBD. *See* Network Block Device
Network Block Device, 239–241
NOARCHIVE mode, 103–104

NOT NULL, 331
NULL, 332
numeric FOR loops, 79–81
Nyffenegger, René, 15

O

OAM. *See* Oracle Application Manager
objects
    auditing, 72
    checking status of, 10–12
OCFS. *See* Oracle Cluster File System
OEM. *See* Oracle Enterprise Manager
oerr utility, 204–208
OFA. *See* Optimal Flexible Architecture
online backups, 332
online redo logs, 332
operating system authentication, 56–57
operating systems, 184
OPS. *See* Oracle Parallel Server
Optimal Flexible Architecture, 18
optimization, 320–321
    See also testing
Oracle 10*g*
    Automatic SGA Memory
      Management, 192–193
    Data Guard enhancements, 246
    DBMS_STATS, 189–190
    Dynamic Sampling, 193
    End to End Application Tracing,
      191–192
    GATHER_STATS_JOB, 186, 188
    Scheduler, 186–188
    SQL Tuning Advisor, 190–191
    tracing enhancements, 185
Oracle 9*i* Lite, 271–274
Oracle Application Manager, 258
    Applications Usage Reports, 261–262
    concurrent manager processing,
      262–263
    configuration information, 258
    Database Status option, 263
    diagnostic log viewer, 259

forms runtime processes and forms
    sessions, 263–264
init.ora parameters, 261
invalid objects, 264
Jserv environment, 264–265
license manager, 260–261
Oracle Workflow Mailer, 258–259
Patch Advisor, 260
site level profile option settings, 265
system alerts, 259
Oracle Cluster File System, 234
Oracle Enterprise Manager, 213,
    250–251, 329
    blackouts, 254–255
    events, 257
    intelligent agents, 253–254
    jobs, 255–256
    standalone use, 251–253
Oracle Error utility, 204–208
Oracle Express, 266–267
    backup and recovery, 269–271
    connecting, 267–268
    querying, 268–269
Oracle *i*AS, 290–291
Oracle Parallel Server, 227–228
Oracle Text, 276–278
Oracle Workflow, 294
Oracle Workflow Mailer, 258–259
OTN, 232
OUNIT, 319

P

packages, 88–89
    bodies, 90–91
    specifications, 90
panic, 216–217
password group parameters, 24, 26–28
passwords
    changing the password file state,
      61–62
    connecting without, 53–55
    creating a password file, 57–59

E-Business Suite, 296–297
maintaining a password file, 59
removing a password file, 60
replacing a password file, 59–60
Patch Advisor, 260
performance, speeding up Oracle on Windows, 184–185
PFILE, 19–20, 236–237
PGA. *See* Program Global Area
physical backups, 101, 332
PL/SQL, 73–74, 332
    BULK COLLECT, 74–75
    controlling loops, 82–83
    cursors, 83–87
    declarations, 77
    error checking and reporting, 87
    exception handling, 78
    executable statements, 77
    FORALL, 74–75
    functions, 87–88
    IEEE floating-point types, 75
    invoker's rights, 76–77
    native compilation, 75–76
    numeric FOR loops, 79–81
    packages, 88–91
    procedures, 77–78
    simple loops, 78–79
    WHILE loops, 81–82
    wrapping code, 91–93
PRIMARY KEY constraints, 332
primary keys, 332
private SQL area, 51
privilege auditing, 71–72
processes, 49
profiles, 23–25
Program Global Area, 51, 332

Q

query-only picture, 125
quick recovery, 125

R

RACs. *See* Real Application Clusters
Rapid Application Development, 274
raw devices, 234
RDA. *See* Remote Diagnostic Agent
Real Application Clusters, 227–229, 230–231, 232, 333
    creating on the cheap, 241
    on multiple VMware nodes, 239
    with network block devices, 239–241
    on a single VMware node, 238–239
    single-node on Linux, 237–238
    trying out, 232–233
real-time backups, 125–126
records, 333
recovery, 98–100, 102–103, 333
    RMAN-managed, 107–108
    user-managed, 105–107
recovery catalog, 129, 132–133
    scripting, 137–139
    See also catalog
Recovery Manager, 127–128, 333
    parameters, 139–141
redo log buffers, 50, 333
redo logs, 333
redundancy sets, 100, 101
referential integrity, 333
REGISTER DATABASE command, 134
regression testing, 316–318
Remote Diagnostic Agent, 220–221
reporting, 137
resource group directives, 24, 25
RESOURCE_LIMIT initialization parameter, 23
restarting, 202–203
restoring, 101
retention policy, 130–131
RMAN, 127–128, 333
    backups and recovery, 107–108, 130
    executables, 129
    parameters, 139–141
    server process, 129
roles, 29–30

rolling back, 333
rolling forward, 333
ROWID, 334
rows, 334

S

SageLogix, 4
Scheduler, 186–188
SCN. *See* system change number
scripting, 137–139
SELECT FOR UPDATE statements, 86
server processes, 49, 334
sessions, 49, 334
SGA. *See* System Global Area
shared pool, 50, 334
shared servers, 334
shared SQL area, 51
shell scripts, to monitor alert logs, 13–14
shutdown, 20–21, 111–112
    abort, 113
    if it doesn't stop, 203–204
    immediate, 112
    normal, 112
    transactional, 112
simple loops, 78–79
software code area, 50
sort areas, 51
space, checking the amount of, 4–10
Spatial, 283–286
spc.sql script, 4–9
SPFILE, 19–20, 235–237
SQL, 334
SQL scripts
    spc.sql script, 4–9
    utlrp.sql script, 10
SQL Tuning Advisor, 190–191
SQL Workshop, 280
SQL*Plus, 334
standby databases, 125, 242–244, 334
startup, 21–23, 114–115
    if it doesn't start, 203
    restarting, 202–203
statement auditing, 71

Statspack, 169–172
suspended backups, 126–127
synonyms, 335
SYSDBA, 20
    auditing, 72–73
    connecting as, 56–62
SYSOPER, 20
    auditing, 72–73
    connecting as, 56–62
system alerts, 259
system change number, 335
System Global Area, 50, 335

T

tables, 335
tablespaces, 335
    putting into backup mode, 116–118
TAF. *See* Transparent Application Failover
target database, 129
tempfiles, 335
temporary segments, 335
temporary tablespaces, 335
test cases, 221
testing
    component testing, 309–310
    defined, 304
    evolutionary approach, 302–303
    examples, 311–314
    functional, 306–307
    integration testing, 310–311
    load testing, 314–315
    planning and organization, 300–303
    regression testing, 316–318
    requirements-based, 303
    as a tool, 304–305
    tools, 319
    unit testing, 307–309
    waterfall method, 301
    See also optimization
TKPROF, 164–167
TNSNAMES.ORA, connecting without, 55
tnsping, 218
Trace Analyzer, 167–168

traces, 149–150
    10032 trace, 161–162
    10033 trace, 162–163
    10046 trace, 157–160
    10053 trace, 160
    10104 trace, 163
    AUTOTRACE, 150–151
    End to End Application Tracing,
      191–192
    finding trace files, 163–164
    Oracle 10*g* enhancements, 185
    TKPROF, 164–167
    TRCSESS, 168–169
transaction recovery, 335
transactions, 335
Transparent Application Failover, 228
TRCSESS, 168–169
triggers, 93–95, 336
    before logoff trigger, 66–67
    BEFORE triggers, 327
troubleshooting
    database links, 218–220
    no Oracle connectivity, 218
tuning
    application tuning, 147
    database parameters, 173–179
    database structure, 179–181
    disk I/O tuning, 147
    memory tuning, 147
    operating system tuning, 149
    SQL Tuning Advisor, 190–191
tuples, 336

U

Ultra Search, 282–283
UNIQUE KEY constraints, 336

unit testing, 307–309
user process failure, 109–111
user processes, 49, 336
usernames, 336
users, 172–173
    limiting user connection time, 73
    profiles, 23–25
utlrp.sql script, 10

V

V$FILESTAT, 173–175
V$LATCH, 175
V$LIBRARYCACHE, 175–176
V$LOCK, 177–179
V$SQL_PLAN, 156–157
views, 336
virtual memory, 50

W

wait events, 169–172
Warehouse Builder, 274–275
warm backups, 116–118, 124–125
    recovering from, 123–124
    scripting, 118–123
WHILE loops, 81–82
whole database backups, 336
Windows, speeding up Oracle on,
    184–185
work areas, 51
workspaces, 279–280
wrapping code, 91–93

X

XML DB, 286–287

Get Certified Fast

Save 75% online and cut your learning time in half.

Looking to jump on the certification fast track? Oracle University s innovative learning methods ACCELERATE the certification process. What might take you 6 months of in-classroom training takes as little as 12 weeks with our online and CD-ROM-based learning methods. And you ll SAVE as much as 75% when you LEARN ONLINE, compared to our traditional training methods. Get the same high-quality material, at less than half the cost in time and money.

Oracle University. Knowledge from the people who know.

Become a certified professional. *Log on to www.oracle.com/education* today.

ORACLE | CERTIFIED PROFESSIONAL

ORACLE

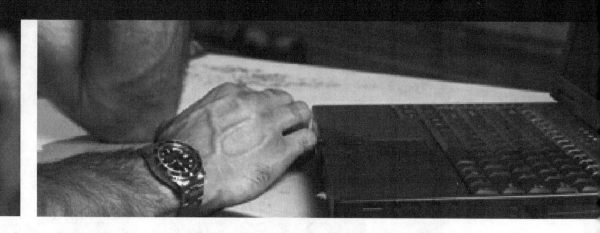

GET YOUR FREE SUBSCRIPTION
TO ORACLE MAGAZINE

Oracle Magazine is essential gear for today's information technology professionals. Stay informed and increase your productivity with every issue of *Oracle Magazine*. Inside each free bimonthly issue you'll get:

- Up-to-date information on Oracle Database, Oracle Application Server, Web development, enterprise grid computing, database technology, and business trends
- Third-party vendor news and announcements
- Technical articles on Oracle and partner products, technologies, and operating environments
- Development and administration tips
- Real-world customer stories

IF THERE ARE OTHER ORACLE USERS AT YOUR LOCATION WHO WOULD LIKE TO RECEIVE THEIR OWN SUBSCRIPTION TO ORACLE MAGAZINE, PLEASE PHOTOCOPY THIS FORM AND PASS IT ALONG.

Three easy ways to subscribe:

① Web
Visit our Web site at otn.oracle.com/oraclemagazine. You'll find a subscription form there, plus much more!

② Fax
Complete the questionnaire on the back of this card and fax the questionnaire side only to +1.847.763.9638.

③ Mail
Complete the questionnaire on the back of this card and mail it to P.O. Box 1263, Skokie, IL 60076-8263

ORACLE®

FREE SUBSCRIPTION

○ **Yes, please send me a FREE subscription to *Oracle Magazine*.**   ○ **NO**

To receive a free subscription to *Oracle Magazine*, you must fill out the entire card, sign it, and date it (incomplete cards cannot be processed or acknowledged). You can also fax your application to +1.847.763.9638.
Or subscribe at our Web site at otn.oracle.com/oraclemagazine

○ From time to time, Oracle Publishing allows our partners exclusive access to our e-mail addresses for special promotions and announcements. To be included in this program, please check this circle.

○ Oracle Publishing allows sharing of our mailing list with selected third parties. If you prefer your mailing address not to be included in this program, please check here. If at any time you would like to be removed from this mailing list, please contact Customer Service at +1.847.647.9630 or send an e-mail to oracle@halldata.com.

signature (required)   date

X

name   title

company   e-mail address

street/p.o. box

city/state/zip or postal code   telephone

country   fax

YOU MUST ANSWER ALL TEN QUESTIONS BELOW.

① WHAT IS THE PRIMARY BUSINESS ACTIVITY OF YOUR FIRM AT THIS LOCATION? (check one only)
- ☐ 01 Aerospace and Defense Manufacturing
- ☐ 02 Application Service Provider
- ☐ 03 Automotive Manufacturing
- ☐ 04 Chemicals, Oil and Gas
- ☐ 05 Communications and Media
- ☐ 06 Construction/Engineering
- ☐ 07 Consumer Sector/Consumer Packaged Goods
- ☐ 08 Education
- ☐ 09 Financial Services/Insurance
- ☐ 10 Government (civil)
- ☐ 11 Government (military)
- ☐ 12 Healthcare
- ☐ 13 High Technology Manufacturing, OEM
- ☐ 14 Integrated Software Vendor
- ☐ 15 Life Sciences (Biotech, Pharmaceuticals)
- ☐ 16 Mining
- ☐ 17 Retail/Wholesale/Distribution
- ☐ 18 Systems Integrator, VAR/VAD
- ☐ 19 Telecommunications
- ☐ 20 Travel and Transportation
- ☐ 21 Utilities (electric, gas, sanitation, water)
- ☐ 98 Other Business and Services

② WHICH OF THE FOLLOWING BEST DESCRIBES YOUR PRIMARY JOB FUNCTION? (check one only)
Corporate Management/Staff
- ☐ 01 Executive Management (President, Chair, CEO, CFO, Owner, Partner, Principal)
- ☐ 02 Finance/Administrative Management (VP/Director/ Manager/Controller, Purchasing, Administration)
- ☐ 03 Sales/Marketing Management (VP/Director/Manager)
- ☐ 04 Computer Systems/Operations Management (CIO/VP/Director/ Manager MIS, Operations)
IS/IT Staff
- ☐ 05 Systems Development/ Programming Management
- ☐ 06 Systems Development/ Programming Staff
- ☐ 07 Consulting
- ☐ 08 DBA/Systems Administrator
- ☐ 09 Education/Training
- ☐ 10 Technical Support Director/Manager
- ☐ 11 Other Technical Management/Staff
- ☐ 98 Other

③ WHAT IS YOUR CURRENT PRIMARY OPERATING PLATFORM? (select all that apply)
- ☐ 01 Digital Equipment UNIX
- ☐ 02 Digital Equipment VAX VMS
- ☐ 03 HP UNIX

- ☐ 04 IBM AIX
- ☐ 05 IBM UNIX
- ☐ 06 Java
- ☐ 07 Linux
- ☐ 08 Macintosh
- ☐ 09 MS-DOS
- ☐ 10 MVS
- ☐ 11 NetWare
- ☐ 12 Network Computing
- ☐ 13 OpenVMS
- ☐ 14 SCO UNIX
- ☐ 15 Sequent DYNIX/ptx
- ☐ 16 Sun Solaris/SunOS
- ☐ 17 SVR4
- ☐ 18 UnixWare
- ☐ 19 Windows
- ☐ 20 Windows NT
- ☐ 21 Other UNIX
- ☐ 98 Other
- 99 ☐ None of the above

④ DO YOU EVALUATE, SPECIFY, RECOMMEND, OR AUTHORIZE THE PURCHASE OF ANY OF THE FOLLOWING? (check all that apply)
- ☐ 01 Hardware
- ☐ 02 Software
- ☐ 03 Application Development Tools
- ☐ 04 Database Products
- ☐ 05 Internet or Intranet Products
- 99 ☐ None of the above

⑤ IN YOUR JOB, DO YOU USE OR PLAN TO PURCHASE ANY OF THE FOLLOWING PRODUCTS? (check all that apply)
Software
- ☐ 01 Business Graphics
- ☐ 02 CAD/CAE/CAM
- ☐ 03 CASE
- ☐ 04 Communications
- ☐ 05 Database Management
- ☐ 06 File Management
- ☐ 07 Finance
- ☐ 08 Java
- ☐ 09 Materials Resource Planning
- ☐ 10 Multimedia Authoring
- ☐ 11 Networking
- ☐ 12 Office Automation
- ☐ 13 Order Entry/Inventory Control
- ☐ 14 Programming
- ☐ 15 Project Management
- ☐ 16 Scientific and Engineering
- ☐ 17 Spreadsheets
- ☐ 18 Systems Management
- ☐ 19 Workflow

Hardware
- ☐ 20 Macintosh
- ☐ 21 Mainframe
- ☐ 22 Massively Parallel Processing
- ☐ 23 Minicomputer
- ☐ 24 PC
- ☐ 25 Network Computer
- ☐ 26 Symmetric Multiprocessing
- ☐ 27 Workstation
Peripherals
- ☐ 28 Bridges/Routers/Hubs/Gateways
- ☐ 29 CD-ROM Drives
- ☐ 30 Disk Drives/Subsystems
- ☐ 31 Modems
- ☐ 32 Tape Drives/Subsystems
- ☐ 33 Video Boards/Multimedia
Services
- ☐ 34 Application Service Provider
- ☐ 35 Consulting
- ☐ 36 Education/Training
- ☐ 37 Maintenance
- ☐ 38 Online Database Services
- ☐ 39 Support
- ☐ 40 Technology-Based Training
- ☐ 98 Other
- 99 ☐ None of the above

⑥ WHAT ORACLE PRODUCTS ARE IN USE AT YOUR SITE? (check all that apply)
Oracle E-Business Suite
- ☐ 01 Oracle Marketing
- ☐ 02 Oracle Sales
- ☐ 03 Oracle Order Fulfillment
- ☐ 04 Oracle Supply Chain Management
- ☐ 05 Oracle Procurement
- ☐ 06 Oracle Manufacturing
- ☐ 07 Oracle Maintenance Management
- ☐ 08 Oracle Service
- ☐ 09 Oracle Contracts
- ☐ 10 Oracle Projects
- ☐ 11 Oracle Financials
- ☐ 12 Oracle Human Resources
- ☐ 13 Oracle Interaction Center
- ☐ 14 Oracle Communications/Utilities (modules)
- ☐ 15 Oracle Public Sector/University (modules)
- ☐ 16 Oracle Financial Services (modules)
Server/Software
- ☐ 17 Oracle9*i*
- ☐ 18 Oracle9*i* Lite
- ☐ 19 Oracle8*i*
- ☐ 20 Other Oracle database
- ☐ 21 Oracle9*i* Application Server
- ☐ 22 Oracle9*i* Application Server Wireless
- ☐ 23 Oracle Small Business Suite

Tools
- ☐ 24 Oracle Developer Suite
- ☐ 25 Oracle Discoverer
- ☐ 26 Oracle JDeveloper
- ☐ 27 Oracle Migration Workbench
- ☐ 28 Oracle9*i*/AS Portal
- ☐ 29 Oracle Warehouse Builder
Oracle Services
- ☐ 30 Oracle Outsourcing
- ☐ 31 Oracle Consulting
- ☐ 32 Oracle Education
- ☐ 33 Oracle Support
- ☐ 98 Other
- 99 ☐ None of the above

⑦ WHAT OTHER DATABASE PRODUCTS ARE IN USE AT YOUR SITE? (check all that apply)
- ☐ 01 Access
- ☐ 02 Baan
- ☐ 03 dbase
- ☐ 04 Gupta
- ☐ 05 IBM DB2
- ☐ 06 Informix
- ☐ 07 Ingres
- ☐ 08 Microsoft Access
- ☐ 09 Microsoft SQL Server
- ☐ 10 PeopleSoft
- ☐ 11 Progress
- ☐ 12 SAP
- ☐ 13 Sybase
- ☐ 14 VSAM
- ☐ 98 Other
- 99 ☐ None of the above

⑧ WHAT OTHER APPLICATION SERVER PRODUCTS ARE IN USE AT YOUR SITE? (check all that apply)
- ☐ 01 BEA
- ☐ 02 IBM
- ☐ 03 Sybase
- ☐ 04 Sun
- ☐ 05 Other

⑨ DURING THE NEXT 12 MONTHS, HOW MUCH DO YOU ANTICIPATE YOUR ORGANIZATION WILL SPEND ON COMPUTER HARDWARE, SOFTWARE, PERIPHERALS, AND SERVICES FOR YOUR LOCATION? (check only one)
- ☐ 01 Less than $10,000
- ☐ 02 $10,000 to $49,999
- ☐ 03 $50,000 to $99,999
- ☐ 04 $100,000 to $499,999
- ☐ 05 $500,000 to $999,999
- ☐ 06 $1,000,000 and over

⑩ WHAT IS YOUR COMPANY'S YEARLY SALES REVENUE? (please choose one)
- ☐ 01 $500, 000, 000 and above
- ☐ 02 $100, 000, 000 to $500, 000, 000
- ☐ 03 $50, 000, 000 to $100, 000, 000
- ☐ 04 $5, 000, 000 to $50, 000, 000
- ☐ 05 $1, 000, 000 to $5, 000, 000

100103